A Song For You

The Quest of The Myddle Class

Kathy West

Library of Congress Control Number:		2010917049
ISBN:	Hardcover	978-1-4568-1791-6
	Softcover	978-1-4568-1790-9
	Ebook	978-1-4568-1792-3

This book was printed in the United States of America.

To order additional copies of this book, contact:
Xlibris Corporation
1-888-795-4274
www.Xlibris.com
Orders@Xlibris.com
88228

A Song For You

... remembering
good, old friends,

Enjoy Going Back ...

Kathy West

Table of Contents

Foreword

I N THE SUMMER of 2010, I attended the Carole King / James Taylor Troubadour Reunion Tour concert in New York City, and in an audience of over twenty thousand fans, I felt special because of my memories of being a close friend with Carole and for knowing how Danny "Kootch," the guitarist in the back-up band, introduced Carole to James Taylor in the late '60s through my friends in The Myddle Class.

I bet everyone my age wants to think back over forty years ago to remember their formative years. Don't we often recall the times in our lives we were more uncertain of our sensibilities about whether someone loved us than we were certain about our self-worth?

The theme of that reunion tour was brilliant and that night among the fans, young and old, I felt like I was a teenager again, sitting in an intimate venue like the Night Owl Café in Greenwich Village, listening to my friends play music and saying, "These guys are going to be big." And it was as if no time had passed.

Dedication

THIS BOOK IS dedicated to my first love, Rick Philp (in memoriam) for all he meant to me, to my dad (in memoriam) for paying attention to me all his life, and especially to my son for encouraging me to remember the times I was privileged to be loved by mentors, caring friends, and a lover who taught me how to love back.

Prologue

GOIN' BACK

IT'S THE SPRING of 2010. I am at the age and stage of my life when I remember more what I did forty-five years ago than what I did last week.

One day during a recent visit with my son, an old friend called to tell me he knows someone who was looking for me. A guy was interested in the lurid death of my high school boyfriend, Rick Philp, who was the admired guitarist with a popular rock band The Myddle Class before he was brutally killed by a troubled college roommate. People knew there was a girlfriend who might know what had happened. I was the girlfriend.

I went to my attic to find a box of memorabilia I saved since the '60s. I started sorting through some of the letters, cards, and pictures from Rick and my friend

Carole King, which I saved for more than forty years. My mind started to wander back to my youth.

It is said you only fall in love for the first time but once.

* * *

My son had heard a lot about this part of my past. As we sat down at my kitchen table for an early lunch, I began to tell him about my discovery: "All these letters* are from Rick, who I've told you was my boyfriend from high school through most of my college years, and Carole King. If I can tell you the whole story about Rick and his band, I'll try to fill you in on all our ups and downs and how I became a close friend to Carole. Look at these promo pictures for the record 'Free As The Wind' released when Carole's husband at the time, Gerry Goffin, was the group's producer. This is how it all began."

As I continued to sort through the poorly protected evidence of one of the most impassioned slices of my assorted life, I started to feel like I had not given these precious documents the proper respect they deserved throughout my many moves. I had simply thrown them in a box in a very careless manner, causing some of the material to become quite disheveled as if the memories held inside would have no meaning in the future. Then I hesitated to beat myself up about that and thought, I must

---

* Letters from Rick were sent to me at varied times we were each away during our respective episodes of starting and restarting our college experiences (Philp 1965-1969). It appears none of my letters to Rick survived his ordeals.

have treasured these things enough that I subconsciously never chose to just empty this box and toss all its contents, like so many other things I decided were not worthy of the cost of moving along with me to my different addresses over these years. As I uncovered each item, I decided to explain to my son the significant, meaningful memories they revealed.

I began to describe what I could recall: "The group's manager, Al Aronowitz, organized several fan clubs and distributed these newsletters. These letters from Rick started in 1965 when he went to Gettysburg College, and I stayed home to save money to start school."

The letters* from Carole King started from when I finally began school a year later in 1966 and continued through several years after the horrific attack on Rick in Boston in 1969.

I found a couple of newspaper articles, and I said, "I've told you that Rick was killed in Boston by a disturbed college roommate . . . look at these. This is the newspaper report of the killer's arrest in May 1969. I called Rick's roommate 'Dog' from the time I met him."

The first report** described how Rick's already-decomposing body was found on a Saturday afternoon

---

* Letters from Carole were sent to me during the varied times I was away for college and continued for several years after Rick's death as we attempted to stay connected. Following our marriages early in the '70s the correspondence ended. (King 1966-1974)

** Emerson Student Found Slain 1969. *The Associated Press*. Used with permission in a Back Bay apartment on Beacon Street. It continued to tell how police booked Dog on charges of murder, saying he had just graduated with honors from Emerson College and, now a student teacher, was living alone in the basement apartment since Rick, being a former roommate, moved out six weeks earlier. It ended quoting the Medical Examiner as saying, "This is a complex homicide." I couldn't read further, and I wasn't sure I could handle remembering more. But I did.

* * *

The really disturbing news article was the one that followed in May 1970 reporting on the outcome of Dog's murder trial. The title alone sadly gave an indication that the truth was not told. It read as such:

Drugs Cited in Student Sentence

> Superior Court Judge Wilfred Paquet today sentenced an Emerson College senior to 8-15 years in Walpole State Prison . . . for the bludgeoning death of his [former] roommate, Richard Philp . . . . The defendant, after two weeks of trial pleaded guilty to a [reduced] charge of manslaughter. (Tarbi 1970)

My son looked at the newspaper and turned his eyes to me to ask: "How did this make you feel?"

I said, "Dog didn't kill Rick because he jealously found his girlfriend fooling around with another guy." Dog's angry rage was more about the rejection of his sexual attraction, which Rick resisted, and his own selfish fears of being left behind as Rick was ready to leave Boston for good. "If he couldn't have Rick for himself, no one was going to have him."[*]

I began to tell the story from my memories. Just the year before Rick's death, I spent the summer in Los Angeles with these guys. Rick and I were invited by Carole to come to LA for Rick to record an album with her and other friends—Charlie Larkey, whom Carole loved; and Danny Kootch, an old friend from New York who had moved to Los Angeles with a new group he joined, Clear Light, after his efforts with James Taylor as the Flying Machine fell apart.

I was a part of this early Carole King inner circle that evolved and held tight from the mid-'60s efforts in New York City to promote hit records by The Myddle Class through the breaking up of Carole and Gerry's marriage and their move to the West Coast, which was replacing New York as the mecca for music publishing and recording.

Dog came along with us to Los Angeles that summer of 1968. His girlfriend, Jane, was supposed to join us, but that was not to be. During that summer, I became suspicious that Dog's obsession with Rick was unhealthy.

---

[*] This sentiment is similar to one expressed by Rick's Emerson College history Professor, Dr. John M. Coffee, who gave an extraordinary eulogy at a memorial service held in Boston's Trinity Church to honor Rick following the incident of his death.

* * *

My son asked me "How did Rick and Dog meet?
I went on to explain.

Rick had pursued his musical talent from our high school years through several efforts to complete a college education to meet his father's expectations. In 1965 he first attempted to attend Gettysburg College in the path of his grandfather, but that was right at the time his group, the King Bees (later renamed The Myddle Class), was beginning the tumultuous journey of likely success as a rock band across the northeast and beyond. Rick lasted only one semester at Gettysburg, which created a long-running estrangement from his dad until Rick decided that going back to complete college was important to accomplish alongside his playing music.

Rick was a good-looking guy with slightly wavy dark brown hair to match his sultry brown eyes enhanced by long, thick lashes that marked his attractive face, darned with lush, thick lips and baby-soft, never-blemished skin. Rick radiated sensitive, gentle features in both his slight build and his personality, but unless you knew him well, nothing stood out more about Rick than his accomplished talent as a guitarist. The deep love for writing and playing music that possessed him was impenetrable when someone would try to get closer to him than his guitars. The desires he held inside to fulfill his own expectations to exploit the talent he knew he had and needed to develop further was almost all that mattered to him. Other needs could be met alongside this mission, but nothing had more meaning to this exceptional guy. However, Rick's preoccupation with his not-yet-fully-defined self-image manifested itself in a serious vulnerability. This was the demon he struggled with, which left him with a naive tendency to ignore most reality around him. Emboldened by his trusting ways, he could never think the pursuit of his true happiness could be thwarted so prematurely. The horrifying ending to his life is still painfully incomprehensible.

Dog was already enrolled at Emerson College in Boston when Rick started back to school there in 1967. He took Rick in to share the apartment he lived in with another guy when Rick didn't know anyone there, and he needed to find the least expensive way to survive living in a city filled with mostly rich New York kids there to pursue even limited talent at a hip college in a hip city but mainly because they didn't know what they wanted from four years of college except maybe to avoid the draft or find a husband.

* * * * *

One of the subjects of human motivation and personality development that intrigued me most during my years as a college psych major is Maslow's theory of Self-actualization[*], the stages of growth experienced along the way to becoming who we are.

---

[*] Self-actualization is the term used by Abraham Maslow in his hierarchy of needs theory defining the stages and achievements in personality development of healthy, motivated people to help define their "self" as they attempt to reach their maximum potential. (Wikipedia, Self-actualization 2010)

20

Maslow begins describing his theories of personality development with his definition of a self-schema which develops into our self-concept of who we are.

> Self-schema* [is] the beliefs and ideas people have about themselves—beliefs which lead us to a tendency for a bias in what we attend to . . . what we remember, and a bias in what we are prepared to accept about ourselves. (Maslow 1954, 1987)

> The self-concept* is composed of relatively permanent self-assessments such as knowledge of one's skills and abilities, one's occupation, personality attributes, and awareness of one's physical attributes. (Maslow 1954, 1987)

Maslow touted that a person can maintain a multischematic approach to defining his or her self by being a computer programmer by day and a wedding singer on weekends. Maslow's native aschematic thinking approach allows someone to realize that if they want to be a musician, they will likely not want to be a businessman.

Rick knew he was not going to follow his father's path into the business world, but he was willing to go to Emerson because he finally wanted to follow his passion for music and writing. I'm sure that many other students

---

* (Wikipedia, Self-schema 2010); (Wikipedia, Self-concept 2010)

there were as well gifted with a voice or the ability to play or write music or act or anything else that could pass one for a performing artist. If they couldn't perform perhaps they could teach. I actually never knew what Dog studied at school or if he had any talent at all except a gift for cunning deception. He seemed more to have the qualities of a wannabe but his effervescent personality and interest in music and journalism were enough to get him by as the insightful type that Emerson attracted.

Perhaps the reality of Dog's motives was to find a partner in his search for his self-identity, including his sexuality, or to find the one who would bring him along for the ride to becoming who he really wanted to be, or who he knew then he already was—a man burdened with a need to benefit from the success of another with qualities and talents he lacked.

Dog had an older, manly look about him; although slightly built, he was muscular, hairy, and had a receding hairline at an early age. Dog's outward appearances helped him, when needed, to mask some of the effeminate tendencies that I sensed, having been exposed to several then closet queens in my own hometown surrounds. Such personality traits were perplexing yet acceptable, especially among the bohemian lifestyle of the '60s when young people were encouraged to find themselves.

Dog always had a wide smile, which often was accompanied by a sinister, sparkly, cold-as-ice stare in his dark eyes, like that of a demonic child caught with his hand in the cookie jar, who could hold back tears in a defiant way without remorse. He was often funny with his sarcastic assessment of the dichotomist lifestyle of the Los Angeles transplants. Those who decided to make the drastic move to the opposite coast wanted to have it all—they wanted to live like there was no tomorrow, with no commitments and little regard for societal expectations, but they also wanted to enjoy a life that only true success would afford them. So it was no surprise that the attraction of real success in the music business was a life that Dog wanted to live vicariously through Rick's talent.

The unforeseen caveat was that Dog wanted to believe that Rick could love him as much as he loved me, his girlfriend. I tried to tell Rick and the others in Los Angeles that summer that Dog was much too enamored, possessive, controlling, dependent, and deceptive, but no one wanted to hear what I had to say. There was enough drama in the complex relationships of meaningful people among the group's environs for there to be any concern with a peripheral personality. Dog's idiosyncrasies went unnoticed by everyone but me.

* * *

Book One: There's Something Special About a First Love

Chapter One

IN SEARCH OF MYSELF

When Will I Be Loved?

A PERSON'S SELF-CONCEPT can correlate directly to one's self-awareness. Maslow defines possible selves as the self-concept that gives each of us our ideas of the person we desire or fear we might become. Often, people will joke that a man must look at his potential wife's mother to find out who the young woman will become. This concept can hold true, although, when an individual finds their self, they may very well choose to be much different than the role models they meet along the way to developing their own identity.

According to Maslow's theory of hierarchical needs, basic needs for eating and sleeping along with needs to feel safe, well liked, and accepted by friends and society in general are easier to identify and satisfy than the more ambiguous needs for belongingness, esteem, competence, and of course, love. Achieving these high-order needs allows one to eventually reach their full potential. So when this search begins and ends is different for each individual. Reaching this self-actualization is the key to understanding when we know ourselves well enough to feel comfortable in our own skin, how well we know what we want from relationships, particularly those with lovers, and how independent we can be of others to define who we are.

When we feel we are in love with one person, at any time in our life—in our youth, in our prime, or even in our twilight years—we choose to invest our time, trust, feelings, loyalty, and devotion in that partner, and we want to believe we have made a right choice, the relationship will last, and our search for the one to share our life with will end. The greatest expectation one can have is that this commitment will be reciprocated with a return of love and assurance in equal magnitude.

What is it that drives us to believe we have made a right love choice? When do we consciously determine we have had enough experiences or points of reference to derive an adequate sense of self—that we know well who we are, what our needs and desires are—to appropriately decide who makes a good life partner? Or do we just decide with our eyes shut tight because at the early ages of eighteen to twenty-one years old, we are simply anxious to resolve all the many nagging questions: What will I do with my life after high school, after college? Who will want me if I am over twenty-one years old and still unmarried?

Who will take care of me when my parents are done with that? Will I or must I satisfy the expectations my parents have of me—to be married, have children, be successful, or at least able to support myself and not rely on them for my rent money? Will I be missing out on what my friends have found in having someone to share everyday experiences with? Will I grow old lonely?

Is there some element of narcissism or just plain vanity that makes us believe that if we give our love to another, that person must stay with us? Do we want it all and expect to deserve every opportunity to find the one with the right stuff even if it means looking at more than one relationship at the same time? Must not we ourselves make the choice: do we stay, or do we go on looking?

I knew I was attracted more to brains than brawn. Over time, the relationships I invested a good amount of time into were with guys who were not necessarily great-looking or muscled men. Instead, I had a strong tolerance for qualities I found interesting enough to be worthy of my ability to appreciate strengths over weaknesses. Did this mean I didn't know myself, or was I just looking for someone to accept me for my better points?

Would I find someone who would allow me to be myself unconditionally?

Is it that, in the end, we get tired of looking for Mr. Right, or maybe we just get plain lazy, and if someone says, "I want you," we just go for it!

I have letters from several of my college girlfriends who returned home after graduation unattached to any of the boys they had invested four years in pursuing. I am amazed even now to read how many of us dated more than one guy at a time, seemingly trying to decide what worked or, at least, what harsh treatment was tolerable. How painful was it to wait for a phone call to be invited out? How badly could I allow myself to feel if he didn't give me nice gifts or if he never sent flowers? How much would I want to satisfy his physical needs if my own were not particularly being met?

What beliefs or aspirations toward the future will we share, or what amount of differences is acceptable? If I am an independent person, will the one I choose to share my future with be comfortable enough with himself to allow me to grow without being intimidated?

And who was going to pass muster with our mothers?

The rationalization for choices to marry pours from these letters along with the anxiety suffered in not wanting to make a bad decision. But how many twenty-one-year-olds really knew all they needed to know to make a right choice in matters of love and marriage? Apparently, by divorce statistics, only 50 percent of these decisions are lasting ones.

On the other hand, some just felt the relationships they developed with a lover, even at the early ages of eighteen to twenty, had the strength to endure even separation. They had determination to overcome obstacles. I once heard from a high school friend who was in a serious relationship with a college boyfriend when, as sophomores, he needed to transfer to another school.

My friend told me that after spending about six hours a day together for a year and an entire summer together, it was hell to be alone. She knew the relationship they shared had developed into something closer and deeper than she ever dreamed would happen. That was it; she was in awe and overwhelmed by the relationship. She had found the love of her life.

The ultimate questions are, when and how do we just know that it feels right? I believe that without overanalyzing all the possibilities, when you make the one you're with laugh, you will know they love you. When they make you listen, you'll know you love them. I believe the relationships that have managed to stay healthy over time have kept this notion a priority every day. I missed out on this for many years after losing my first love.

* * *

People tell me my home is beautifully designed with a unique sense of charm that goes beyond a single style with just-enough in number and variety of collectibles. I've decorated with hues of red, gold, and green. Living in the South, I learned that the pineapple is a sign of welcome. My aunt taught me that every room should have a touch of yellow in it. My home is balanced in such a way that furnishings fit just so on walls and in spaces, but many pieces are one-offs that just go together to display—just what I am all about—a warm yet colorful, neatly kept but comfortable with a sometimes-messy, with too-many-magazines-on-the-coffee-table, lived-in feel that reflects my open and inviting personality.

My various attempts at self-actualization have had me dabbling in my passions to express my somewhat artistic talent in amateur decorating, resulting in accumulating many pretty objects in place of one beautiful relationship. I have way too many sets of dishes and glasses, platters, pots and pans, and serving pieces for all seasons and occasions, which came in handy when I entertained more and for large crowds. Now I feel a need to purge much of this no-longer-useful stuff I have gathered in my life because, although my adult life has been blessed with a wonderful son, a successful career, a good deal of travel, and a general sense of well-being, the fact is suddenly now, in my early sixties, I want to lessen my load in life.

Chapter Two

THE BEST OF TIMES

Rick And Kathy Are More Than Friends

WHEN MY SON probed with questions of when I first came to be Rick's girlfriend and how I got to know Carole King, I began to recall my high school years when Rick and I became close friends. I knew Rick played the guitar and he was writing his own songs. I had written what I thought were love poems and when Rick and I ended up in the same English class, we both worked on writing for the school newspaper, *The Folio*.

Everyone knows where they were on November 22, 1963. I was sitting with my sophomore guidance counselor, Mr. Burritt, intending to have one of our many chats about how I was doing with my classes. He had become my confidante, and I became close to his family—his wonderfully sweet wife and his four daughters whom I would babysit from time to time.

I stepped into his office at 1:00 p.m. and started a conversation, which quickly became one of my more typical ramblings about the dysfunction I endured at home. Suddenly, we were interrupted with an announcement over the school wide PA system telling us the fact that at 1:33 p.m. that afternoon, President John F. Kennedy died from gunshot wounds he suffered during his motorcade ride through the streets of Dallas, Texas. This day marked a historical moment in my life and the lives of an entire nation of people who had enjoyed nearly two years of high hopes and dreams for a bright future of trust in our government under the leadership of a president loved for his charm and good looks much more than for experience and values we would come to learn he seriously lacked. We were enamored by the beautiful first lady, Jackie, and the adorable children, Caroline and John Jr., barely three years old at the time of his father's death.

I was just a young high school student, barely understanding that GOP was an acronym for Grand Old Party to represent the Republican politicians that mostly received the 1960 votes of the college-educated white-collar parents of my newly formed conservative friends. I was hardly aware of the Bay of Pigs and the naval blockade of Cuba when these events occurred, let alone what they meant to the destiny of my friends just a few short years later when they would need to fear being drafted into a war in Vietnam. Who the hell ever heard of Vietnam?

As we learned the horrifying news that a president of the United States could actually be assassinated in his own country and tried to process the meaning of such a tragedy, Rick and I, along with other friends, met with our drama club and English teacher, Ms. Swigert, to acknowledge that, in just one day, we were scheduled to give a two-night performance of our school play *Dino* to what might very well be a half-empty audience. Ms. Swigert gathered the cast to tell us that in spite of the tragic event that we faced, "the show must go on." The next day, my parents were only interested in their plans to actually drive to Washington DC to see the procession of President Kennedy's funeral. My parents, my sisters, and my aunts did come to see the first night's performance of the play. I was the secretary, behind a desk at a youth center for juvenile delinquents, who had to answer a ringing phone with the play's opening lines. I was as nervous as anyone could be even though I had rehearsed my part a thousand times. I got through the second show, and when I returned home, my parents and five family members drove through the night to get to DC.

It was a remarkable time in the life of a sixteen-year-old girl. I was just starting to build some semblance of self-esteem, aptitude, and what I thought was talent. High school was getting good for me. It was at least improving from the way I started as a freshman. Attending Watchung Hills Regional High School (WHRHS) presented the challenge of meeting and learning the lifestyles of more than the kids I grew up with in Passaic Township[*]—an area of eight square miles connecting five small towns of mostly shortsighted ethnic families who only had, as a frame of reference, their backgrounds of hardly making it through high school, let alone college. They were mostly families of Italian or German immigrant heritage. Our fathers were hardworking blue-collar craftsmen—mechanics, carpenters, painters, masons, mailmen, perhaps as advanced as electricians or as fortunate as butchers, shoemakers, or restaurant owners. Our mothers, if they worked at all, were waitresses or seamstresses or worked in family businesses greeting customers. These were the family centric believers that they didn't need many friends because family was all-consuming and deserving of their free time because they would help raise their children in times of need.

Their strongest belief was that their children, particularly the girls, would get out of high school, get a nice job as a waitress or a secretary; they would live at home and contribute to the family income until they would bring a nearby family's favorite son into the mix and get married young to bring their parents grandchildren to spoil, if not raise, like their own. Who needed college—and certainly, what girl needed a college education? This was not planned for nor funded with the

---

[*] Passaic Township New Jersey was renamed Longhill Township in the 1980s. It consists of roughly eight square miles connecting Meyersville, Millington, Stirling, Gillette, and Homestead Park.

scarce money that could be better spent on a new car or a weekly, if not daily, trip to the racetrack for a day's earnings to be wagered on win, place, or show bets on the favorite horse in three out of six races and perhaps a few two- or five-dollar bets on a good long shot that could bring in a week's or month's worth of cold hard cash.

When the principal of my middle school, Mrs. Cashman—a waspy matron who wore her hair in a tight bun at the back of her neck and who had taught my parents in grade school—was responsible to recommend the Stirling kids to a choice of college prep versus a vocational curriculum at the high school level, it was an easy choice. All the Stirling kids were sent to high school assigned to secretarial, home economics, and machine shop classes without any consideration for a foreign language, algebra, or an advanced English literature course. So I arrived at the high school attending my first week of classes alongside mostly all the same kids I had graduated eighth grade with.

In English class, we were instructed to take desks in alphabetical order from the front of the room to the back, which was where I ended up. I was nearsighted, and I asked the teacher, Mr. Chesler, if I could move up to the front of the class, and he agreed.

Mr. Chesler was the very first mentor in my life—someone who took interest in my well-being. He was a handsome, recently out of college himself young married man with a new baby, enthusiastic, incredibly sensitive, and an incurably naive believer that being a teacher would be a most fulfilling career as he endeavored to influence young minds to appreciate classical and modern literature.

Who among this group had ever read Shakespeare or heard of *Catcher in the Rye*? Our first assignment was to read this book, and during class, we would have to give our interpretation of the characters, the story, and the tragedy that would unfold. I remember the class, one by one, being called upon to answer serious questions, returning ridiculously ignorant answers through their innate abilities to only encourage the rest of the class to deliver congratulatory out-loud laughter, with intent to waste time in order to possibly avoid their turn at the embarrassment. I was the only one in the class that took Mr. Chesler's assignment and interest in my sensibility seriously and gave fairly intelligent answers.

By the end of week one, Mr. Chesler took me aside and said, "I am taking you to the guidance office to have you moved out of this class." The result of this good fortune was that all my classes were changed to college-prep courses, and I was being sent to Mr. Chesler's honors English class. Rick Philp was in this class. I knew Rick from middle school, but he was from Gillette, and he was college material. There I met Brenda Smith, Linda Iulliano, and Dave Palmer.

Brenda Smith was one of the most beautiful girls in the entire freshman class. She was from Watchung, the town of upper middle-class, mostly white-collar, college-educated lawyers, doctors, businessmen, and the like. Brenda had been a middle-school cheerleader and was as smart as she was pretty. Her best friend from grade school, Linda Iulliano, was also pretty, well-to-do, and a cheerleader for certain with all the apparent confidence to go with all that.

Dave Palmer was a leader, outspoken with confident intellect and raw, sexy looks that matched his wit. He could be called arrogant and self-serving but, intriguingly, under the display of overconfidence was a vulnerability, which I later learned was the effect of being raised without a father figure to dispense the love needed by a young adult male, and that was strongly missed in forming Dave's personality.

Rick Philp was always quiet, pensive, and studious looking with soft brown eyes that pierced your heart like an arrow transporting the message, "If you're lucky, I will let you get to know me."

I entered this classroom terrified. My first thoughts were that I might not measure up to these classmates in capabilities. However, I was quite gregarious, never shy, and not at all afraid to express myself. I could be formidable, even at this young age of fourteen.

According to Maslow, one obtains self-actualization by the following:

> the desire for self-fulfillment . . . a yearning for ever realizing one's capabilities. It gives the individual a longing, or motivation to achieve budding ambitions. Common traits of those who have reached self-actualization are: they embrace reality and facts rather than denying truth . . . Upon reaching a higher

level of development, [this] person possesses qualities of independence, autonomy, a tendency to form few but deep friendships, a "philosophical" sense of humor. (Maslow 1954, 1987)

I believed I had already acquired many of these characteristics early in my personality development.

Mr. Chesler gave me my sea legs on the passageway to self-actualization, and I was determined to never let him down. I soon came to realize a lesson I attribute to back then—the best way to succeed is to surround yourself with people who know more than you and learn from them. I ultimately found I could hold my own with these kids. Somehow, I sensed that in spite of the magnitude of their good fortune in excess of mine, we were all equals in this new frontier of learning, not only about English literature, but also of who we were becoming as individuals, our developing bodies, and how to be fearless yet cautious young crusaders in a quest for knowledge, confidence, popularity, and perhaps, along the way, some sense of purpose. Entering this class was the first truly significant turning point in my life and the beginning of a long journey with this circle of friends.

Dave Palmer and I seemed to become the closest with Mr. Chesler. I would babysit his newborn baby, and Dave and I helped Mr. Chesler put out the newspapers *(The Folio)* filled with stories we had written. I remember many days when Dave and I would be in the classroom after school to collate the paper for distribution and we would sit around sharing our personal woes with Mr. Chesler. He seemed to understand more than anyone that Dave and I had little to go home to after school, except on the days when I needed to go to my mother's friend's house to clean for five dollars, working from three o'clock in the afternoon until sometimes eight o'clock at night. But that was OK—if it would please my mother and possibly have her think of me as a daughter who shared some of her values, I was in. Dave and I would spend time visiting with Mr. Chesler and his wife, Carol, at their home. They just seemed to want to watch us grow and hope we would succeed.

Dave sang in his church choir, and he was beginning to become the lead singer in a band of high school friends Rick was forming. Rick and Dave wrote songs together, Rick played lead guitar, and Chris Irby played bass guitar. The band would practice at Chris's house—in the garage. This was the essence of what is now referred to as the days of garage-rock* bands—back then, a new era in the music business.

---

* (Wikipedia, Garage Rock 2010)

Chapter Three

TIMES—THEY ARE A CHANGIN'

Changes And Chances

IN THE EARLY '60s, my sister Linda and I were young teenagers collecting the single records we listened to nightly on the radio while doing our homework. I remember the few times we made the trek to New York City to see the singers live in the famous music review shows at the Apollo Theater, produced by Alan Freed, and at the Brooklyn Fox Theater hosted by the popular radio DJ Murray "the K" Kaufman. These shows featured multiracial rock and roll artists who performed several times a day for a full week, a few times a year, usually during the Christmas and Easter school recesses. Kids would stand in long lines stretching around the corner of the theaters, knowing they would get in to one or another of the repetitive ninety-minute shows of the day, if you could stand the cold of the year-end or the spring rains. Those shows featured the top performers of the early rock and roll era always introducing new acts, such as Little Anthony & the Imperials, Patti Labelle and the Bluebells, Wilson Picket; the great James Brown as well as Buddy Holly and Chuck Berry. Later to join were Jackie Wilson, Gene Pitney, Ben E. King (with and without the Drifters), Dionne Warwick, the Shirelles, the Ronettes, the Chiffons, Bobby Vinton and even new artists bringing to New York the Detroit Motown sound of the early '60s: Stevie Wonder, the Marvalettes, Four Tops, and more. Throughout his radio career from the 1950s through the 1970s, Murray "the K" released numerous LP record albums, often compilations of hits by the acts that appeared in his famous Brooklyn Fox shows. These albums were titled *Murray the K's Blasts From the Past* and *Murray the K's Holiday Review-Live at the Brooklyn Fox*. In the late 1960s, Kaufman also produced and hosted a television variety show featuring many of these early rock performers. His best known was a national broadcast entitled "It's What's Happening, Baby." The show featured performances by many newcomers to the business as the pop artists of the day much like the live theater shows did before. It was on Murray "the K's" late '60s TV show that later friends Charlie Larkey and Abigail Haness played and sang in the house band as a

way to meet artists they admired as they hoped for their
own breaks into fame.

* * *

As we rang in the new year of 1964, the music
on the radio of solo artists we followed with loyal
purchases of 45-rpm records of rock and roll singles
released with B-side filler songs was changing. Now,
even more important than a new sweater or a six-pack,
we became obsessed with collecting 33- and 1/3-rpm
vinyl albums holding twelve to fourteen songs, most
of which we never heard. We were mindlessly lured
by colorfully artistic jackets and liner notes, giving us
all the enticing stories we wanted to know about these
new artists who could produce recordings of the unique
words and music they had written themselves. With an
insatiable curiosity to explore the sounds emanating
from Los Angeles, Detroit, and still New York's own
Greenwich Village from the likes of the Beach Boys
("God Only Knows"), The Supremes ("Baby Love"),
Bob Dylan ("Mr. Tambourine Man"), we were attracted
to these new artists by their telling stories of free spirit
and lost loves or a prolific stream of consciousness
to pronounce political affirmations to denounce the
unpopular war our country would not escape for a
long time to come. The common threads were the
steely sounds of the Gibson and Fender guitars and the
poetic prose of self-expression by singer-songwriters
who were swiftly replacing the assumed endless appeal
of the steady output from the modern-day Tin Pan

Alley* songwriters of the early '60s whose music we had previously followed resolutely.

It became a new dream of bands that practiced in their garages to stretch our senses with dueling guitars, drum solos, and vocal harmonies. New musically talented groups, like the one Rick and Dave were forming, took to the stages with reckless abandon and fervent hopes of becoming famous and maybe rich in the process by exploiting their command of the electric sound and their rebellious jilting of the establishment.

To add encouragement, along came the British invasion. The Rolling Stones and the Beatles, with unprecedented group appeal, captured the hearts of millions of teenage girls who all truly believed that Mick Jagger and Paul McCartney would surely leave their girlfriends to consider their love. I know; I was one of them. These groups imprinted the minds of many new folk or rhythm-and-blues-turned-rock bands who quickly took to emulating the mop-tops by covering their new releases at the performances they booked at high school dances and private parties, hoping to make themselves

---

* Tin Pan Alley is the nickname given as the starting place for the gathering of New York City–centered music publishers and songwriters who dominated the popular music of the United States in the late nineteenth century and early twentieth century. Tin Pan Alley was originally a specific place in New York City: West 28th Street between Fifth and Sixth Avenue. Its start is usually dated to about 1885, and Tin Pan Alley is considered to have continued into the 1950s when earlier styles of American popular music were outdone by the rise of rock and roll. The origins of the name are unclear. With time, this name came to fondly describe the U.S. music industry in general. (Wikipedia, Tin Pan Alley 2000)

known, feeling just as entitled to success given the new phenomenon of making it big overnight.

*   *   *

In February 1964, Rick had just turned seventeen years old. One day, I met up with him at his school hallway locker to say I was sorry he had lost his mother to her long illness. We talked for a long time, and Rick invited me to join him in getting tickets to a summer concert by the Beatles in Atlantic City. Rick knew how to get advanced tickets, so I said I wanted two. I planned that my older sister Linda and I would join him. I had those tickets in my hot little hand for four months when my mother decided in early August that we were going to go to Miami, Florida, on a family vacation. I told my parents there was no way I would go and miss the Beatles concert. They would have nothing to do with me staying home alone while they were away, so I was forced to give up the Beatles concert tickets to my married sister and her husband.

On the August day I should have been in Atlantic City, I was in Miami, Florida experiencing a severe hurricane. I sat in a motel room in the pouring rain, listening to the radio telling the news of the Beatles concert in New Jersey. The reporter said something like, "It was the first time you could actually hear what they were singing above the screaming crowd." I immediately got sick to my stomach. When we returned home from the vacation, my brother-in-law had taken movies of the show. It was pretty amazing, and they bragged about going to that concert for years to come.

During the summer of 1964, Rick and Dave had their band, the King Bees, playing quite a number of events. I returned from Florida looking good with my hair frosted and my skin very tan. I went to see the band play at the Stirling Firehouse shortly before the start of our senior year at WHRHS. I remember exactly what I was wearing: green madras plaid, Bermuda shorts, and a yellow blouse. I just stood there watching and listening to these guys make great music and having all the younger high school girls scream at them as they covered songs by the Rolling Stones and Bob Dylan along with some original music they had written together. They had become quite good and very popular.

Shortly after our senior year in school started, I was going to have an operation on my eye—the one I do not see out of—to correct the lazy eye I lived with for seventeen years. I had found an ophthalmologist who would fix the wall-eyed defect in my appearance that always had people look over their shoulder to see who was behind them that I was looking at when I spoke to them. It took just $250, a few days with a patch on my eye, and a week of wearing dark glasses in school, and I was a new woman. I felt my five feet eight inches tall and proud of my dark brown eyes and my black hair that I took meticulous care of. The improvement in my appearance was not talked about much, but I finally felt somewhat attractive.

As part of a select group of senior members of a service club, Rick and I would get out of classes five minutes early to get to our hallway monitoring stations to keep students moving to their next classrooms. It was a cool thing to be an authority figure to a bunch of underclassmen, especially being on the same post with Rick. We started to become close friends, and we hung out a lot. I had been told that he had a girlfriend at another high school, and I knew Rick took guitar lessons in Plainfield.

One day, Rick drove me home after school, and he asked me if I would be his girlfriend. I said I didn't want to come between him and the girl he was dating. He said he had decided to break up with that friend. We started to be a couple. I remember one afternoon in Mr. Chesler's homeroom talking with Dave Palmer about going out with Rick. Dave said he had told Rick, "You better not hurt her."

After school, I would sometimes go with Rick to his home in Gillette where we would spend time in the basement den while he practiced the guitar. He would play rhythm and blues riffs to mimic B.B. King and jazz-chords plucking with just his thumb like one of his music heroes, Wes Montgomery, who we once saw play at the Copacabana (and who also died prematurely). When Rick would reach the harmonic notes, which sounded like an angel playing a harp, I would think to myself, "This guy can do anything to me, and I will always stick".

Sometimes we would go upstairs to the living room, and he would play songs he was composing on the family piano. I think this was his way of communicating with his mother, asking her opinion of his latest creation.

Maslow's hierarchy of needs theory says people have lower-order needs, like eating and sleeping, however, it also notes:

> . . . the higher level of needs mostly apply to the need to be loved, starting with the belongingness needs for emotionally based relationships and . . . the esteem needs for social acceptance . . . by which we gain a sense of competence, recognition of achievement by peers, and . . . our seeking of fame or glory, which depend on respect from others but must start with self-respect. (Maslow 1954, 1987)

I remember wondering if Rick was playing for just me and for my acceptance or respect. But I realized soon that Rick was so absorbed in his playing that it didn't matter if I was there or not; he just needed to play, and I was thrilled to listen.

Along with being focused when it came to playing his music, Rick had a very playful side to him. Rick's dad commuted to New York by train, so his hot sports car was always available to Rick after school. Unfittingly, his dad had a classic muscle car—a Chevy Malibu SS convertible—black with a tan soft top and red leather interior, with bucket seats, a four-speed-on-the-floor transmission, and a 350-horsepower 327 engine. In 1965, that was a pretty suped-up car.

One afternoon, Rick took me in that car to the parking lot of our old middle school to teach me how to drive a stick shift. It was fun and scary at the same time. I couldn't do much more than drive in a big circle on the blacktop, but handling the heavy clutch and gas in perfect synchrony was more than a challenge; the car bucked like a bronco, and I thought I might just be leaving the transmission on the pavement. While Rick wanted to patiently give me some rope, the terror in his face was unmistakable. My driving lesson that day seemed to only last about thirty seconds, but I had learned all I needed to know about balancing a clutch, gas pedal, and the break of a sports car. The most exciting part of it all was how much Rick trusted me with his dad's most prized possession.

Rick had a placid manner that often seemed incongruous with the passion that emanated from the music he created. We laughed a lot when all we wanted to do was share each other's humorous interpretations of issues we faced that we knew we could do little to change. Rick seemed to get great relief from some of the tension he faced at home when he could project a playful disguise of his feelings of helplessness over things he could not control. I learned this technique from him and applied it routinely in my approach to my life's frustrations. He was a great role model.

I was invited to stay for dinner at Rick's house a few times. I got to see how Rick's dad related to his children. Mr. Philp was a good-looking, charismatic man with obvious conservative values and a strong sense of pride and security in the status he had achieved from his hard-work ethic. He was a sales executive at Hanes Hosiery and travelled into New York City on the Lackawanna Railroad train line that routinely swallowed the New Jersey commuters every morning and evening. He had lost his wife at a very young age, and in spite of cordial small talk that he attempted to control as the allowed light conversation, I could tell that becoming a single father of three young kids was daunting to this man only in his thirties.

I never met Rick's mother before her death, but it was clear Rick had to have her genes because he was far from the persona his father portrayed.

We only have the points of reference we derive from our experiences as we develop our life goals. At this point in time, Rick and his dad, on the surface, had shared little and had extremely disparate goals for Rick's life ahead. But didn't every teenage boy and his dad in the '60s have different points of view?

Chapter Four

THE MYDDLE CLASS DREAMS—HOW IT ALL BEGAN

The Turning Point

D URING THE SCHOOL year of 1964-65, as Rick's girlfriend, I had become embedded in the activities of Rick and Dave's band, the King Bees. They had been working with an organ player from Plainfield High School, Danny Mansolino. Danny was a quiet, shy, intellectual type who didn't have much to say. I got to know Danny by talking with him one-on-one. He was a very solid organ player who knew his place in the group was to be a sleepy giant. He would later contribute to original songwriting and background vocals.

The band's drummer, Myke Rosa, was from Governor Livingston High School (GLHS) in New Providence. Myke was slight in size, but he had a relentless, mighty spirit. Myke always had a smile and a sense of humor, which masked a nervousness that would raise its ugly head every now and then by causing him to throw up after a performance that expelled the energy of three people.

For whatever reason, Chris Irby didn't want to be part of the King Bees.

The group was planning a very important winter concert scheduled at a Berkeley Heights Catholic school auditorium. Hundreds of tickets were sold for this show, and they didn't have a bass player. Myke Rosa's good friend in high school was Charlie Larkey, whose father owned the upscale local Larkey's men's clothing store. Myke said Charlie wanted to join the band, but he didn't play an instrument. Rick said he would teach Charlie to play the bass. In less than a week, Charlie learned enough chords to get them through the hugely successful CYO concert. What Charlie lacked in talent, he made up for with McDreamy looks; his parted-in-the-middle, chin-length, silky black hair practically covered his long face except to expose his deep-set strikingly black eyes that caused hearts to throb.

Dave's long legs and broad shoulders gyrated as he straddled the pole of a microphone hugged by a harmonica on which he wailed with enough sexual passion to rival Mick Jagger himself.

Rick was the quintessential performer married to his guitar like a faithful lover. His boyish good looks captured onlookers with mesmerizing skepticism of how someone so focused could ever be aware of their awe.

I followed the band everywhere they practiced and everywhere they played. As Rick's girlfriend, I was in the front row the night of the Berkeley Heights concert. The auditorium was filled with mostly screaming girls only a few years my junior. The police that were summoned to control the crowd couldn't stop the dozens of girls who rushed the stage to get a piece of Dave's shirt and a whiff of Charlie's scent. The guys thought this had to be as good as it gets. This was a new turning point in the lives of all of us.

We soon came to find out that among the crowd at this concert was the one and only Al Aronowitz. Al who? Here was this burly middle-aged man with thin red curly hair he wore in a bohemian ponytail. Al was a somewhat scary man until you got to know his quiet, calm, at-first-glance-unimpressive ways; until you learned his gift for penning images of the trickery that permeated the music industry. A journalist since the fifties, Al Aronowitz had written stories and reviews of the elite in the music business, most notably Frank Sinatra, Duke Ellington, Miles Davis, Louis Armstrong, Johnny Cash, and Ray Charles. More currently at the time we met him, writing for the *Saturday Evening Post* magazine, Al was as much a fan as he was a flattering reporter of the destined-to-be icons Jimi Hendrix, Mick Jagger, Bob Dylan, and the Beatles. Al had developed close friendships with many of the artists he covered in the early '60s, namely Bobby Darin, Dylan himself, and particularly the Beatles' George Harrison. Al writes about his opportunity to meet and interview the Beatles upon their first U.S. tour. Al describes how he introduced the Beatles to both Bob Dylan and marijuana, saying, "The '60s wouldn't have been the same without me."*

In recent years, following the death of Al Aronowitz at age seventy-seven in 2005, Al's children shared many of his writings on a Web site titled *The Blacklisted Journalist*. Here, one can find an article Al wrote in August 1963 for the *Saturday Evening Post* titled "The Pre-Beatles Pop Era: 'The Dumb Sound.'"** This lesson in a segment of rock and roll history details the evolution of a phenomenon resulting from the mass production of 45-rpm singles recorded by one-hit wonders, like "Locomotion" by Little Eva Boyd (babysitter to Carole and Gerry Goffin); or successfully sustaining single artists like Connie Francis singing "Everybody's Somebody's Fool," 1960, and "Where the Boys Are" (penned by Neil Sedaka for the movie by the same title), 1961; Dion (DiMucci) recording "Runaround Sue" and "The Wanderer," 1961, in his

---

* Al Aronowitz has often been credited with introducing Bob Dylan and other close friends to the Beatles starting with their 1964 visit to the United States. From this and other connections Al developed with major music business personalities at the height of their careers, through his early reputation as a respected rock music columnist, Al proclaimed himself as the "Godfather of rock journalism."

** The Al Aronowitz Web site *The Blacklisted Journalist* displays this example of his awe-inspired commentary on the pop music of the '60s as he followed the success of Carole King and Gerry Goffin as early singer-songwriters who sprang from the famed Brill Building "Tin Pan Alley." "The Pre-Beatles Pop Era: 'The Dumb Sound'" © 1963 is used here by permission from the *Saturday Evening Post* magazine for which Al wrote at the time.

solo career separate from Dion and the Belmonts[*]; or group artists like the Chiffons' "He's So Fine" and "One Fine Day," 1963; the Cookies' (featuring Jeanie McCrea) recording "Don't Say Nothin' Bad (About My Baby)" and "Chains," 1962; and the Drifters (originally including Clyde McPhatter, later replaced by Ben E. King before he went solo) known best for "There Goes My Baby," 1959, "Up on the Roof," and "On Broadway," 1962 and "Under the Boardwalk," 1964. The repeat of hits for these well-known performers was, in large part, due to the prolific output from behind-the-scenes songwriting teams who were happy to spend every free minute after college classes pairing up their musical and lyrical talents to simply pump out product for the famed Brill Building at 1619 Broadway in New York City.

> Home of the music publishing industry . . . once ruled by balding men with cigars in their mouths, [a contemporary] Tin Pan Alley is packed with so many kids, they've started calling it Teen Pan Alley. (A. Aronowitz, "The Pre-Beatles Pop Era: 'The Dumb Sound'" © 1963 Used by Permission.)

---

[*] Dion and The Belmonts sang their hits, "Teenager in Love" and "Where or When," in the late 1950s as part of The Winter Dance Party tour with Buddy Holly, Ritchie Valens and the Big Bopper. On February 2, 1959, after playing in Clear Lake, Iowa, Dion decided he would not join the others on a flight out of town, which crashed in the snowy night killing the three headliners.

The Brill Building was supplemented by the offices of Don Kirshner's Aldon Music (publishing company) at 1650 Broadway. This was the actual fox den for the young, talented songwriting teams of Goffin and King[*] (later husband and wife), Barry Mann and Cynthia Weill (later also married), Ellie Greenwich and Jeff Barry, and Neil Sedaka and his early writing partner Howie Greenfield and Mort Shuman who wrote with Doc Pumus. The Brill Building ultimately housed these pairs along with the talented Burt Bacharach and Hal David; Jerry Leiber, and Mike Stoller[**] (the latter being the thrust for the successful Broadway musical *Smokey Joe's Café* featuring songs written for the Drifters); as well as Phil Spector, before he became a qualified producer in his own right, and Neil Diamond, before he elevated his writing talents into a long-lasting career as a solo recording and performing artist. This historic list of collaborators

---

[*] (Wikipedia, Carole King 2006); (Wikipedia, Gerry Goffin 2010)

[**] Songwriters Leiber and Stoller wrote the Drifters' first hit, "There Goes My Baby," in 1959. Other hits were "This Magic Moment" and "Save the Last Dance for Me." Ben E. King left the group to pursue a solo career in 1960. The Drifters had major pop and rhythm and blues hits provided by Brill Building songwriters. These included Carole King and Gerry Goffin's "Some Kind of Wonderful," "When My Little Girl Is Smiling," and "Up on the Roof" and Barry Mann and Cynthia Weil's "On Broadway" and "I'll Take You Home." In 1964, early Drifter Johnny Moore took over the lead for the group's final pop hits "Under the Boardwalk" and "Saturday Night at the Movies." The Drifters were inducted into the Rock and Roll Hall of Fame in 1988. Several different groupings of Drifters perform today. Johnny Moore died in London on December 30, 1998, at the age of sixty-four. (Wikipedia, Jerry Leiber and Mike Stoller 2010); (Wikipedia, The Drifters (American Band) 2010)

enjoyed nearly five consecutive years of producing hits
for the artists that had maneuvered their names into the
lexicon of the teenage upshot of the baby-boom births
that started in 1946.

> Rock and Roll got its name from Cleveland
> disc jockey Alan Freed, who became its
> champion after Bill Haley and his Comets
> Rock Around the Clock electrified the kids of
> the world. (A. Aronowitz, "The Pre-Beatles Pop Era:
> 'The Dumb Sound'" © 1963 Used by Permission.)

Before rock and roll was prevalent, I remember listening
to my mother's collection of Frank Sinatra's 78 and 33-1/3
records which began to fade from popularity.

> . . . the sounds of popular [60s] music are
> not designed for the parents, [but] designed
> for the kids . . . more specifically, for that girl
> at the counter of the Pop Record Business.
> (A. Aronowitz, "The Pre-Beatles Pop Era: 'The Dumb
> Sound'" © 1963 Used by Permission.)

Those counters were at the distribution outlets for
hundreds of 45-rpm singles popping up as local
businesses in the early '60s like head shops would at the
end of the decade. The record stores like Scotti's Records
in Summit, New Jersey, were the places you could spend
hours perusing the latest Top-40 hits and ask to hear the
records played in advance of your purchase if it wasn't

a song played on the popular AM radio station, WABC, where New York DJs Scott Muni and "Cousin Brucie" played the top ten records once an hour—which racked up the royalties for not only the recording artist but also for the songwriters at anywhere from one to ten cents a play. Even during the days of payola (favors and/or money paid to DJs who would promote an unknown or mediocre record), these record plays over the airwaves as well as copies sold were reported to either BMI or ASCAP, the royalties agencies responsible to track and fork over the earnings to these entertainers.

I remember the endless collections of 45 rpm records my cousin Claudia had acquired during high school days. She later had a full-fledged jukebox to house her records—one you could make selections from without depositing the dime for a single play or a quarter to hear three songs. By the way, jukebox plays were not traceable to BMI and ASCAP, so songwriters and artists knew for many years they were missing out on big bucks in royalties, which they could do nothing about without taking on mobsters.

> [The most likely purchaser of singles was the] sometimes tomboyish and sometimes entirely feminine creatures with an identity as vague as her years and as elusive as her tastes . . . cursed with the catastrophe of parents and boyfriends, . . . desperate, unhappy, and [to] complete her misery, too young to drive.
> (A. Aronowitz, "The Pre-Beatles Pop Era: 'The Dumb Sound'" © 1963 Used by Permission.)

The millions of dollars per year spent by kids buying 45s were not lost on the old moguls of the biz who keenly identified the ease of producing demos by songwriters working out of the Brill Building. The success of this production line was epitomized by the insight and A&R (Artist and Repertoire) genius of "the Man with the Golden Ear," music publisher/record producer Don Kirshner, and later, Jerry Wexler, who gave birth to the unparalleled Atlantic Records and all that followed for that empire. Donny (as Carole and Gerry called him) had the knack for peddling potential hit songs to the most popular recording artists. Kirshner started his own label—Dimension Records, published under his Aldon Music. The earlier record production business was monopolized by several major publishers who managed to compete with a few independents. Technological advances allowed for a cultural revolution describes by the following:

> [when] . . . for a few hundred dollar investment . . . if the record sold and got radio-play as a 'hit,' thousands in profits could be derived . . . . Fairy tale that it may be, The Pop Record Business is still a business and for every dollar and a half that the public spends for a movie ticket, it also spends an estimated fifty cents for a record. In 1962, these fifty-cent pieces added up to a grand total of six hundred and fifty-one million dollars which is another explanation

of why a whole generation of stage-struck teenagers is now frantically engaged in recording demos/'dubs' in such makeshift studios as cellars, attics, garages . . . where for upwards of a quarter, any aspiring singer can have his voice handed back to him on an acetate [proverbial] platter. (A. Aronowitz, "The Pre-Beatles Pop Era: 'The Dumb Sound'" © 1963 Used by Permission.)

The songs that became hugely successful met the criteria for a catchy beat teenagers could dance to and subtle words that were indiscernible by parents of those dancing. Carole and Gerry Goffin were the first highly driven collaborators to marry and become parents during their early years of college. It was the words of "Will You Love Me Tomorrow?" recorded in 1961 by the Shirelles that subtly told the story of why high school junior classes of the early '60s lost four to five girls over the summers to intimate friendships among young steady couples who believed that you must love who you sleep with. Carole King and Gerry Goffin were the first of the Brill Building brass to hit number one in early 1961 with "Will You Love Me Tomorrow?" on the charts of the industry metric *Billboard* Magazine.

In a 2001 *Vanity Fair* magazine article titled "The Hit Factory," David Kamp gives a comprehensive accounting of the history of New York City's Brill Building as a launchpad for the highly successful careers of some of the most distinguished song-writing teams who became icons of the early pop-music era. Complete with early pictures and interviews with the colleagues giving detailed in-their-own-words recollections of how their careers unfolded, Kamp describes how:

> Goffin and King were the first to hit pay dirt [and] the Brill Building songs which week in and week out dominated America's Top-10 [proved] its quality is the reason . . . why the Righteous Brothers' "You've Lost That Lovin' Feeling" is the most played song in radio's history (reportedly having over fourteen million plays). (Kamp 2001)

This superbly written history is a testament to what came "before . . . the stigma of [singers] not writing their own material."

When the King Bees met with Al Aronowitz a few days after the Berkeley Heights CYO concert in December of 1964, he told them that his babysitter had described to him how much exuberance they drew from a screaming crowd who saw them play at the traditional summer festival held at the Berkeley Heights Mount Carmel field. She told Al how the King Bees had original songs that were more popular than the covers of the Rolling Stones ("I'm a King Bee") and Bob Dylan ("Gates of Eden") they performed in their show.

Al told the skeptical Rick and Dave he wanted to manage the group into a recording contract that would make them rich and famous. He wanted to introduce them to the songwriting team of Carole King and Gerry Goffin. They learned Carole and Gerry had written "Locomotion" for their babysitter, Little Eva; "Hey, Girl," by Freddy Scott (one of my favorites, including the later cover by Billy Joel); "Chains" (later covered by the Beatles); and "Don't Say Nothin' Bad About My Baby" by the Cookies; "Take Good Care of My Baby" by Bobby Vee; "Oh No, Not My Baby" by Maxine Brown; "Every Breath I Take" by Gene Pitney; "Go Away, Little Girl" by Steve Lawrence; "One Fine Day" by the Chiffons; "Some Kind of Wonderful," "When My Little Girl Is Smiling," and "Up on the Roof" by the Drifters; and on and on.

When Rick told me he was going to meet Goffin and King who wrote "Will You Love Me Tomorrow?" I was amazed. All I could think of was how much I loved that song. In January of 1962, my sister Linda gave herself a sweet-sixteen party in the family room newly added to the back of our house. The room was still empty, and we had a big group of the kids from school at the party. I was a fourteen-year-old high school freshman with a big crush on Tommy Symons, a co-member on the WHRHS football team with my best cousin, Doc. Tommy danced

---

* The '60s period of Goffin and King song-writing collaboration, mostly over the years elapsing the duration of their marriage, produced the songs most prominently identified in the Carole King 1980 album, *Pearls*. Many of these classics have been covered extensively over decades through the admiration for their music and lyrics by music elites no less than the Beatles, Neil Diamond, Billy Joel, James Taylor, and Phil Collins as recently as 2010.

with me to that song, and I was in love. When kids danced to slow music in 1962, the boy grasped a girl's right hand in his left hand held down at his hip, and he tightly held his right arm around the girl's waist. The girl held her left arm high over the boy's shoulder and softly placed her hand around his neck so they would touch cheeks in a daze of lust. I'll never forget the thrill I had thinking that maybe Tommy could actually like me as he whispered the words to that song, "Tonight you're mine completely," and feeling the chill that travelled my spine as I listened intently to the violins in the background. I would come to learn when I met Carole King that she was not much more than my age at the time when she wrote that string arrangement.

Goffin and King were legends, and I was about to enter into the inner circle of their life together and encounter the impact it would have on me and my best friends. As she wrote the music and he wrote the words to some of the most memorable songs of the early '60s, their newfound gold mine motivated the city dwellers to wander to the suburb of West Orange, New Jersey, to be neighbors of their mentor and unrivaled publisher, Don Kirshner. The house on Waddington Avenue, while sparsely decorated on the inside, had a white Cadillac in the driveway and a pool in the backyard. The most impressive thing was the doorbell that rang the eight notes to the words "will you still love me tomorrow." Rick and Dave went to meet Carole and Gerry at their West Orange home in the spring of 1965. These music geniuses were to listen to the original songs that Rick and

Dave had written that were so well accepted by their fans. The plan was to see if Carole and Gerry would take a shot at producing one of their favorites as a hit record.

The group was fully aware of the success this duo had enjoyed and how much being pursued by this couple could mean to their future chances for the King Bees to get the break that dominated their hopes and dreams. Soon after their first meeting, I was allowed to tag along to meet the Goffins on a day they were going to share some of the songs they had in waiting (on a discovery of a group to record with them now somewhat independent of Donny Kirshner). They planned to assess what Dave's passion and vocal talent could do to interpret some of the new material Gerry was generating to compete with the newly emerging, not-so-ready-for-prime-time songs of Dylan and other writers that evolved less from doubts about lasting love and more from the influence of mind-altering drugs. After the British invasion, the music of the Brill Building whiz kids had reached a drought, and if their songs were being produced, they were of a new ilk and being recorded by new unproven names in the business. This was a bit unsettling for Carole and Gerry after the dumb sound had been so good to them.

Carole King's gregarious personality worked to advance an inviting atmosphere in the opulent home of this couple. Carole's looks were a bit ethnic, but her naturally curly, dirty blonde hair and blue eyes added to her sensual, thick lips and petite build to give her a sexiness that could have caused the somewhat evident look of jealousy in her husband's discomfort around these younger guys who would make up this newfound partnership. Gerry was seven years older than these boys, and he and Carole had yet to meet Charlie Larkey, the declared sex symbol of the King Bees. Carole always had a big smile to complement her efforts to be funny when she expressed her dry Jewish humor, which stemmed from her deep-rooted Brooklyn upbringing. Her voice was raspy when she spoke with purposefully measured articulation of her words, but this guttural tone when she sang enhanced her ability to herald the melodies she wrote.

But it was the song lyrics' fierce sensitivity she would express that grabbed the heart and ear that listened intently to get all the meaning that needed to be understood in their songs. Carole and Gerry were the yin and the yang in personality. As at ease as you felt upon first meeting Carole by her outgoing friendliness, Gerry's somewhat timidly quiet, introverted ways could be quite intimidating. Gerry often had a depressed look showing in his eyes and on his face. I always thought there was a thin line between genius and crazy. He had strikingly good looks with dark wavy hair and dark eyes that often stared into space. When he did smile, you could tell he was having a rare moment of letting himself go from some kind of constant dwelling on the next prose he would unleash.

It didn't take long to know that Carole was vulnerable to criticism, especially to Gerry's low-keyed, heavy-on-his-mind judgmental concentration over the way Carole's expression of his personal thoughts—and perhaps, weaknesses—came across to a listener. In spite of their differences, you could see the chemistry they shared, and it was a successful formula.

The room that had the piano Carole created her music from was decorated in black and white with red filtered, recessed ceiling lights that could be dimmed to a sexy atmosphere. Over the next couple of years, Rick and I spent several overnight visits together in that room wishing the next day's light would never come.

It was in this room I once asked Gerry if he would look at several love poems I had written as a teenager. I sat with him one day with a knot twisting in my stomach. After reading the pages and without commenting on the quality, he gave me a polite smile and said, "I can't use these," and he kindly handed them back to me. When I left the house that day, I immediately tore up the writings I had done, feeling they merely were rhymed words on paper. Although a little hurt, I adoringly admired Gerry Goffin after that day.

* * *

In May of 1965, Brenda Smith and I were co-chairmen of the junior-senior prom committee. We selected the venue, the meal, and photographer and led the other committees through production of a prom program and memorabilia. Peggy Luppino and Linda Iuliano were responsible for decorations. Rick was to provide the entertainment. I would come to learn that, as a child, Rick had played piano in a trio with his mother for musical events at his church. He set the prom theme to the song "Rhapsody in Blue" after the sultry music of George

Gershwin designed to be played by a solo pianist as part of a jazz band. None of us knew then the significance this had for Rick; it just made the night so romantic, we were all very impressed.

Brenda was still my cousin Doc's girlfriend, but she was not going to sit out our senior prom while he was away at college in Florida. So Brenda went to the prom with Dave Palmer. Dave had pined for Brenda since freshman year, but he was not going to compete with a football icon and the 1964 class' Most Popular kid. So it wasn't until our senior year in school that Dave let it be known how much he longed for Brenda's unattainable attention.

Everyone remembers their prom night. Brenda and I had shopped together for just the right dress, shoes, and long white gloves and planned to have our hair done at a salon. I picked out this dress that had a blue and white flowered design along the bottom which meant it could not be shortened. Then I bought these three-inch spiked white patent leather heels. After deciding not to style my own hair, a hairdresser gave me this pompadour hairdo. I ended up looking like I would tower over Rick, who was actually no more than a couple of inches shorter than me. I remember my mother's lack of any compliment and stares implying she hated the way I looked as I prepared for the night. I thought, how could she want to make me feel so bad? What she actually meant to do was spare me of the realization that I was going to look ridiculous next to my date, who was not a big guy. It was a disaster when I looked back on the pictures that were taken. But that night, we all felt like queens and kings. Linda Iuliano was Miss Watchung Hills, but the prom king and queen were Peggy Luppino and Norman Hewitt. They are married to this day.

The prom didn't end until after two o'clock in the morning, and the idea was to be out the entire night. I remember Rick and me intimately passing time in the car as a soft rain warmed the night until sun-up.

The plan was for a crowd to spend the next whole day at the shore beachfront home of the Nagles. Eddie Nagle was one of six children of a reclusive mother and a handsome Irish Catholic father who was apparently quite successful. Mr. Nagle was a well-liked frequent patron of the Lake Edge restaurant, where my mother worked as a waitress. The Nagles had a large home in Watchung at the top of the mountain with a gorgeous view of New York City. Everyone envied Eddie Nagle, but few knew of the heartache and demons that lead this popular guy to a suspicious, serious drinking problem.

That day in May at the Jersey Shore was a letdown. It rained, and it turned cold. Everyone tried to sit out on the beach, but we were wrapped in sweaters and jackets. It was a memorable day but less than fulfilling of the expectations that were built around prom weekend.

We soon came up to graduation ceremonies. I don't recall much about it except that, as a graduation gift, I gave Rick a silver ID bracelet that simply was engraved with "Rick" on the front and "Remember Me" on the inside. That night, the King Bees played at a packed crowd of nearly every graduate at Jeanie Elder's house near the high school. The Elder's English Tudor home sat on a hill surrounded by large trees through which you could barely see the castle like stone turret that resembled the tower where the Miller's daughter in *Rumpelstiltskin* remained captive for three days to spin gold or lose her life. With neighbors far off, the band played loudly in the well-appointed courtyard where everyone danced and drank all night long.

At the end of our senior year, my year-book picture included a caption saying I was considered a talented writer, but the only claim to fame I remember was being voted best dancer. Graduation was the milestone that forced us all to make our first choices for the future. To be college bound was now becoming a reality no one was quite ready for.

English

"People interest me."

S. ALAN CHESLER

English.
Union College, AB., Seton
Hall University, MA.
Folio Advisor.

DAVID E. PALMER

Dave . . . his records will bring
fame to Watchung Hills . . .
digs the Rolling Stones . . .
participant in life . . . "Sarcasm
is the weapon of the weak" . . .
Baseball 1; Track 3; Chorus 1;
Folio 3, 4, Co-editor 3; GLC
1, 4 Ex. VP 1 . . . College.

Mr. Chesler: Folio newspaper advisor and Freshman year English teacher to Kathy, Rick and Dave who all were Folio contributors. Used with permission by WHRHS

Dave Palmer: 1965 Graduation / *Lenape* yearbook picture and caption. Used with permission by WHRHS

Kathy . . . talented writer . . .
England can have the Rolling
Stones . . . great dancer . . .
anyone for a party? . . . "Finki-
doo" . . . GLC 2, 4 Secretary 2;
Drama Club 3, 4; GAA 1; JSC;
SSC; *Folio* 3, 4; *Lenape* 4 . . .
College.

I hate signing
yearbooks

RICHARD H. PHILP JR.

Rick . . . likes guitars, drums, and
Ernest Heming___ . . . avoids
madras and s___ socks . . .
"It's lovely" . . . Drama 3, 4;
Folio 3, 4; A___head 4; SSC
Capt.; Orientati___ Chairman 2;
JSC; Saints 2, 3 . . . College.

Kathy and Rick H.S. graduation 1965 *Lenape* Yearbook pictures and captions.
Used with permission by WHRHS

KING BEES CHANGE NAME

the myddle class

The King Bees, five 18-year-old musicians from New Jersey's Passaic "filter suburbia, have been forced by circumstance to change the name of their group. From now on, they'll be known as The Myddle Class.

Heralded by their fans as the most exciting new group since the advent of The Rolling Stones, The Myddle Class had to give up the name they were born with because it conflicted with that of another group, The King B's.

"The other King B's released their record before Myddle Class did," said manager Alfred G. Aronowitz. "It's as simple as that. Now we have letters and phone calls congratulating us on our record, and it isn't even ours. Various people are calling the King Bee name throughout Long Island and New Jersey and the other King B's are cashing in on it. If you hear a King B record on the radio, it's not ours. We're now The Myddle Class."

FANS TO PICKET FOR SCOTT ROSS

Scott Ross, Long Island's No. 1 disc jockey, has been fired from WBIC, and his fans are planning to picket the station in a demand for his return to the air. WBIC has its studios in Bayshore, N.Y.

No reason was given by the station in its dismissal of Ross, but there were reports that the station management was annoyed with the type of records he played.

"Scottie was too far out for them," commented one friend. "He liked the Rolling Stones, Bob Dylan, the Myddle Class and all those people that reflect the modern trend in pop.

Any way you look at it, it's Scott Ross

Fan Club Organized

A National Myddle Class Fan Club is being organized. The national club will use the funds to promote records that reflect the modern trend in pop.

Local chapters and the national club is being organized in Berkeley Heights, N.J.

the myddle class

FIRST CONCERT DEC. 11TH

With its first record, "Free as the Wind," already on its way toward becoming a nationwide hit, The Myddle Class will launch a series of coast-to-coast concerts on Dec. 11 with a performance in the Summit High School auditorium.

Tickets will cost $2.50 each. The concert will begin at 8 p.m.

Also appearing on the program will be two other groups, the Velvet Underground and the Forty Fingers, both of whom will soon have records on the market.

Emcee of the show will be Scott Ross, the Long Island DJ who first played the Myddle Class records on the air when the group was known as the King Bees.

"Free as the Wind" was released last week to radio stations across the country and the record has been acclaimed by disc jockeys as a sure shot. "Gates of Eden," by Bob Dylan, is on the flip side.

Orders already are pouring in to Atco, a division of Atlantic Records, which is distributing the Myddle Class record on the new Tomorrow label.

Aronowitz, the city of Summit was chosen as the location for the inaugural concert of The Myddle Class because, "This is where we grew up, this is where we live, this is our home. Summit is the geographic center of all the original Myddle Class fans.

"If we play for anybody, we've got to play for our own people first."

The last performance of the group was at the Football-Soccer Dance of Pingry School, Hillside, last Nov. 20, with Scott Ross also present. It was his

26th birthday and he celebrated it at a party thrown by The Myddle Class.

If you are or want to be a Myddle Class fan, you can do your share by helping publicize the concert. Simply post the reverse side of this newsletter on the bulletin board of your classroom.

If you wish to sell tickets for the concert to your school, write to The Myddle Class Fan Club at its new address, Post Office Box 221, Berkeley Heights, N.J. Make sure to include your name, address, age and telephone number.

THE MYDDLE CLASS CO-OWNED PINGRY SCHOOL AT DANCE

the myddle class

IN CONCERT

Summit High School Auditorium
125 Kent Place Blvd. Summit, N.J.

8 p.m. December 11, 1965   Admission: $2.50

The Velvet Underground

The Forty Fingers

the myddle class

FIRST RECORD RELEASE !

★★★★

FREE AS THE WIND
(Screen Gems-Columbia, BMI)
GATES OF EDEN (Witmark, ASCAP)
THE MYDDLE CLASS—Tomorrow 7501.
Arresting arrangement, song and new group should shoot the Myddle Class up charts.

Left to Right: Myddle Class Newsletter No.1—p.1;No.1p.2; Myddle Class release of "Free As The Wind" review by Record World magazine—1965;Myddle Class Newsletter No.2; Myddle Class Newsletter No.3 p.1; No.3p2.

Left to Right: (Top) The Myddle Class Newsletter No.1—name change; —fans picket for Scott Ross; (Middle) The Myddle Class Newsletter No.2—first record release of "Free as the Wind"; Newsletter No.3—First Concert announcement; (Bottom) rating of "Free as the Wind" by Record World magazine—1965; Newsletter promotion—The Myddle Class in concert December 11th with the opening acts, The Velvet Underground and Forty Fingers.

Book Two: I Would Lay Down My Heart

Chapter Five

SUMMER IN THE CITY—1965

Off To College

THE KING BEES spent the summer of 1965 almost constantly in New York City. The City was about an hour's ride from where we lived in Jersey, and I knew the route across Highway 22, over the Route 1 and 9 Pulaski Skyway to the Holland Tunnel to downtown like the back of my hand. Most nights I made the trip that summer the band was playing clubs in Greenwich Village, going between the Café Wha? and the Café

Bizarre. Later they would gravitate to the Café Au Go Go* and ultimately, the Night Owl Cafe.

Bleecker, MacDougal, and West Third streets were always packed with young kids moving from club to club to catch the bands that stacked their performances three and four deep for forty-five minute sets that would go from 8:00 p.m. to 2:00 a.m. or later. Sometimes a group was popular enough that they would play at 9:00 p.m. and come back at midnight. Fans would get in to at least one set and were lucky to be allowed to stay to hear a second group before being made to give up the precious few tables to the line of new patrons that piled up outside, ready with their cash to lay out to not only pay to get in but pay for the required two-drink-minimum cover that funded the groups' minimal pay per night for four or five musicians.

As we left to walk the streets in between sets, thinking it was a chance to get out for fresh air away from the dark, smoke-filled rooms, the street lights were blinding

---

* See the picture (used by permission) showing a promo poster billing The Myddle Class at the Café Au Go Go with the Blues Project, Richie Havens (weekly regulars) and the Seventh Sons with Buzz Lenhart circa 1966. The Cafe au Go Go was located at 152 Bleecker Street. Between its opening in 1964 until closing in October 1969, the club featured early performances of the Grateful Dead, Jimi Hendrix, Van Morrison, Tim Hardin, Tim Buckley, Joni Mitchell, Judy Collins, Muddy Waters, John Lee Hooker, the Youngbloods, John Hammond, Jr., The Paul Butterfield Blues Band, Michael Bloomfield, Jefferson Airplane, Cream, The Chambers Brothers, Canned Heat and The Fugs when the group included Charlie Larkey. The Au Go Go was originally owned by Howard Solomon, who was once arrested along with Lenny Bruce for Bruce's obscenities in his comedy act. (Wikipedia, Cafe Au Go Go 2010)

for a minute, and the outside speaker noise on the streets was as loud as the indoor amped sounds we just came from. The air was thick with humidity, and the number of people in the way of getting where you wanted to go was annoying. With two hours between sets, we often stepped inside a couple of clubs to catch other acts. Then you could find Jose Feliciano and Richie Havens* playing to small crowds, passing a hat to make their bread for the night. In spite of the frustration this hot town could present, it was New York City in all its glamour and raining with all the excitement of music everywhere.

If we weren't in the Village, the guys were in an uptown recording studio where Carole and Gerry planned to cut their teeth on producing a first record with the band. Most sessions were booked at the Dick Charles recording studio to start at no earlier than 10:00 p.m., which was the cheap time. I would attend many of the sessions to observe the process of creating the demo of "Free as the Wind"—planned as the band's first release on the new Tomorrow record label started by Carole and Gerry.

Carole and Gerry basically revised an early original song written by Dave and Rick to make it more commercial. I remember Rick always thinking it might not do very well because it neither really represented them as the group they had become nor for the music they really liked to perform.

---

* Richie Havens played songs he would make famous years later opening the famous Woodstock Music and Art Fair (Woodstock Festival) on August 15, 1969 when he performed for three hours filling in for other artists delayed in arrival. (Wikipedia, Richie Havens 2010)

One night, Gerry spent over two hours just trying to get the drum sound he wanted. Myke would play and replay the same drum solo over and over and over again until Gerry would say, "OK, let's move on." Then it was Dave's turn to sing the first verse of the song, and when it wasn't what Gerry wanted to hear, Dave would start over, and the guitars and organ would need to repeat and repeat their parts in the introduction until they couldn't take it anymore. They would take breaks and get more coffee, and this would go on for session after session. Finally, one night, the song reached a point where Gerry was pretty satisfied with the sound and Dave's performance altogether, and the song was mixed and cut.

Sometimes I would drive into the city twice a day to spend time with Rick just wandering around and then again to go to an all-night session. One night, we didn't leave the recording studio until morning. It was never the next day until the sun was up. I remember driving home and getting into the house as my father was leaving for work, which meant it was about 6:00 a.m. I stood in the bathroom doorway to talk with my dad while he finished shaving. Then we went to the kitchen, and I proceeded to tell him about the previous night while he made himself some breakfast. He never said a word about being concerned that I was out all night. He never seemed to mind that I was hanging out in New York. He always trusted me and Rick, and he appeared to understand that this was what came with the boyfriend who was in a band.

I had quickly started a close friendship with Carole. My parents met Carole and Gerry and their daughters. One day, near the end of the summer Carole brought the girls to my house for my mother to babysit the three-year-old and five-year-old sisters. I remember Louise and Sherry sitting down in front of the color TV we had in our family room to watch *The Wizard of Oz*. Gerry came by with the new, kelly green, 1966 Buick Riviera he had just bought. I always felt that my parents were good with the crazy summer we were having. They never told me they didn't approve. I was supposed to be planning to go away to college in the fall, but we didn't talk much about that either.

During this summer, Al Aronowitz managed to book the band into steadily playing weekends in the Village alternating at the Café Bizarre and the Café Wha? on MacDougal Street. The (original) Café Wha? was known for being the place where

> various musicians and comedians—Bob Dylan, Jimi Hendrix, Bruce Springsteen, The Velvet Underground, Kool and the Gang, Peter, Paul & Mary, Woody Allen, Lenny Bruce, Joan Rivers, Bill Cosby, Richard Pryor, and many others all began their careers.[*]

---

[*] The New York magazine "Night Life Profile" reports that while the Cafe Wha? official Web site claims the current location to be the birthplace of legends like Jimi Hendrix and Bob Dylan, the truth is that they actually got their starts at the original location next door. Manny Roth, owner of the original Cafe Wha? and uncle to David Lee Roth, sold the bar in1988. The original Cafe Wha? is now a comedy club [Comedy Cellar]. Cafe Wha? is located at 115 MacDougal Street, between Bleecker and West 3rd Streets and is about two blocks from Washington Square Park. (Wikipedia, Cafe Wha? 2010)

One night, while the group was playing in the Village, the guys met Danny Kortchmar. Danny went by the nickname "Kootch." Danny was seeing the popularity of the King Bees in the New York area and he came to tell the guys that he had a group also with the name King Bees that had already released a record. Their song was getting some air play on New York radio mostly because a band member's dad was a DJ. Although not particularly successful, Danny's band was the one out there with the name and a record, causing the New Jersey King Bees to soon become known as The Myddle Class—a name intended to reflect their roots with an old English spelling to have them appear as cool as a British group.

It is said, we all make our own hell. The group was feeling very good about the contracts they planned to sign with Carole and Gerry's new record label, Tomorrow. Al decided to throw a party at a friend's summer home on Fire Island one Friday night. The entire group, along with Carole and Gerry, was to go out there to talk about recording and promoting the band and to just have some fun. I had to work the weekend waitressing, so I did not go.

When everyone returned to New Jersey on Saturday, I met Rick at his house after work around 9:00 p.m., and we just sat in my car to talk. He was a nervous wreck. He started telling me about the night on Fire Island. What he described was a disaster. It was assumed that Al slipped Gerry LSD, and Gerry was tripping so badly he was taken to a hospital. That wasn't all. In the midst of the entire trauma while Gerry was freaking out on a powerful hallucinogen, Carole was demonstrating an attraction to Charlie by singling him out for her needed solace during a scary experience. This added more drama for everyone to deal with on top of Gerry scaring the shit out of all of them.

Rick was beside himself. He figured that was the end of it all. How could they survive this and have any kind of professional relationship with Carole with or without Gerry recovering from a psych-ward hospitalization? This could not be a good thing; it could only spoil the group's opportunities for Gerry to be taken seriously by the connections they had hoped would shop their recordings. Now as individuals this group had crossed over the line of professional relationships and had become entwined in the personal liberties of these people who might lead their future. At least that was our perspective. We were probably the only two who thought a professional relationship was all that was needed. Little did we know then how commonplace the web of partner sharing and wife swapping would become for many among this circle of friends in later years.

As we approached the end of the summer of '65, The Myddle Class was primed for their newfound road to stardom. Al Aronowitz, Carole, and Gerry and all the shit that surrounded getting contracts formulated to move along a record release were dragging agonizingly slowly. Gerry Goffin was seeing a shrink between his bouts with depression and residual hallucinations and the guys were getting anxious and nervous at the same time. They were seeing their popularity rise to the point of fantasizing laughing all the way from the stages to the banks. However, the reality of their urgent situation was that, at least for Rick and Dave, in the wings were the parental expectations for them to travel the roads to their respective college educations.

Chapter Six:

DON'T FORGET ABOUT ME

Sitting Out That First Year (1965-1966)

I STAYED OUT of school that first year (1965-1966) because I needed to work to save money to pay for college. My dad was raising five children on a good salary for those days, but there was no savings account or long-laid plans for college expenses. So I was headed to a job for the time being. Ultimately, I started college the next year, and I earned half the expenses, and my dad scrounged up the other half for the next four years. Money was scarce, but the cost was relatively low. That is, you could actually work your way through or save enough in a short amount of time to pay for college. Today, not so much.

Dave Palmer followed Brenda Smith to college in eastern Pennsylvania, which led to a future irony. In their first year there they met two classmates, Sue and Peter, who were a couple. In short order, Dave was dating Sue, and Doc had lost out to Brenda dating Peter, who she would later marry.

Rick was heading off to Gettysburg College. His grandfather had gone to Gettysburg, and it was naturally expected that Rick would go there, get a great education, and come away with a bright future in the business world. That, as it turned out, was a major conflict in Rick's self-schema. While he wanted deep down to meet his father's expectation of him completing college, the turn of events that could very well lead to a recording contract for The Myddle Class was tugging him toward his passion for playing the guitar and, maybe, just maybe, making a success of it. Soon it was September.

Once Rick first left New Jersey for Gettysburg, I sometimes went to a pay phone at the Millington train station to call him at school. I would make the call, talk for nearly an hour, tolerating the cool breeze blowing through the crisp leaves falling from the trees. When the operator called back for me to deposit coins to pay for the call, I would drive off from the desolate location, leaving the phone ringing in the fall darkness. One night on the phone, I told Rick I was having a problem with my vision, and I had gone to see my ophthalmologist. I told him I was seeing halos around everything I looked at.

I had been working two jobs—my day work editing user manuals for an electronics company and still waitressing a couple of weekdays and weekend nights at the restaurant where I had worked during school and the summer. As would be my luck, I was getting run down. When I visited my eye doctor, I learned I had developed dendritic ulcers on the cornea of my eye (a likeness to sores from sun poisoning I once had or the fever blisters I would get on my lip when I was catching a cold). What made this a real threat was that I only had vision in one eye, and this was the eye infected with the ulcers. My doctor treated me with a series of massive-dosed smallpox vaccinations and used a cornea scrapping method to try to fight the virus in my body. This left me for a couple of days with a patch over my only good eye, but it got me out of work for awhile.

In our long phone conversation that night, Rick told me, "Baby, you gotta take care of yourself . . . God! I miss you, and I want you to be happy and healthy . . . when I do get home . . . I hope you realize how much . . . I mean if anything ever happened to you . . . well . . . please, just take care of yourself."

He changed the subject to tell me all about how excited he was to receive bids to pledge three fraternities: Phi Kappa Psi (Phi Psi), Alpha Tau Omega (ATO), and Tau Kappa Epsilon (TKE) and how much of an honor that was because typically only one frat would pursue a freshman.

In a matter of weeks, he was already popular on campus. Rick pledged TKE for its being known to be one of the few fraternities that never had a discrimination clause in its membership requirements to prevent acceptance of men because of their race, color, or creed. TKE is where Rick made friends with a fellow musician,

Jim, one of few black kids at Gettysburg and Alex Kaye, a very cool upperclassman.

Rick and I wrote each other frequent letters during that one semester he spent at Gettysburg. By mid-September I received his first letter to me. It was written on his roommate's Gettysburg College stationery. He wrote about how, when all the guys wanted him to join them going into town to celebrate the frat bids, he told them he needed to study; instead, he was writing me, and he wrote, "Clever, huh?" When Rick didn't plan to take any date to a big football-weekend frat party, Alex Kaye was the one who understood Rick's plans to stay loyal to his girlfriend back home. When other brothers would give Rick some grief about not wanting to meet girls in the sister sorority, Alex told him, "That's all right, Rick, if you have a girl back home, and you like her . . . don't screw around."

He ended his first letter, telling me the following:

> Keep writin' baby; just scribble on the paper
> if you have nothing to say . . . just as long
> as . . . With all my . . . Rick.

I had to read between the lines. I guess I didn't think at the time how actually difficult it was for Rick to put in black and white the word "love." I just knew what he wanted to say. With or without making a commitment, at least at this stage of our relationship, he planned to be faithful.

What made us so bold as to make sure we told a boyfriend or girlfriend who was miles away that while we were trying to enjoy college life as a free-spirited, young-blooded teenager, we were being faithful and expected the same in return? Did he think I needed to know that so that I would not give up on him? Did he need the sense of security of a girlfriend he could come home to in case this new environment—college—might never materialize any alternative? Or was he genuinely not interested in looking beyond the bond we had formed? At the time, I didn't even know to ask myself these questions; it was just nice to be needed like that. So I tried to keep letters to Rick flowing so that when he went to the mailbox every day, more often than not, a letter from me would be there. I expected the same in return, and for the most part, he was a pretty frequent letter writer.

Rick and I wrote back and forth about every other week during that one semester he spent at college. In his second letter to me, he described how he was discovering the Student Union Building as the place where kids hung out during the precious time when they did not have to study and where he was going to be a DJ on the school's radio station.

He followed this with an explanation that was supposed to ease my mind, telling me that he had formed a jazz group with his new friend Jim and that they played at a sister sorority party, saying:

> I played piano most of the night. What I'm
> trying to say mainly is that I'm keeping out
> of trouble. Nobody can quite understand

it when I say that I have no intention of getting a date for this big weekend. I miss you, naturally . . . I can't wait to get home. Love ya', Rick.

There, he said it, the words "love ya" were finally in writing, and I was thrilled.

Rick had a younger sister, Bonnie, who was less than two years younger than us and still in high school. She had cute looks with a bubbly, witty personality, which often came across in her own funny sarcasm about her struggle with her weight and how she would always look twelve years old. Bonnie had a crush on Charlie and truly thought that she could compete for his affection with all the girls that threw themselves at him for his attention. When she didn't get anywhere with that, she turned to the friendship Mike sometimes offered her and would misinterpret it for a fondness defined by her own visions. As Rick's sister, it was easy to feel involved in the lives of the group, but the reality of their world was very different than her conjured fantasies.

In October, Rick wrote again to say:

> Hi dear, . . . Say . . . it have been many sittings of sun since I got-um letter from paleface girlfriend . . . . Oh . . . I went into town yesterday and some little ol' lady cleaned my bracelet for free. It looks great . . . hope it stays that way for a while. Hey . . . just got-um letter from paleface girlfriend . . . also groovy

guitar strings . . . Squaw really on the ball . . .
got a French lab, baby . . . take it easy . . . Love
ya' as always, Rick.

Rick said he was concerned about my telling him
that Bonnie and I had gone to a party with band friends
including a girl Karen who had a crush on Myke. Rick
told me how upset Myke was that Karen followed
him around, emphasizing that he wished his sister
wouldn't get involved in all that nonsense because he
felt she would get hurt. Knowing she would not listen
to his advice, Rick wanted me to tell her to stay away
from these girls who wanted to get close to the band
members.

What made Rick think I could influence Bonnie
or that I would want to throw water on the fire in
her heart to feel close to the band? She had as much
a right as anyone to pursue her own infatuation with
these guys; after all, every girl her age felt she could
become attractive to any one of them if they gave her
half a chance—so why not Bonnie? The guys were
like family—she should feel entitled to access to them
more than anyone. It is a brutal reality knowing that the
way you see yourself may not be at all the way others
see you. I couldn't spoil another young girl's beliefs in
a chance to have some kind of emotional connection
with one of these boys, although it was a far-fetched
illusion. I could understand the desires, and why not
let it play out? It would soon fade without anything
needing to be said.

Rick's next note to me was sent in a cute card asking me to come to Gettysburg for a big fraternity weekend; he wrote:

> How y' doin' Baby . . . It was great talking to you nite before last . . . I'm glad you called. IFC weekend starts Fri Oct. 22. It's quite a big deal actually . . . you have to get off [work] for that weekend . . . Bonnie called me last night . . . she was a riot . . . I'm beginning to think everything you said about her was right! . . . Love ya', Rick.

I was so excited over being invited to make my first visit to see Rick at school that I couldn't sleep that entire night. The next day, I immediately made my plans to get to Gettysburg for the big IFC weekend. Being invited by my boyfriend to attend a major college fraternity party was packed with thrilling promises and huge anxiety. In high school, the only lovemaking kids did was in a car. This weekend would mark the first opportunity for Rick and me to stay behind closed doors together as a couple. Rick had become close friends with his upperclassman fraternity brother Alex Kaye. Alex lived in an apartment off campus, and we were going to stay at Alex's for the weekend. So I needed to think about all that came along with agreeing to spend two nights alone with the love of my life.

I went shopping for new outfits to wear along with something to wear to bed. I was in no way ready to sleep with nothing on. I made plans for a ride to Port Authority to get the bus to Gettysburg. Rick borrowed his friend's car to pick me up in town. He proudly showed me all around Gettysburg and the school campus when we finally arrived early that evening of Friday, October 22, 1965. We eventually went to his friend's apartment, and I met Alex Kaye for the first time. Alex was a good-looking, high-spirited, funny guy who I liked right away.

We all went out to get a bite to eat until it was time to go to the fraternity dance. It was held in a school auditorium with a stage and an open dance floor. The band that was to open for the celebrity act, the Isley Brothers, was a local group that Rick considered to be really good. We had some beers and were enjoying the show. It was time for the main event, and the Isley Brothers came out on the stage. They were great performing their hits—especially "Twist and Shout." What caught our attention was this guy in the band who started playing the guitar with his teeth and behind his head. The guitarist turned out to be Jimi Hendrix. Of course, Rick was so impressed with this guy, he had to go backstage and meet him. So during an intermission, he did exactly that. I stayed out on the dance floor and listened to a second performance by the frat band that opened the show. Neither Rick nor I knew then who he had just met, but that was a night to remember in more ways than one.

* * *

Rick's next letter included several pages his grandmother sent him from a Reader's Digest article: "Going

Steady—Who Needs It?" It was advice from Ann Landers as she made reference to a cartoon picture of a teenage couple with the girl showing a very bulging middle, saying, "Henry, I think you and I will have to start going a whole lot steadier." Ms. Landers was well known for giving her opinion in answers to inquisitive letters she often received about love and marriage. Her comments in this article suggested that "going steady" gave young teenagers a false feeling of security and the worst thing that could come of it was that, out of making a habit of being each other's only partner, young people got married. Her final advice offered to people who were so unattractive and dreary that it was amazing even one person would go with them was consenting—suggesting, by all means—"go steady".

Did Rick's grandmother know I was going to visit him at school? Did she remember what it was like to spend a college weekend with a boyfriend? She was a grandmother, but her curiosity was right on the money. Rick and I had gotten pretty close all throughout the previous year in high school, but did we just cross the line into going steady? Were we ready to make this commitment to each other now that we agreed to consummate our relationship? If we didn't know, we needed to figure it out.

Later in October, Rick wrote:

> Hi hon, It's really raining like a bitch down here . . . God, I just figured it out . . . I hate this place . . . I really do . . . . I called Al last night and come to find out he's screwing

around as usual . . . . [I wish] we could get that damn record out . . . . Well . . . I love you and miss you very much . . . . Cheerfully yours, Rick

Al was stalling the signing of the recording contracts with Carole and Gerry because he was told, if he encouraged the guys to leave college, he was facing a lawsuit for essentially contributing to the delinquency of minors. Rick described how the contracts were all drawn up, just awaiting signing by the group members, and Rick was getting very upset with Al wanting to have more meetings with the parents, and Carole and Gerry were getting very frustrated with Al dragging his feet. They told Al that Rick was speaking as the leader of the group and that he was willing to sign the contracts, which he was, and Al needed to allow the commitment they all wanted to make.

Al Aronowitz assumed that the glory of a promise of fame came for the asking, but he was not ready for the challenges that came along with the opportunities. Al thought it was enough to be a purist, a believer, a dreamer, and he didn't seem to understand that he was about to be swimming with sharks in this biz. Rick knew that Al didn't have much business sense, but he also recognized that Al was well connected to people in the profession that could help them. However, more often than not, Al's lack of concern for the business protocol caused more harm than good. He hesitated when he needed to act, and acted, sometimes foolishly, when he needed to patiently hesitate. For example, under Al's haphazard tutelage, having never registered the band's name for copyright protection while their first record was about to be contracted for release, the King Bees had to relent to the other New York area band who legally claimed the name when their record hit the market first. Thus, the name The Myddle Class was adopted, although reluctantly, and Al was excused.

When Al chose to overcompensate for this loss and hastily tried to single-handedly get into the distribution business, he ordered several thousand copies of that first Myddle Class release, "Free as the Wind," from the record label at a cost to be charged against future royalties, only to simply give them away to fans at events, leaving the coffers empty of any revenue.

Al did all his network building on handshakes and with a sense of arrogance thinking "How would anyone dare give these talented guys a hard time?" Back then, deals in this business that were made on a basis of faith and trust had the potential to wind up resembling warfare. It wasn't until later that there were tightened rules to the game that defined the legitimate money-making propositions of honored contracts and rightly paid royalties.

Rick was trying to be patient with the looming fate of his ambitions to play music while he was feeling stifled by his conflicting obligation to stay in school. However, that conflict was about to resolve itself. Rick and Dave both were planting their feet deeply into walking away from their respective colleges, where they were decisively unhappy, to take the plunge into the abyss of unknown passages toward proving themselves worthy of the musical reputations that preceded them.

Chapter Seven

YOU'VE GOT A FRIEND

And I Love You

I HAD TO earn and save the most money I could in order to help pay for my start at college, which I had planned to be in the fall of 1966. I continued working the two jobs. I was getting myself sick again. Before I knew it, from my one good eye, again I was seeing the halo rings around everything.

I made a return visit to see my ophthalmologist. After an exam, he told me the dendritic ulcers had returned. He put me in the hospital to scrap the cornea again, but this time, while I was being tested for a better diagnosis, they found that I had an unrelated bone growth in a sinus cavity, and this needed to be removed surgically. So now I was in a hospital room with a patch over the only eye I could see out of, and nurses didn't understand why I could not feed myself. I would try, but I couldn't get a spoonful of food from the plate to my mouth. I was very frustrated, and I was getting pretty sad. In fact, the doctors told my parents that I was having the problem with my eye because I was rundown and depressed. What the hell would depression have to do with the dendrites of my eye?

Carole came to see me in the hospital at the Saint Barnabas Medical Center. It was in Livingston, which was very near West Orange where she lived. Carole brought me a Panasonic portable clock radio as a gift. She knew that if I could not read, I would at least pass the time listening to the radio. It was pretty cool.

I always had light perception in the eye that wasn't covered—I just couldn't make out images due to scar tissue on the retina, which caused the blindness (from whooping cough as a three-month-old baby). I remember one night feeling my way along the walls of the hospital hallway and finding the pay phone to call Rick. I could feel the numbers on the rotary dial, so I was able to make the call. This just frustrated the nurses who didn't believe me when I said I couldn't feed myself.

In our conversation, Rick told me Carole had called and told him that I would soon be going home. He thought he didn't' have to worry too much anymore, but he had already written me a letter to say:

> I swear I just can't take stuff like that . . . strong I'm not. God, baby . . . it's such a helpless feeling knowing that you are miserable and I can't do anything for you . . . . I'm sorry . . .

> OK . . . I'll stop . . . . I love you! I just thought
> you'd like to know that.

With that, I felt one-hundred percent better. This was one of the first times Rick seemed vulnerable and particularly so where it came to expressing his feelings for me. I began to feel like he really did care about me not only for what I was going through but also for how my sadness made him sad; that made me feel very loved. I was glad I called.

We continued to write letters to each other late in the semester. Although Rick was trying hard to concentrate on schoolwork, it wasn't easy. Although learning came easy to him and he didn't really have to work hard at studying, he still needed to put forth some effort to get through his classes. As much as he wasn't very motivated by being there, he felt responsible to get good grades, and it upset him to not be making the best he should of the opportunity for a great education.

In November Rick wrote, saying, "I haven't done anything in the last two days." He had received a call from Dave saying he was running away from school and was on his way to Gettysburg. Rick couldn't believe it. He wrote me, saying,

> So often I considered doing the same . . .
> but, I think ahead too much . . . . I want to
> get out of here . . . but I couldn't go within
> 50 miles of home . . . therefore I wouldn't
> see you, which is the only reason I hang on.

All the guys traveled to Gettysburg to see Rick and
Dave. That, in and of itself, caused quite a stir on that
school's campus. They were all going to run away; they
talked about going to Chicago. Maybe that seemed just
far away enough to be a manageable car ride and a place
they could get back from easily; after all, it wasn't all
the way across the country, and it might not take much
money, which none of them had.

> I'll tell you honey, I really wanted to leave
> with those guys, but I guess I've always been
> the sensible one . . . . I may be passing up an
> opportunity to do exactly what I want.

Rick was much too practical to believe that quitting was
a good idea.

> Something just wasn't right . . . yet, in a way . . .
> if we are going to try to make it playing, we
> shouldn't be kidding ourselves—we should
> be playing.

He had received a letter from Carole saying she was
surprised he was going to stay at school until the end of
the semester; she wanted him to get back to playing and
recording sooner.

Rick considered all that he would be leaving behind
at Gettysburg—the school his grandfather had revisited
with him, appearing to be enchanted by the thought
that his grandson was repeating in his footsteps. He

considered his sister, Bonnie, and his brother, Steve, and then he thought of us.

> The big problem is . . . where do we fit into this mess? . . . if I actually did run away I'd probably see you less than I do now . . . perish the thought . . . well, that's the title for another discussion. I love you and "I Can't Make It Alone" . . . so . . . Take care, Rick.

The reference to "I Can't Make It Alone" was an innuendo for me to think of the song The Myddle Class had been recording for Carole and Gerry. It was a torchy apology from a lonely guy repenting over a decision to leave his lover, admitting that he was happy before he left her. The song was intended for the Righteous Brothers as a follow-up to the 1965 hit, "You've Lost That Loving Feeling," but this time, the guy realizes that what he felt in his soul would always bring him back to the one he loved.

As much as Rick felt he might have been letting go this great opportunity to have his ability promoted to a higher level, he always felt there would be another time for his music to be a priority. He had that much confidence in himself. The fact that he was putting his feelings and love for me into the equation was very comforting. It gave me a great sense of security even if it might be fleeting.

Rick came home from Gettysburg as often as possible during his brief four-month stay there. I was happy to spend time with him when he was home, but he was back mostly to fit in playing at some promotional gig the group was expected to perform.

As their first record "Free as the Wind" was about to be released in December 1965, a major concert was planned by Al and the gang for a sold-out crowd at the Summit High School auditorium. There were hundreds of young fans that couldn't get into the show, and it was a tremendous success. Al managed to book as an opening act the Velvet Underground who he had started to manage before they left him to connect with Andy Warhol. This group was known to be one of the most esoteric musical acts getting exposure playing at the Greenwich Village Café Wha? It is said that some of the Underground group members felt they were selling out to perform at a high school gig in the suburbs of New Jersey, but this billing has gone down in the history of The Myddle Class as a real triumph.

Rick needed to see as great number of people in that two-day weekend. I ended up combining my own plans with the craziness of this concert without realizing how big a deal it was and hoping to maintain a sense of priority within Rick's plans for the visit home. I don't know what I was thinking, but I must have reached one of my rare that's-it moments and later decided to let my feelings be known, which I seldom did. I guess I took my paranoia out on Rick and told him I felt like I was being neglected all weekend. I knew I couldn't do much about all the attention other girls were getting from all the guys in the band, including Rick; after all, this was part of the mystique—they all had to appear accessible and available to the fans—whether it was just to give an autograph or perhaps seem attracted to the point that they might want to meet one of these chicks.

After that concert in December 1965, Rick called me to talk about feeling his own frustration with how the concert weekend had created an apparent conflict between us that he felt he needed to apologize for. He said: "This past weekend . . . I know I was wrong sometimes . . . but we both knew that it would be a hectic weekend . . . somehow my plans never quite work out. All I am asking is that you put up with all this nonsense . . . actually, that's a lot to ask . . . I mean . . . I know no other girl would put up with what you already have. Hey . . . you don't have to worry about losing me . . . I want to say . . . I'm sorry."

Rick was trying to make me feel that he understood my frustration with having to share so much of his time while he was home. I wanted to be a big part of the reason for his being there. But the reality of it all was that, on that particular weekend, I was relatively insignificant, but he would never make me feel that way. He did everything he could to make me believe I was just as important to him as the group, his music, and his goals for that particular concert to be a major milestone in his life. How could I have missed the point? How could I have thought that I could compete with that event and all the meaning it presented? Now I was intuitively realizing that I could never hold a candle to this excitement and the promise it held. Without confessing, I was grasping the fact that our love relationship, although vital, was relegated to occupy a level of importance much lower than the one this event held and others like it would likely always hold. However, neither of us wanted to accept that thought.

Near the end of the semester at Gettysburg, before dealing with the anguish he would have to face as he needed to tell his father he was leaving school, Rick called to tell me, "Kath, I talked to my advisor about quitting school, and he was pretty upset . . . he said I am walking away from something because it is distasteful to me . . . and I'll just continue to walk away from things which I get tired of. I hope he is wrong, baby . . . that sort of shook me."

I wanted to reply with a sense of confidence that I knew that would never be anything I should fear. Maybe I was reassuring enough to ease his concerns that he just might one day get tired of me and decide to walk away, but he felt he needed to try to make it certain that he would never treat me with such disdain. It was more upsetting to him than it was to me, and to stop thinking and talking about it, he said, "I'm sorry . . . this is probably upsetting you . . . but if I can't tell you this, who can I tell . . . I love you very much-please remember that. I realize that we both need convincing every once in a while . . . so I guess it's my turn to convince you . . . I miss ya, babe."

These words kept my hopes up. As much as Rick wanted to believe he was making the right decision to leave life as he then knew it to take a new fork in the road to his future, he wasn't ready to tell himself or me that he was letting go of all his senses. He was going to maintain his loyalty to what came before the potential for fame and a whole new way of living; he was determined to make me feel I would always be a part of it—whatever it would become.

Chapter Eight

YOU GO ON

The Myddle Class And Kathy Take Flight

RICK AND DAVE both only lasted in college for the one fall semester of 1965. By January of 1966, they were both back home in New Jersey. Rick accurately knew he could not go to live at home while his father was furious with him, not only for giving up college but also for the fact that he hated the world of music that had engulfed his son's ambitions. So Charlie's parents welcomed Rick to live in their home in Mountainside where he and Charlie shared a room in the basement that was Charlie's personal space.

Dave came home to live with his mom and his aunt, but he didn't come alone. Dave brought home his college girlfriend, Sue, and he vowed to marry her.

Rick needed to work for spending money and to offer a contribution to his living arrangement at the Larkey home. He got a lot of work as a studio musician by networking with Carole and Gerry's colleagues from the Brill Building. I remember Rick telling me how he was invited to play with Neil Diamond on the B-side of what became a huge hit, "Cherry, Cherry." The record was being produced by songwriters Jeff Barry and Ellie Greenwich. Rick thought Neil Diamond was kind of uptight. But I guess at the time, he was just as much hassled with anxiety and doubt as the rest of these newcomers because Neil Diamond has told his own story of the days when he struggled to be a legitimate writer for the music publishers of the famed Broadway mecca before he became one of the earliest to realize that recording his own songs was the best way out from the jaws of the old-timers who only really wanted to exploit young talent. Diamond describes in the *Vanity Fair* "Hit Factory" article by David Kamp how he needed to pack a pistol when he received threats for bucking the way some artists often were not paid for their work or were forced to put their record arranger/ producer's name on a song as a writing partner in order to cut into the royalties that could be paid for years to come.

Phil Spector was known for this and took co-writer credit for the song "Be My Baby," written by Ellie Greenwich and Jeff Barry, which turned out to be a huge 1963 hit for the Ronettes. Phil Spector later married the lead singer, Veronica, mostly known in the biz as Ronnie

Spector[*]. That may stand as the ultimate marriage from hell as seemingly, by her own admission she was made to tolerate Phil Spector's madness for years after the group fell apart. I recently learned of how Nedra Talley broke from the Ronettes at the height of the group's newfound success when she married Scott Ross, the shock jock DJ who had MC'd The Myddle Class 1965 Summit High School bonanza concert. In the 1960s, as a DJ, Scott Ross became friends with Al Aronowitz. Al introduced Scott to the Beatles, Bob Dylan, Carole and Gerry Goffin, and ultimately, to The Myddle Class.

Scott fell heavily into drugs in the '60s. His self-directed defiance of authorities caused him some pain, which was quickly eased by the influence of acid, pot, and anything else he could digest that allowed him to dismiss the jeopardy he was putting himself into by supporting struggling artists, like The Myddle Class, whom he believed had potential for greatness and deserved all the influence he could rally.

Later Scott Ross was fired from his job at the WBIC radio station on Long Island for self-promoting the unapproved "Free as the Wind" record. Al Aronowitz launched a big campaign in a Myddle Class newsletter to provoke the group's fan base to besiege the radio station with protest hoping for Scott Ross to get his job back, but most outrage fell on deaf ears in those days.

Scott Ross was born in Scotland, where his father was a minister, so as a "PK"—preacher kid—he had been

---

* (Wikipedia, Ronnie Spector 2010)

raised with God in his heart. In his own words, Scott tells the story of how, one day, while tripping on acid, he called upon his God once again, and the hallucinations just stopped. He describes how that experience renewed his faith in God, and from that day on, "[he] never again smoked pot nor ingested another pill."

Nedra tells her personal story of fighting demons when the pioneering girl group hit it big with Phil Spector and the single record release of "Be My Baby," which sold millions of copies, shot the group to the top of the *Billboard* charts in 1963. The group was very popular in 1964 in Britain where the Rolling Stones opened for a concert they performed in London. The Ronettes also toured with the Beatles at the height of their early fame.

Being connected to the Brill Building crowd, Scott actually dated two of the Ronettes before he chose to marry Nedra Talley. After being married, they attended a church service near his mother's home in Hagerstown, Maryland. At this service, Nedra tells of how she heard a calling for her to stand up, and she saw God come before her with a chalkboard and a gesture to erase all her sins. She decided that she needed to give up all the fame and fortune she had derived from her recent musical success for her willingness to have God lead her through her future. Soon thereafter the young married couple departed NYC to move bravely into the heavily prejudiced South, even if as born-again Christians. Nedra and Scott Ross both describe the power of inner strength that the incredible influence of taking God back into their lives has bestowed upon them, and she does not regret a thing.

The couple settled in eastern Virginia where Scott accepted a job as a radio DJ for the station formed by well-known evangelist minister, Pat Robertson, as the Christian Broadcast Network. Scott Ross somewhat jokingly said he wished his wife had stuck with singing for the fame and fortune it likely would have meant, but in fact, she has enjoyed a very different, more satisfying path in her life as a happy wife, mother and grandmother, restaurateur, and business owner.

The couple has remained in the Chesapeake coastal area for their full forty-plus-year marriage enjoying their family of four children and three grandchildren. You can see and hear Nedra and Scott Ross on the *CBN 700 Club* Web site. Nedra was interviewed in 2007 by Pat Robertson as, for being one of the Ronettes, she was inducted into the Rock and Roll Hall of Fame in recognition of the group's musical achievements of the early '60s.

On the same Web site one can watch and listen to a four-part interview of Scott Ross by Craig von Buseck that chronicles Scott's career from the early '60s as a shock jock DJ in New York during the low points of his life influenced heavily by the clenches of drugs and alcohol through the path he followed to redemption. Scott Ross has devoted a prominent career as an enthralling Christian radio (WXRI) and TV talk show host (*Straight Talk*) to challenging the culture he and his wife faced as New Yorkers, and northern liberals at that, living in the "Bible-Belt-Buckle" in the 70s.

Scott tells the story of a time he was ridiculed by his audience when, after Martin Luther King was killed in the aftermath of the social divide that followed the assassinations of John F. Kennedy and Bobby Kennedy, on his radio broadcast, he said, "Let us pray for this man." The near last straw of supporter tolerance came when Scott Ross invited into the studio a group of grubby, vagabond musicians for an on-air interview. This caused donors to the newly renovated fortress of the fledgling CBN ministry to rally before Pat Robertson to demand the return of their monetary contributions. Robertson faithfully supported Ross and his guests during this encounter when he addressed his congregations, saying, "When this building means more than these people, I will personally burn it down to the ground myself."

Scott Ross has continued his contentious journalistic interviews challenging the inner angels and demons of some of society's most celebrated political, religious, and extremist groups and individuals that made news in the '70s and '80s, including Itsak Rabin, prime minister of Israel (over controversial detention and terrorism of his own country's citizens); and the "Son of Sam" serial killer, David Berkowitz, who Scott believed—in spite of his rant of multiple senseless killings in New York City—was forgiven by the God Berkowitz came to believe in. All this was Ross's tribute to his calling to reach out to the "culture he could relate to"—the maturing protagonists of the '60s—now older, with children attempting to bring them the messages of God's omnipotence. The telling histories of Scott and Nedra Ross is the most heartwarming and inspirational story I came across in my research for this book.

* * *

As The Myddle Class traveled in early 1966 outside of the city many times to upstate New York, Philadelphia, and as far as DC and Pittsburgh, they were gaining exposure and popularity. The record "Free as the Wind" with Dylan's "Gates of Eden" on the B-side was being played on WPTR in the Albany market, but it was the second single release of "Don't Let Me Sleep Too Long" with the B-side favorite, "I Happen to Love You," written by Goffin and King, that got its break in Albany, New York, with equal airplay on WTRY in Troy, New York. In February 1966, The Myddle Class was enjoying radio exposure and fan admiration up and down the East Coast. They played an Albany High School gig on the same stage with the Lovin' Spoonful. The group spent a good deal of travel time playing to fans in Albany, Troy, Kingston, Lake George, Glens Falls, New York, and a college campus circuit throughout Pennsylvania.

In spite of this growing reputation for being a great band with a promising future, the needed exposure of airplay on New York City's WABC radio, that which would have really counted, remained elusive. In his own heartfelt declaration of a futile experience managing The Myddle

Class[*], Al Aronowitz affirms by self-admission the ways in which he force-fed copies of "Free as the Wind" to many radio show hosts and how, to no avail, he swarmed the WABC station with fan mail and postcards requesting the record to be played, only to piss off the gatekeepers. Once again, Al's arrogant, self-fulfilling prophecy to fear success as much as failure had prevailed. It seemed safer to Al to not make any money with or for these boys.

By the spring and summer in 1966, Al had propped up The Myddle Class to performing alternating weekly gigs between the Café Au Go Go and the Cafe Bizarre clubs, where they drew consistently large crowds to see and hear the loudest group in Greenwich Village. The Café Au Go Go advertised a steady stream of some of the most notable musicians and bands playing the Village at the time, who went on to broad and long-lasting achievements in the business: Richie Havens, Stephen Stills with Neil Young in tow to join in his original Buffalo Springfield; Muddy Waters, John Lee Hooker, and Al Kooper's Blues Project who even took the singing

---

* The Al Aronowitz Web site, *The Blacklisted Journalist*: Column 83; How I Nearly Made A Million Dollars In The Rock And Roll Business sums up Al's own accounting of his impassioned efforts to manage the anticipated stardom of The Myddle Class. After introducing the five eighteen year olds to Carole King and Gerry Goffin in 1965 as a highly popular local band he found near his home in the New Jersey suburbs, he forged an unrelenting quest to promote the talented group. Al's self-critical exposé tells of his personal high hopes and dreams of acquiring a King's ransom, which tumbled down a path of lost opportunities and an awakening to a yield of little more than noble sacrifices by many.

waitress, Emmaretta Marks[*], on the road with them, settling in San Francisco for several months before returning to the New York scene.

Many of these confident musicians experimented with trial-run group members and allowed various artists to jam with them as commodores, all in the name of mutual respect but mostly to find the one magic formula of talent that could create a winning compound. Many thought they had the right recipe to grab the attention and favor of a new producer under a budding or established label to press an album containing one or two really strong cuts to put the group on the charts and in the public eye. They hoped to attract loyal fans to follow them, not for just a few appearances but for their duration. If they didn't have the right stuff on their first attempt, they would try, try again.

Stephen Stills, always known for his folksy "Bluebird," would form one group after another before settling into

---

* Emmaretta Marks was (along with The Night Owl Cafe waitress, Shelley Plimpton) an original cast member of both the off-Broadway and Broadway productions of *Hair* (musical director, Galt MacDermot). As a member of the "Tribe," Emmaretta, along with Melba Moore and Lorie Davis, played the "The Supremes" singing "White Boys" among other songs in the show. It is Emmaretta's silhouette that covers the poster to advertise the musical for the Biltmore Theatre. A 1969 Playbill for *Hair* can be found on the internet showing autographs of Ms. Marks, Ms. Moore, Ms. Plimpton, with other cast members—Keith Carradine, Geraldine Griffin, Natalie Mosco, Erik Robinson as well as James Rado and Gerome Ragni (writers and lyricists). (Autographed Playbill 2010) Diane Keaton is also listed in the cast as a "waitress. "Emmaretta Marks was also known to travel as a backup singer with The Rolling Stones, Jimi Hendrix, and Ike and Tina Turner. She is also credited as a singer-songwriter member of the group, Mambo Daddy.

his greatest success as part of the soft harmonic electric blues rock sound of Crosby, Stills, Nash, and Young along with releases of several later solo albums (showcasing "Love the One You're With").

The Myddle Class played the Café Au Go Go several weeks in March 1966, sharing the stage with other up-and-comers at the time like Ritchie Havens and the so-called house band, The Blues Project. The Myddle Class became well known for their new recording, "Don't Let Me Sleep Too Long," which was a creative version of an old gospel theme considered in the public domain and to which they had extended composer credit to all the band members, given they were performing the song since their early start in 1965. This song somehow simultaneously was released on the recording of *The Blues Project—Live At The Au Go Go* as a hot rendition they titled, "Wake Me, Shake Me." This time, it was The Myddle Class claiming their version of a song came first.

To settle a dispute to the rights to the song, the popular Myddle Class record was later rereleased on the Buddah Records label, and they granted Al Kooper of the Blues Project with credit for the arrangement. I don't know who called that shot because the distinctive jamming, particularly between the guitars and the organ on this record, featured Rick's purely signature riffs and established his versatility as a guitarist capable of crossing over multiple genres of style. It's been written that this recording marked his excellence as a guitarist who many chose to learn from and mimic.

The record was a hit in and around NYC and particularly in upstate New York. It even made it to number one on a weekly chart of the fifty-thousand-watt radio station WPTR-1540 in Albany, New York, while the Beatles' "Yellow Submarine" was only number four. In spite of the popularity of the A-side of the record, the B-side, a sultry ballad written by Carole and Gerry, "I Happen to Love You," was mostly considered the better cut.

The Café Au Go Go and the Café Bizarre are best known for hosting the early Chicago-style rhythm and blues groups who played heartache riffs turned into rock melodies, and the likes of the Velvet Underground billowing avant-garde lyrics suggesting flirtatious trysts with every conceivable drug. The shortcomings were that these clubs were either off the main drag of Bleecker Street or could not survive without the receipts of liquor by the drink.

The rival Night Owl Cafe gained the most prestige after scoring the main attraction everyone wanted to see and hear in the summer of 1966; the jug-band-turned-pop-rock Lovin' Spoonful with John Sebastian drew the crowds performing their recent big hit "Do You Believe in Magic" and their newest release getting play on the radio, "Summer in the City" which rose to be a number one seller for the group.

The Night Owl must go down as the hottest gig for the many then almost-famous bands that graced that small but hallowed stage, which fronted less than fifty doting fans per set. Those were the days when the audiences couldn't get enough early glimpses of the endless register of young, raw, unsophisticated talent presented by these fearless warriors who simply wanted their music to be appreciated for what it was—evolving from its embryonic stages of development and headed toward pure muscle.

Peter Sando, lead guitarist of Grandolf, was the guitarist of the Rahgoos in the mid-'60s. He recalls the band to see in the place to be was the "Spoonful" at the Night Owl Café. Peter's group later auditioned and got a gig playing at the club. In the following, he aptly describes the venue saying:

> "It was a unique room, a long and narrow storefront. The stage faced straight at a wall in the center with one church pew at the foot (the 'crotch watchers bench'), an aisle, and then another pew against the wall. All the other seating was to the left and right of the stage . . . The music crashed into the wall and died, leaving the vocals bare to the bulk of the crowd to each side. You had better sing on key or else it was a disaster. The waitresses said four letter words we never heard before; . . . the cook was openly gay and the Night Owl served Thanksgiving dinners for all the bands . . . The Mothers of Invention served and we still believed in the magic." (Sando 1997)

Although a tough place to play, the Night Owl was a site of legends[*]. Sando gives props to those he remembers well: James Taylor from The Flying Machine as one who "never stopped getting better," Garry Bonner and Alan Gordon (of the Magicians) who went on to write many hit songs for other pop artists, and to The Myddle Class's Charlie Larkey and Dave Palmer for later working with Carole King and Steely Dan.

During this time, while The Myddle Class played steady gigs downtown, they resumed recording sessions uptown laying down demos with Carole and Gerry who participated when he wasn't in one of his frequent cycles of unbearable sadness. With Gerry in and out of a hospital psych ward, Charlie and Carole had covertly managed a steamy relationship that would wane on-again, and off-again throughout 1966 into 1967 and stayed rocky even after Carole and Gerry split at the end of '67, and each left to live separately in Los Angeles in early 1968.

So if the summer of 1966 was thrusting The Myddle Class into orbit, and we had survived the air pockets of leaving school, tumultuous contracts, name changes,

---

[*] Peter Sando lists some of the bands of The Night Owl Cafe (not in any particular order): Tim Hardin, Felix Pappalardi, John Sebastian and the Lovin' Spoonful, the Magicians, The Myddle Class, James Taylor and the Flying Machine, the Blues Magoos, Tim Buckley, Richie Havens, Cat Mother and the All Night Newsboys, the Rahgoos (Gandalf), Jimi Hendrix, the Overland Express. Peter Sando perfoms as a currently active member of the group Gandolf. His blog can be found on the Web at www.petersando.com

records, road trips and hobnobbing with potential celebrities; now it was time for the fist-clenching turbulence that was yet to come. With The Myddle Class trying to make it in this crazy business, Rick and I would have to survive all the swapping of friends and lovers that came with the territory and a new round of separation that we faced with my first effort at attending college. By the end of the summer of 1966, we once again were dealt the challenges that time and distance between our everyday lives presented to our loyalty to one another.

Rick thought of the meaning he held for the ID bracelet I had given to him before he left for college, which he faithfully wore every day, and he decided it was his turn to offer a token of assurance of his vow of dedication. For my nineteenth birthday in September of 1966, just before I left for school, Rick bought me a gold, pinky signet ring that had my initials engraved on top in old English script. I have never gone a day in the past forty-plus years without wearing that ring on my left hand. I remember the day he gave it to me like it was yesterday. It marked a promise that I would always keep a pledge of my love for him in my grasp.

* * *

September came quickly that year, and I was headed for Virginia—yes, there were parts of the United States south of Philadelphia, Pennsylvania—always considered godforsaken country to all my NYC buddies. It was actually an eight-and-a-half-hour car ride, which I always referred to as the point of fatigue. My parents drove me to my school, and as I remember it, they didn't even get out of the car. They did not have the money to stay in a motel for a night—especially somewhere with nothing to do—so they just dropped me off in the middle of this campus I had never seen before, and there I was, a college freshman.

The first night of my arrival, there was a mixer, which was a gathering of the new kids to meet the upperclassmen. There was a band, so anyone who didn't have much to say could just stand around with a cup of beer and not mix much at all. But I had made friends with my new roommate, and we ventured out to the party. She was what they called a townie—she lived in a dorm, but her home was just miles away, and she left campus every weekend. I made good friends with some sophomores who shared rooms near mine, and I was better off for that socially. At this party, on the first weekend away from home, my new friend and I went outside to get some fresh air (it was still very hot in the south even in September), and we met a couple of guys who were also townies, but they were funny, polite, and nicely dressed. I always had a tolerance level to try to get to know a person before just writing them off. The really funny one was a guy named Rick. OMG! Did I need a Rick in Virginia and a Rick in New Jersey? As it turned out, I started to go out with southern Rick, but he always knew I had a boyfriend, Rick, at home.

When I started at school, Rick wrote me letters every other week.

In his first letter he told me:

> It's only been a week. Well . . . I miss you
> a little more than I expected to [although]
> I anticipated some amount of regret that
> you're so far away, (once again!) . . . I'll never
> finish this . . . Charlie says hello by the way.

They had just returned from a pretty tiring two days in
Allentown after playing a dance at a firehouse and a new
supermarket, which Rick described as getting his vote for
the draggiest jobs ever. He told me it was pretty exciting
to get a letter from me and nice to have it waiting there
when he got home. He continued to say the following:

> I have just told you that I miss you . . .
> Someone must have a list of my faults around
> somewhere and near the top is the fact that I
> take things for granted . . . fail to appreciate
> things when I have them. I always knew
> that you were about ten minutes away if I
> needed you . . . . Somewhat selfish though, I
> wanted an amount of freedom and you when
> I wanted you . . .

Being far away and a bit depressed, confined to a place
and people both very different from those from which I
had come, these words were like music to my ears. I didn't
go away to prove any point or to test whether Rick would
realize how much he would miss me when I wasn't right

there anytime he wanted me. I had to take this opportunity
to map out a plan of my own. I truly believed our love
could survive another round of separation just as I had
endured Rick's time at Gettysburg. So many of my friends
were enduring the tests of time and distance, and I felt
it was just another road bump, and the shock would be
minimal. What I did not envision was how extremely
opposite the slow-motion pace in the new South I had
discovered was compared to the NYC pace Rick was about
to experience in the new daily grind he was taking on. Was
it too different? Was it the kind of difference that would
destroy our bond? Was I going to be left in the dust?

> Kath, I decided to start over . . . congratu-
> lations . . . if you couldn't find anything
> major wrong with the school in your first
> week, chances are you're going to be happy
> there . . . . Probably the most painful experi-
> ences are those "mixers" . . . but don't miss
> out on meeting people.

We were going to be apart again, and Rick was trying
to give me his permission to meet other people—to have
some sense of freedom. Was it because he wanted a little
rope in return? We both knew that such freedom was
maybe just to avoid any guilt we would feel if we actually
were unfaithful, but we didn't mean we were letting go.

> Some pretty exciting things are happening to
> us, by the way . . . the record is being played

regularly on WOR-FM (that new station). So
we're getting play in New York . . . . It's not
very original but I'll have to sign, Love, Rick

WOR-FM was the new radio station Murray "the
K" had gone to when WINS-AM radio had elected
to convert to an "all-news-all-the time" format. He
brought along with him Scott Muni who later became
a favorite night-time DJ along with "Cousin Brucie"
[Bruce Morrow] on the industry benchmark WABC radio
station. This was a big deal for the band's second record
release. Rick made every effort to keep me informed of
what every new day of his adventures brought his way
so that I would feel like I was right there beside him,
experiencing the ups and downs as he was. That was
Rick's way of helping me to feel that, although out of
sight, I was not out of his mind. It worked. I always felt
really good that he found it essential to keep me a part
of his every day.

Virginia Rick and his friend Bobby were welcome at
any party my friends and I had on or off campus. Rick
was a good dancer, and as a crowd, we used to go to
this place out of town called Dicky's that had a bar and
a dance floor and live music.

We also hung out at the bar close to campus called The
Lounge. In Virginia in 1966, there was only beer (or wine
if you had the money for it) served in bars. There was no
liquor by the drink served, not even in restaurants. You
needed to buy liquor in ABC (Alcohol Beverage Control)
stores that were run by the state. Restaurants did allow

you to bring a bottle of liquor in to have with your dinner, but the bottle was kept by the bartender, and you could only have one glass of an alcoholic beverage per person on your table at a time. When a waitress would bring you a new glass of whatever, the glass you had with you had to be taken away. That remained the law as long as I was in Virginia, and that was up until 1974. So one of the first things I learned in Virginia was how conservative it was, and the second thing was that they were still fighting the Civil War. My school had actually recruited kids from DC to New York, trying to not be just a state school. I took a lot of heat about my New Jersey accent, but I learned to say "ya'll" a lot. I even learned to play bridge, which was a favorite pastime of all the girls. I have not played that game since I left college, but back then, whenever we didn't want to study, we either played bridge or listened to Temptation albums or played bridge while we listened to the Temptations.

I received letters at college from Carole, who also felt obligated to keep me aware of the goings-on back home where she felt I belonged.

Chapter Nine

ON-AGAIN, OFF-AGAIN

Tentative Relationships

CAROLE WAS A good pen pal to me when I finally went away to college in September 1966. Her correspondence was always full of news about the progress of The Myddle Class activities aimed at their big break through with the record releases and playing around the city. But there was seldom much spin on the stress and strain being shared by all the victims of the complex circumstances that surrounded this group. Anyone who was involved in these working and interpersonal relationships was beginning to lose any sense of privacy and was destined to less and less independence from the tentacles that surmounted as the personal misbehaviors and weaknesses on the part of individuals imposed negative impact on the group as a whole.

Over the course of a year Carole and Charlie were sharing their secret attraction to each other. Gerry had become more and more terrorized by the slowdown of easy placement of his songs with artists then growing independent of their Brill Building marketers. He was not always proud of the writings he and Carole could muster amidst the competition of the singer-songwriter dominance of the likes of Bob Dylan and the Beatles.

I had witnessed many of the changes Gerry was going through during the year that I remained in New Jersey before leaving for college and particularly while Rick and Dave were away at school. They didn't get to see as I did the everyday stress that was felt by Carole, Gerry (and Al) as a result of waiting for these guys to pursue the foundation that might quickly pave a fresh pathway to vicarious success as producers (and manager) of an exciting new talent as an extension of themselves. Gerry was hoping for a little relief from the responsibility he and Carole had to bear for the total burden of creativity, and when the endgame was slow in developing, he turned to self-indulgences to ease his pain.

This, along with the possible awareness that his marriage was being threatened, was becoming too much for the man who had a fragile personality to begin with. Gerry had succumbed to the temptation of daily use of pot and Lord only knows what kinds of chemical concoctions. He had suffered what was then considered a nervous breakdown as each day Gerry's mood swings were manifested by more and more frightening reactions to even commonplace events he would need to deal with.

Gerry's doctors convinced Carole that he required several lengthy hospital stays before they would properly diagnose his deep depression countered with fits of outrage and figure out an effective treatment. Human behavior marked by extreme uncontrollable cycles of depression and delusion, in those days, was for the most part diagnosed as a disorder thought to be partly due to a chemical imbalance (too much serotonin) in the brain and partly due to excesses in self-destructive habits that often came with the genius of artists who struggled with fluctuating self-esteem.

To the artistic self-schema, the esteem needs become a driving force in development of a healthy and realistic self-respect. In many cases, particularly with creative people, the striving for acceptance needs to be bolstered with reassurance from peer approval repeatedly and repeatedly—with a need for almost every product of work to be great rather than to accept the fact that sometimes work in progress is the necessary means to an end. This type of person is hardest on themselves always chasing excellence as their goal. Maintaining these high levels of expectations of oneself is often a curse, manifested in debilitating frustration, but also a blessing in that it continues to create drive and motivation to ever improve one's skills. That was a good thing, if one could take the pressure by keeping one's self based in reality and stability.

Carole called me by phone the first week I was away at school. She explained all the confusing information she was getting from Gerry's doctor as they agreed to allow him visits home from a hospital stay. Gerry's unpredictable behavior was being treated by his doctor with large doses of vitamin C and frequent doses of individual therapy. With all that, his doctor helped Carole with ways to handle Gerry's visits with her and their children.

I knew Carole was bearing a difficult burden pretty much alone. Although the many people around her may have tried to appear to understand her fears, I sensed that she was telling me that no one really knew the thoughts that plagued her mind as she would try to sleep peacefully at night. She was saying, in not so many words, how difficult it would be to begin to trust herself and Gerry with trial returns back into their family life together that was now going to be different than he previously knew it.

Carole's first correspondence to me now, away at school, was to say that Gerry had come home from the hospital, and surprisingly, it was a really good visit. She said he laughed a lot and seemed in very good spirits. They began to talk through a lot of things they had been through when he lost control of his emotions, and he really wanted to try to get better. Carole wanted to believe he was better and hoped he could stay that way. In spite of her hoping, the honest confession was that she could not go through more bad times and certainly not without me around to talk to. Carole was good to tell me about these difficult times with Gerry. I felt honored that she considered me such a good friend and that I could comfort her as she shared her deepest emotions about very painfully personal matters.

* * *

Soon in Carole's next letter to me, she would return to sending me news about the band. She explained that the guys were playing a "freebie" for a disc jockey in Allentown on the upcoming weekend and the following week they were going to play a gig in Glen Falls in upstate NY. She hoped that when The Myddle Class came back they would know whether the second record was going to make it.

Carole was intent on making me feel like I was right there with her as if she was my proxy in the activities of The Myddle Class and our circle of friends that were at the core of the group's connectivity. Often her words put me in the moments, as if it was not her experience, by my own. Maybe this way of putting another's feelings into words was her gift for songwriting.

Carole ended her letter saying:

> Kathy, I'm glad to [hear] that there are some halfway decent people there at your school. Leave it to you to find them!

Carole had her own way of making me feel I was not wasting my time in Virginia, although I imagined she could not see how I could be enjoying it there. She just knew me well enough to know that I was determined to make the best of any situation I found myself in and that I could see the forest for the trees.

By late fall, Gerry had come home from the hospital for good. His doctor said he could function outside now if he kept on his medication, but he continued periods of uncertainty and downs. In a phone call, Carole told me she wasn't sure how to feel, but for now, she had to stay with Gerry and see if they could make it. She said, "But I'm being myself more than ever . . . not giving in to him on every little thing . . . It's all very confusing."

Carole was perhaps fortunate on one hand to have the abilities to be artistic within the boundaries of sanity at the same time as being cursed with simple, sensible capabilities to forge an attitude that enabled her to avoid facing the reality of Gerry's wavering. She felt she had no choice at times. She was his wife, the mother of his two children, his lover, and his professional partner in a successful career—all this was way too difficult to turn away from easily.

In spite of all that, she was mostly a sensitive girl who would give it all up for a simple feeling of sharing love with someone who could deliver even a low level of security, flattery, and acceptance of her for who she was: talented, ambitious, mostly self-assured, and willing to be independent. She would put up with a lot if only she had someone in her life that was capable of being comfortable just being her equal.

Carole called me at school to tell me some news on
The Myddle Class. As Tom Shannon[*] (DJ on the Detroit
AM-CKLW radio station) was reaching a significant
Midwest audience playing the second record release for
several weeks, the guys agreed to do a promo for him
as a spoof on a friend and colleague. The guys recorded
a satire on "Don't Let Me Sleep Too Long," singing,
"Wake him, shake him, don't let him sleep too long,
Joey Reynolds in due time is bound to do something
wrong." On that afternoon they prepared this tape, they
discovered that Joey Reynolds[**] was fired from the radio
station! I couldn't believe their bad luck?!? Carole wrote
to say:

> I miss seeing you . . . , if anything drastic
> happens, you will hear from someone up
> here. Write soon and stay up!

Carole's updates always left me with a sense of
security that I could count on her to keep me prepared
to respond to anything that might happen eight hours

---

* Tommy Shannon moved to the Motor City in 1964 for a job with a
50,000-watt AM radio station, CKLW. The physical station was in Windsor,
Ontario, Canada (just across the river from Detroit). It had a long reach at
night to Detroit, Toledo, Ohio, Cleveland, Ohio, and many nearby states.

** Joey Reynolds was a pseudonym of Joey Pinto who rose to fame as a
Top 40 radio personality during the '60s and '70s in Hartford, Connecticut;
Cleveland, Ohio; and Detroit, Michigan; as well as New York City, New
York. Joey was known for his on-air antics and was considered the originator
of shock-jock radio. (Wikipedia, Joey Reynolds 2010)

away; if it was necessary to show up in person—especially for my man—even if it meant traveling all day to get to where I was needed, Carole knew I would do whatever it took. This bond we shared served me well in later dire situations.

Rick wrote to me from out on the road at Glen Falls, New York saying:

> Kathy, It's been raining since we got here and I've been thinking what that does to you and it depresses me too . . . we're practicing some new things from Carole and Gerry . . . we're going to record when we get back home . . . we're pretty excited. I'd like to get back home 'cause it's been raining since we got here and I've been thinking what that does to you and it depresses me too . . . oh well . . . I love you, Rick.

I could feel Rick's depression in his words. He knew I hated how I felt when it rained. He remembered how much I hated when fall came, and we needed to change clocks back one hour, causing it to be dark by 5:00 p.m. I used to spend all day and night playing with friends in the streets during summer months, and I thought nothing of walking home nearly a mile as late as 10:00 or 11:00 p.m. at night. But when the early darkness and rainy days of the fall would come around, I would get so depressed and frightened of the wind I hated to even walk to the corner store for errands for my mother.

There was something very sad about the leaves dying on the trees and the eerie whisper of the chilling wind that seemed to take away the comforting spirits of hot summer nights. The fall always brought the most significant change to things that were enjoyable before its arrival. Fall blues could easily transition into winter doldrums, but by then, there was snow and ice-skating to enjoy. An end to winter brought the promise of spring showers in a warm inviting way because flowers would rise from the earth, and trees and grass would return to the green that was so vivid, it painted a soothing contrast against the yellow forsythia blooms and the bright blue skies. Spring allowed me to think about all that summer would soon bring: the end of a school year, the freedom of summer months away from books and confinement to little else but TV watching or reading in my bedroom. Summer was the time for constant sunbathing and swimming that allowed me to tolerate the hot, humid nights as long as I was catching lightning-bugs or staying outside until dark, playing wiffle-ball or hide-and-seek with my boy cousins after a Little League Baseball game.

But September rains marked the time to put away all the summer toys, and the unavoidable fall changes were harsh, scary, and pretty depressing. Fall marked a stronger end to a season than any other because it was a time to worry about what came next. To minimize worry, my mind played the game of returning me to memories of things from the past—short term and long term—which brought comfort in the face of change. Fall brought a certain kind of change that was hard to take.

In October of 1966, Rick wrote me to say the following:

> I'm sitting here watching "Dino" on the
> Late-Late-Show. Wow, it really brings back a
> lot of things. Hey . . . you know I'm not usually
> that much of a collector of used sentiment
> but . . . anyway greasy Sal Minio is a gas.

Rick had received my letter before leaving for Albany, so he wanted to tell me the latest of what was going on. The guys had gone into a studio session to record two songs Carole and Gerry had written for the Monkees. Rick describes it as

> unbelievably great . . . it lasted nine hours . . .
> and we all had a great time. Donny Kirshner
> really loves us . . . the guitar sounds are
> fantastic. Donny is showing interest in
> signing us to a new contract . . .

Oddly though, Rick also was explaining how the group finally decided to produce a couple of songs by themselves. The group was so pleased with what they could do independent of Carole and Gerry that Rick accepted responsibility to go to them with the songs they had mixed to tell them the following:

> Listen, the group was falling apart and we had
> to see what we could produce for ourselves
> working together as a group . . . I'm sorry we

had to do it this way; but look at what we can
do and will you back us up and help us, etc.

This made me think that, perhaps without knowing
it, Rick was experiencing the very conflict that resulted
from serious change, like what I always felt when fall and
a new school year set in. The movie *Dino* took him back
to the uncertain times we all shared as high school juniors
starring in the school play *Dino*—the one we had to put on
when President Kennedy died. Now Rick was facing the
potential change in destiny of The Myddle Class. They were
either going to go it alone, producing their own records
without total reliance on Carole and Gerry—whose illness
was robbing him of his authority—or the group was
possibly going to fall apart and adopt a very different set
of independent goals for each of its members.

Rick explained that apparently, Al told Carole and
Gerry about the whole independence thing, and they
were pretty hurt. He told Dave it was a lousy thing for
Al to do, and Dave got upset with Rick for criticizing Al.
Dave somehow always found it in his heart to defend Al
no matter how much jeopardy his actions created for the
group. Al was the father figure Dave was always seeking,
and like an admiring son, he never chose to find faults in
Al Aronowitz. Rick wrote the following:

> Right now the whole thing turns my
> stomach . . . sorry to give you such a happy
> letter . . . Love, Rick

P.S. God, honey . . . how could anyone fail
a trig test?

I thought it was very interesting that, in the midst of
a life-changing dilemma of his own, Rick didn't forget
that I had told him I was struggling with my trigonometry
course, which I didn't care much about. He wanted me
to know he would be disappointed in me if I didn't make
a noble effort to pass the course.

In October, I received a letter from Carole with similar
news about the group. She told me:

> I haven't written because . . . the group has
> been threatening to break up, so they initiated
> a new project among themselves. They went
> in to Talentmasters to cut "Fun and Games"
> by themselves, without us.

Dave had gone to Carole and Gerry to inform them
the group wanted to produce themselves, and Dave's
encounters with Carole and Gerry were not typically
handled diplomatically.

Carole could only describe the news as such:

> You can imagine what changes I went
> through, not to mention Gerry. It's sort of
> like what mothers go through with children,
> I guess—you sort of know [something] isn't
> going to work out well, but you have to let
> them find out for themselves.

By the end of Carole's letter, she sounded more upbeat.

I remember feeling especially very sorry for Carole and also for Gerry. Everyone, including myself, seemed to be going through some serious growing pains. It was a time when The Myddle Class felt strengthened by growing independence from Al Aronowitz yet strangled by Gerry's declining interest and Carole's need to delicately treat Gerry's motivations or lack thereof. It was a natural tendency for the group to believe they could spread their wings and capitalize on Don Kirshner's interest in moving Rick and Dave into a new contract for their songs. They felt the need to be loyal to each other, but perhaps there was not enough loyalty at hand to continue to be dedicated to Carole as a solo producer given Gerry's absenteeism. But going-it-alone producing was possibly a stretch.

Maybe we all really knew that perhaps this call for independence by the guys would just pass and nothing much needed to be said. Carole's parental analogy made me think back to my mother and the night I got dressed to go to my prom. My mother showed outward disappointment, but her unspoken words were actually meant to ease my pain and guilt. Maybe parents just know when it is and isn't necessary to say anything when a child has a dream. Maybe saying something would be saying too much because even one disappointing comment in the midst of a difficult situation is remembered most and can often be more damaging than the event itself.

By Carole's next letter, there was no more mention of The Myddle Class parting ways. This time, Carole was telling me more about her personal struggles in her marriage. The fact that she had fallen in love with Charlie was complicating things greatly. She was telling me she had talked to many people about Charlie: her mother, Gerry's doctor and Gerry himself.

Gerry was home to stay, but during Gerry's hospitalization, Carole had become deeply engrossed in her attraction to Charlie, and she now had decided to split from Gerry. While Gerry's early days home were spent trying to get back to his life with Carole as a family and as a partner, both in their marriage and their writing, Carole was ready to tell Gerry she did not want to stay married and they could no longer live together.

She described to me that at first, listening to her declaration, Gerry got upset—he was crying. He started out asking why, and was there any chance she would stay? Then he got angry, saying she would regret giving up on him. Finally, he said he understood her feelings that she could not rely on him given the state of his instability. He started to realize what Carole was telling him about was a problem he caused, and then he said he would try to get better if she could still believe in him. Gerry told Carole he didn't think he could love anyone else, and he didn't want to lose her altogether. He asked her, if they couldn't be married, could they continue to be friends and still write together?

Carole was determined to have the strength to tell Gerry the truth in spite of his sensitivity at this vulnerable time in his recovery. She kindly told him that maybe someday they could get married again. But she honestly told him he would have to be better for a long time, and before they could be together again, she would also have to be good for him.

She explained it to me saying she told Gerry she would always love him—that was true—and that Charlie or anybody else that she would ever get involved with would have to know that.

I could tell that Carole was very torn by the choice she was trying to make decisively. If it took falling in love again with another to force Carole to face her fears about the man in her life, the time was at hand. She was making the most courageous decision of her young years, and it would take a long time before it would unfold into its impact, magnitude, and ultimate outcome.

* * *

I took a look at my bewildered son after I had been rambling for some time about all these entangled events in the lives of this crowd who had shared so many twists and turns in their personal and professional relationships. As he sat at the table, my son was keeping track of my story albeit somewhat froth with digressions. Noticing that I was noticing his concentration, he felt obligated to let me know he understood much of the torment I was describing that existed in the feelings of my friends.

He asked me, "How did Carole handle the conflict she was feeling over these two important men that meant so much to her?"

I went on to explain that Carole decided to move with her children out of the Waddington Avenue home they shared with Gerry. As Carole had shored up this courage to move out, Gerry called Charlie to say he had better back off because he wanted to get back together with his wife. Oddly enough, Carole wrote, telling me that rather than being furious, she felt touched by Gerry's actions. But she worried over Gerry's potential behavior and didn't trust what might happen at home "if he [got] sick again, or changed his mind." Carole was telling me how utterly scary her life had become, and all she could worry about was the safety of her children. Although I couldn't do a single thing about it, I was worried with her.

At the same time Carole told Gerry she was in love with Charlie enough to end her marriage, Carole dredged up the courage to tell Charlie she wanted to date publicly. The caveat she faced was that, while Charlie convinced her he would "be there" for her if she needed him, he still wanted to date other people.

Charlie was somewhat afraid of Gerry, so he told Gerry he wouldn't see Carole anymore. Finding this out, Carole began to realize Charlie possibly could not be relied on, and she admitted the following to me:

> What I need is some tall, dark, handsome guy . . . who won't get hung up about my work . . . [and] has his own thing . . . [that] I won't get hung up about . . . Do you know anyone like that?

Soon Carole wrote me, "I thought I'd send you a letter with good news." She had decided she had nothing to lose by talking things out with Charlie. Soon he agreed to see her publicly. Sounding very relieved, she said, "I don't want to have to sneak around anymore." I was happy for Carole, although skeptical about Charlie's sincerity. She sounded finally happy and settled into hoping that she could make Charlie believe that sharing a loving relationship with her could make all the stress and pressure worthwhile.

We all want to believe in our own rationalizations, especially when it comes to matters of our hearts. The error in this logic is that a conversation we have with our self is exactly that—a one-sided conversation when we don't allow ourselves to listen to what we don't want to hear from the other party in the equation. As happy as I was for Carole, I was afraid she had made this decision alone. As I heard her describe how hard it was to face the most difficult time of her life, I could only cry for my friend because I only heard pain where there should have been joy, hurt where there should have been happiness and disappointment where there should have been thrills.

Carole would remain engulfed in these feelings and an unresolved, on-again, off-again triangular struggle over who deserved her love, devotion, and commitment for years ahead. I think it took well into a time when she decided she could no longer love either one of these men before it was a story that found an ending. But I'm only guessing.

* * *

Near the time I would be heading home for holidays, Carole called to tell me The Myddle Class was getting a gig to play at the city's trendy upper west side club Ungano's[*]. This was a big step up from the grimy clubs of the Village to where a fan following and record-company promo men came to see the group nightly. Ungano's was later known as a showcase club [where] celebrities could hang out and perhaps perform under the radar. Supposedly the Grateful Dead played there during a time when they were booked to play at Bill Graham's Fillmore East[**]—a converted Village theater that became a landmark early venue for small concerts of the early '70s up-and-coming psychedelic acid rock bands like the Dead.

The Fillmore hosted the Allman Brothers Band (known for their *At Fillmore East Live* platinum album); Derek and the Dominos (a new group featuring Eric Clapton); the Fugs (for whom Charlie Larkey played for about a year); the Chambers Brothers, and the Jefferson Airplane (when they were not playing the counterpart concert hall, Fillmore West, which promoted the heaviest of psychedelic groups of San Francisco) just as starters.

---

* Ugano's nightclub at 210 West 70th Street (between Amsterdam and West End) was open from 1964 to 1971. It was run by two brothers, Arnie and Nicky Ungano, and was thought to be under the watch of a mafia like group of protective people.

** (Wikipedia, Fillmore East 2010).

During this time, The Myddle Class continued to record with Carole serving as the principal on producing without Gerry; they were still perfecting a complex arrangement of a song, "Fun and Games," that Carole and Gerry had written during one of their times of struggle.

* * *

The next question my son posed to me had me remembering more about my days at college. He asked me: "And how were you able to stay focused on your own school experience when you were mostly concerned about what was going on with all your friends back home?"

I described one of the letters from Rick I had that reminded me of how by nearly the end of the school semester, I was admitting to Rick that I was worried about all the work I had to do to prepare for exams before I could leave for the winter break that came during the Christmas holidays. He decided to give me his funny but honest advice, writing:

> Kathy, It seems from your letter (thanks, by the way, that was nice to wake up to) that you have a lot of reading and a lot of tests and that you're starting to f___-up a little . . . no good! (Envision my laughing) . . . take it from me (I know you do) I don't want to scare you . . . but . . . if you start to get behind you will flunk all your exams and they'll throw you out of the school and nobody will ever talk to your because you're a college dropout

and your father will hate you for spending his money . . . . And you'll be the lowest form of life and . . . I'll be stuck with an idiot. I know . . . that's what they told me! All my love, (and whatever else you need) Your pal, Rick

P.S.(and I'll really be mad if you don't) take that trig exam.

I was a little bit flattered that somehow, Rick was still concerned about how I was doing with my classes, yet I was a little bit intimidated by Rick's lecture to me about my grades. On one hand, he was being dramatically sympathetic and supportive—telling me he would stick by me even if I flunked out of school, which was unlikely. One the other hand, he was telling me not to dismiss the opportunity I had to get a good education because I didn't have reason to. He felt he had squandered his opportunity for college, and he regretted it, even though he had a good reason for doing so.

Rick's next letter came just before I was heading home for Christmas. He was visiting Dave and Sue at their apartment in the city and he tried to type a letter.

It started out saying:

DEAR KATH',
. . . i'll have to start over again—
DeaR Santa cLause,
Fpr XMAS I wOulD like aBig read fir ENGIN and smallBlckPUpPy anD as3bScription to

Play boy mag. beCause MY Dadduy Readsit a lot andHewont let me looke at it and If you Wont gIve me what iwnat i8ll write to God becouse H'll give me aNYthing I want. Love, RIcky . . .

He changed to handwriting the letter and said "forgive my ridiculousness." He said he couldn't hack the typewriter and he continued with news about recording some songs and being depressed by some gig he just played.

To insulate myself a bit from the chaos of the New York scene, I found it was pretty easy, however lonely, to get lost in the cocoon of my southern campus life. I always worked in some kind of job on campus the whole four years I was in college. I mostly liked the classes I was taking, except trigonometry. I had been getting Ds on all my trig tests the entire semester. It came to time for the exam; I was going to have to stay at school three extra days to wait to take the damn exam.

A choice I faced was between going home three days earlier and staying to likely fail a test. I went to my teacher and asked him, "What are my chances of passing this course?" He said I would need a "B" on the exam; I said, "I'll see ya." I left for home and took an "F" in the course. That screwed my GPA for the next four years, but I couldn't see the point of worrying about it at the time. The fact that I would be letting Rick down bothered me more.

My best course was my Psych 101, which decidedly became my major when I earned the trust of my professor, Dr. Cone.

You see, it was just before Christmas break, and my roommate (also a psych major) and I wanted to go to a basketball game the night before our psych exam. We went out to the game and returned to the dorm by our midnight curfew. We decided to stay up all night to study for the test, taking No-Doz—the drug of choice in those days. When it came close to 9:00 a.m. and time to go to take the exam, we had a four-floor walk up to get to the classroom. My roommate was so out of it, she couldn't make it up the steps.

I went to take the test, which was a four-question essay. We were to write each question's answer in a separate blue book—these small notepaper booklets. I got through two of the questions and drew a blank. I couldn't write anything for the other half, so I just handed in the two blue books, and soon I left for home and to see all my friends and family for Christmas.

When I returned to school, Dr. Cone called me into his office to say "Kathy, I am so sorry, but I lost half your exam booklets from before the holiday." I couldn't deceive Dr. Cone, so I confessed. I told him what I had done and that I only handed in two booklets. He let me take a make-up test, and that's what made me a psych major.

* * *

My son let me know he was curious if Carole received from Charlie the encouragement she had hoped for that might make her feel she had made the right decision to leave Gerry. He soon asked me: "Did Charlie decide to live with Carole while she pursued her independence?"

I had to answer him describing that, as it turned out, Charlie's actions didn't thoroughly back up his halfhearted commitment.

In 1967 Danny Kootch (of the other King Bees) had formed his group The Flying Machine with his friend James Taylor and their long-time friend, Joel O'Brien. Thanks to the well-to-do upbringing these guys enjoyed, Danny and James had spent summers playing music on Martha's Vineyard and they had stayed in touch with each other's interests in writing and performing their own original songs. During this winter, James and Danny's group had followed the departure of the Lovin' Spoonful and they were playing the Night Owl Café in the Village.

In the brief period when Charlie was willing to be seen in public with Carole he took her into the Night Owl to hear The Flying Machine playing there. Danny and James were impressed to meet Carole King, knowing of her Brill Building successes. That visit marked Carole's introduction to James Taylor.

It didn't take long for Charlie to become distant from his entanglement with Carole, so she decided to move back into the house, and she was going back to Gerry. She looked forward to what a new year would bring. Once they were living together again, she started to fall back in love with Gerry. He was regaining his confidence, and Carole began to believe he could be more trusting about her spending time with The Myddle Class while married to him.

Carole and I spoke on the phone one night, which we had not done in a long time. She told me Gerry got upset after one visit the group made to the house, thinking it was only to see Carole, but she said it was mostly to return her Cadillac she had often lent to all of us. They talked it over. She told me Gerry expressed to her that he felt more at ease when they shared time with Rick and me, like when we went out to eat at a favorite Japanese restaurant together, because Rick was with his girl and Gerry felt like he was with his girl. She made a point to tell me, "He said that." I think Carole always knew that it meant a lot to me to think that Gerry liked me and, even more, that he liked me being Rick's girlfriend.

She described that they had been having a lot of good times. They had gone skiing with the children. She was being more of a marriage partner to Gerry by cooking and doing things for him and she was enjoying him enjoying it.

She said they had talked about each wanting to be more independent. She told Gerry she intended to produce by herself. He said, although he realized that made him a little uptight, it was OK with him, and he'd try to accept it. Carole had told Gerry she was over Charlie.

She hoped she had livened up my campus life with a bit of news from New Jersey. It was good to talk with Carole again like we used to when I was home. It was like I was there.

I wanted to believe what Carole was saying was true; she was feeling happy again in her marriage, even if there was a tinge of caution in her words. Carole and Gerry tried hard to face the difficulties of recommitting to their relationship, and if it didn't work out again, Gerry agreed he would take an apartment and let Carole stay in the house because he said he wanted the children in it.

By the next letter I received from Carole, in the midst of that winter it seemed she was feeling more convinced she had made a good decision to stay with Gerry. She said it felt very good when she would meet Gerry at the end of a day. He was giving her all the things she wanted: a feeling of security, affection, consideration and love; "it was really great."

She said my last letter clued her in that most of the people she had talked to about the situation had been wise and really good friends (especially me). She wrote to tell me:

> Your letter was the first clue I got that most people knew I would (and should) go back to Gerry . . . which is wisdom beyond what the world expects of people under twenty-one. Anyway, I'm grateful to have a friend like you.

I felt extremely relieved by this news. Carole had worked this highly disruptive episode in her life with Gerry to a point of apparent closure and remarkably positive results, and I felt I had helped her through it. We had exchanged our personal doubts, uncertainties, and reservations about our love for the men in our lives whom we knew would be much too much to handle for any average chick, and we came out of the storms all the stronger and ready to weather even more intensifying tempests.

Chapter Ten

A SEASON OF DISCONTENT

Not What Was Expected

THE TIME I was spending with my son in this one afternoon was getting me to relive so much of the stalemate we were all in at the time when I was away at school, needing to vicariously experience the progress and setbacks that The Myddle Class was enduring, waiting for their second contract and third record release, "Don't Look Back[*]," to climb the charts (with flip side, "Wind Chime Laughter"). My son was now asking about just that.

---

[*] "Don't Look Back" by The Myddle Class, was arranged by Rick as an up-tempo, rock version of the Temptations recording written by Smokey Robinson and Ronald White, also covered by The Rolling Stones. This song was included in the anthem of greatest Motown hits selected by Phil Collins in his 2010 tribute to the Detroit sound of the 60's and 70's.

I started to reveal some of the letters that came from Rick while the band was juggling gigs in the city, road trips, and a possible tour with the Animals along with more demo sessions of recordings that were not meant for them to release. It was a quite turbulent time.

During the winter of 1967, The Myddle Class worked mostly as studio musicians recording demos of Carole and Gerry songs they continued to write for Screen Gems/Columbia for Donny Kirshner to place with other artists.

Carole told me Gerry was feeling really good (knock on wood), except he still needed to appreciate how great he was and how great the things he was writing were. Some of Gerry's latest songs were really heady lyrics as he continued to transition his writing style. They were beautiful in their meanings, but they were pretty much uncommercial with the exception of the bubblegum songs written specifically for the Monkees, the latest focus of attention for Donny Kirshner.

The Myddle Class was recording the demos for "Porpoise Song" and "Pleasant Valley Sunday," which would later be released nearly unchanged on a Monkees album when primarily Peter Tork was the only one with any musical talent.

Some of the other demos The Myddle Class were recording for Carole and Gerry were the bleeding-edge songs they were struggling to place with known artists all during the heyday of Bob Dylan, the Beatles, and more British groups.

Some of these songs, while risky, were taken on by British newcomers trying to break into the U.S. market; particularly "Don't Bring Me Down" by the Animals, "I'm into Something Good" by Herman's Hermits, and one of my favorites, "Goin' Back," which was recorded by the Byrds. The biggest compliment to this installment of honesty-from-the-heart songs written by Carole and Gerry at the time was the selection of four greats cut in Memphis, Tennessee, with the Memphis Cats backing up Dusty Springfield on her first album released for the rhythm and blues niche of Atlantic Records. This album known best for her single, "Son of a Preacher Man," includes Carole and Gerry's "No Easy Way Down," "So Much Love," and "Don't Forget about Me," which were beautifully performed by Ms. Springfield with taste, at a time she self-describes as "[when] I sort of grew up as this album progressed."

Also tackled on this album was "I Can't Make It Alone"—one of the toughest lyrics and melodies from this down cycle for Carole and Gerry; a song The Myddle Class was able, much earlier, to get down as a demo that Carole and Gerry desperately wanted the Righteous Brothers to record. This song was a gem but too difficult even for their talent, which had made a huge hit of Barry and Cynthia (Weill) Mann's "You've Lost That Lovin' Feeling." The Righteous Brothers ultimately recorded Goffin and King's "Just Once in My Life"—another difficult yet beautiful song—as a subsequent hit for the duo.

It took years and many covers for appreciation to grow for these songs, more currently referred to as some of the best in the Goffin and King library. But at the time, they were not as commercially successful as their prolific output from the first half of the '60s. It was only after a divorce in 1968 and recurring periods of hiatus from writing with Gerry Goffin that Carole King came into her own and literally smashed all barriers and all stats in the industry as a solo artist with her album *Tapestry*, which still relied on the recognition of a couple of early standards: "Will You Love Me Tomorrow?" and "(You Make Me Feel Like) A Natural Woman."

* * *

Rick wrote me in January telling me:

> Our future seems to change from day to day . . . . Donny [Kirshner] seems to have liked the material we presented, (which was performed rather well, I might add).

Apparently, Donny had never really heard Dave sing before, and all of a sudden, after he heard the group's performance on the Monkees' dates, he was interested in The Myddle Class. At the same time, new contracts were pending signature with Cameo-Parkway records with young Neil Bogart[*] at the helm. After Cameo-Parkway brought in the British mastermind, Alan Klein who had worked with the Beatles to replace Neil Bogart to head up the label, the deal between The Myddle Class and Cameo-Parkway never happened. Amidst heavy debt, mismanagement of resources and federal charges of fraud, the record label folded leaving the group's third record release, "Don't Look Back" with "Wind Chime Laughter" on the B-side, decaying on the empty desk of Bogart after he was ousted.

Since everyone was fairly dissatisfied with the contracts Neil Bogart was presenting and later disappointed by Cameo-Parkway anyway, they soon had a promise from Donny Kirshner that he would sign the group on the Colgems label. He was quite certain he wanted to sign Dave and Rick as writers.

Rick happily wrote to tell me:

> Kath' . . . on the strength of this latest development and a possible opening at

---

[*] Bogart is credited with being a key player in the rise of bubblegum pop music. After moving from Cameo-Parkway and Buddha Records, he started Casablanca in 1973 when he first signed KISS and later promoted the disco career of acts such as Donna Summer and The Village People. Neil Bogart died of cancer and lymphoma at age 39. Both KISS and Donna Summers dedicated record albums to Bogart in his memory. (Wikipedia, Neli Bogart 2010)

> Ondine* (quote from the Manager, Brad Pierce—"the greatest group on the east coast") and a possible tour with the Animals, The Myddle Class is again practicing . . . . If you can get home I imagine I'll be around . . . I miss you very much, Love, Rick.

This was the most excited I had heard Rick sound in a long, long time, and I was thrilled for him. I somehow felt vicariously encouraged into feeling it was now finally approaching a dream come true as if I was signing a contract myself. I was still integrated within the group of friends enough that I was entitled to feel the pangs of success. After all, I had lived through it all as a sidekick, and it was fabulous to finally see a possibility of pay dirt.

During that winter back at college, I decided I was completely committed to the love I left behind at home.

---

* The Ondine was an Upper East Side New York City nightclub/discotheque at 308 E. 59th Street known for its private attendance by the posh mid-'60s celebrity city-dwellers like Andy Warhol, Jackie Kennedy, Faye Dunaway, and more to witness well-known acts like the Doors' first New York gig. After a year or so of it being opened to the public, the then manager, Brad Pierce, having connection with industry types and being a fan of The Myddle Class, began to book the acts that were "pioneers" of the popular music scene around the city, setting a new trend in "happenings" of the era. The attraction of the Ondine led to the success of The Cheetah, Studio 54, along with the Fillmore East as the hot venues in the city for the hottest talent of the late '60s and early '70s. In August, 1966 Rick and I met up with Carole and Gerry at the Ondine after they had visited with the Beatles in their hotel room, while the group was in town for a repeat performance at Shea Stadium on their last U.S. live concert tour.

I told Virginia Rick that I wasn't going to date him anymore, and even if it meant I would sit in a dorm room on weekends, I had my friend Laura who did the same while she waited for the times she could go to visit her boyfriend who was a cop in DC. I thought I stressed over the life my boyfriend lived while I was separated from him, but I never had to worry about him being killed like she did every day. She talked about it so much that I could only visit with Laura if she wanted to listen to music.

I was back at school, feeling very happy for Carole and Gerry as their relationship seemed to be stabilizing and solidifying. Things were looking up for everyone involved with The Myddle Class, and all the future plans were promising, however tentative. Could it be as easy to all work out well as it was to describe the ecstasy of its promise? There was not a lot of luck in the history of these notables in spite of their flair, hard work, and good intentions. Time would tell, and I awaited my next update.

* * *

In February, Carole wrote one of her newsy letters. The most important part of Carole's message was to say the Animals' concert was coming up that Friday night. She was all enthused to tell me:

> They're all excited . . . send your spirit, if not your presence, and pray that they're as good as we know they are, and that the equipment doesn't let them down! Anyway . . . stay well, Love, Carole

Carole always wanted me to feel like I was at these performances I was missing. She knew I loved being part of the satisfaction when the gigs resulted in a good outcome. I was always so appreciative that she understood how meaningful it was to me to keep up with the progress of promoting the group and her songs.

Rick's letters would be equally informative but always with a personal touch to make his messages about us as well as about himself.

In February, just before his twentieth birthday Rick wrote to say:

> Kath' I was pleasantly surprised to wake up to your letter this morning . . . This [Animals*] concert ought either to be a smashing success or a compete bust! Unusually, we have most of the details fairly well worked out. Dominic took us to eighth street to buy clothes . . . you can imagine what a fiasco that was . . . all my love, Rick.

---

* At the same time The Myddle Class was looking forward to an opportunity to travel with the Animals, Jimmy Hendrix had been discovered playing the Café Wha? in Greenwich Village by the Animals' bassist, Chas Chandler, who later signed Hendrix to form a new band in London. Becoming his manager, Chandler changed Hendrix's name to Jimi. In 1967, Jimi's newly formed group with drummer Mitch Mitchell and bassist Noel Redding became known as the Experience, releasing the hit album, *Are You Experienced*, featuring the popular tracks "Purple Haze," "Wind Cries Mary," "Foxey Lady," "Fire," and "Are You Experienced?" (Jimi Hendrix Biography 2010)

As quickly as I was allowed to hold exhilaration in my head about the possibility of a world tour for The Myddle Class, the letter I received a week later from Carole punched a hole in my heart as I read about the terrible disappointment that resulted from the debut performance opening for the Animals. She wrote:

> First of all, let me begin by saying I sat down Sunday evening, wrote you a six-page letter telling you all about the concert, and then I tore it up [because] the way everyone was feeling, I knew if I wrote you on Sunday, you would worry and wish you could come up, or even come up! Rick said you had called so I figured he told you the concert was a nightmare.

Carole went on to describe how the worst thing that could happen did. The Myddle Class went out on stage looking out of sight with authority and sounding great as they started to play "Fun and Games." But after just the first verse, all three microphones gave out, and all you could hear was the instruments. Dave was singing his heart out, and the audience could not hear a thing. She said that Dave and Rick tried to call for a stop to start over, but the other guys continued to play, and Bruce finally brought out new mikes, but by then, they had blown their entire cool. As I read this, I thought to myself, "Good God, how could you invoke such bad luck on these poor souls? They don't deserve this."

Carole continued to say the rest of the set went over surprisingly well. The group got a pretty good reception and applause in spite of the foul-ups. She added a funny story about how she and Sue were practically in tears when some girl behind them in the crowd started making nasty cracks about The Myddle Class being really shitty. Carole said she and Sue told the girl to shut up, and when she continued to be obnoxious, the guy she was with hauled off and socked her one right in the face! In spite of wanting to cry, I had to laugh picturing Carole or Sue giving some girl the finger as if she insulted their babies. They must have felt miserable to have some jerk add insult to injury.

By the end of the Animals' set, Carole and Sue took the plunge and went backstage. All the guys had the attitude of, oh well, it was atrocious, it was a nightmare, but it's over, it was not an indelible experience for them, except for Rick. Carole explained how she found Rick smoking a cigarette, leaning against a wall, seeming totally incommunicado. Nothing anyone could say would reach him.

Carole said that when she wrote to me on Sunday night, although she was determined not to worry me, she couldn't shake the image of Rick for two nights, and it came through all over the letter. That's why she tore it up. She could just see me down in Nowhere, USA, reading about my guy going through all these changes and wanting to rush up there on the first train or plane. She knew I would be upset, and she couldn't do that to me. Well, all I could think of was how bad the original letter she had written could have been because if she was trying not to upset me, she had failed.

Her letter went on to tell me about her own frustrations with all the delays in the Cameo-Parkway contracts, the people that were screaming for money, Donny's involvement with the Monkees' problems to the exclusion of ever listening to the demos she and the guys had done the prior weekend, and the general standstill of the music business as far as she and Gerry were concerned. She said she was trying not to think of all those things, but she obviously was not succeeding.

She ended this long sad story with "take care of yourself, Love, Carole" as if she could possibly think I was caring about myself at such a time of disappointment for all my friends and especially having to wonder how Rick was getting past this failure without wanting to give it all up.

All I could do was cry as I read through this account of the night Rick looked forward to more than anything in months, and as Carole predicted, all I wanted to do was go running up to New Jersey to see him, hug him, and relieve his hurting somehow. I wanted to think that I could still help him feel better as I would have done immediately when it happened if I had only been there that night.

As it turned out, it was in our earlier phone call that I was scarcely able to reach Rick with the insipid attempt I made to ease his self-deprecation. All I could think to say was that the concert didn't mean that much, that he should shake it off, and there would be other chances to show how great The Myddle Class actually was. But I was left feeling minimally effective as I spoke, if I was being heard at all. All I could hope was that time would pass and Rick would forget the scorn.

It didn't take me long to make another monthly schlep up to New Jersey. This time I wanted to only see Rick, and I didn't even tell my family I was near home. We stayed at Carole and Gerry's for two nights and roamed around the city. Rick was feeling much better since the group was ready to go back into a studio to work as hard as ever on more demos for Carole and Gerry. The Animals gig didn't happen for The Myddle Class, but he was shaken, not stirred, and he just planned to go on with what would come next.

* * *

By March, when I next heard from Carole, things were on an upward swing of the roller-coaster The Myddle Class was riding. She wrote saying:

> Rick and Dave were over the other night to sign the Colgems contracts for "You Go On" [a song they had written]. The guys are working on "Snow Queen" and want to do "Goin' Back" over the original track. Also, they liked "Angel Walks Beside Me" and I think they may be working on that. It was great seeing you and Rick . . . it was like old times-you two over here. You must do that more often.

Carole's newsy correspondence always helped me to feel I didn't need to worry so much about how well Rick's motivation was holding up. I felt a lot better knowing Rick and Dave had signed new contracts, and they had a new, however possibly more independent, opportunity for writing and playing to look forward to.

As we approached spring break of 1967, Carole's next letter said Rick told her we would be spending several days in the city during my next trip home. She said she was proud of me getting "A"'s in psych and in sociology and that I should call her when I got into New York.

Carole always made me know she looked forward to seeing me, and it made me feel good to remember it was only a short time before I could be home to see her again and to make plans to spend a lot of time in the city.

Rick and I at home together in March of '67 had an offer from Danny Kootch and his wife, Joyce, to spend time in the city staying at their apartment. We went to see The Flying Machine at the Night Owl, but while we talked with Danny, James was off stage with the other members of the band.

Rick and I had come to be friendly with Danny and Joyce as well as their friend Stephanie Magarino, who once dated James Taylor but now fell hard for Charlie. At the time Charlie was simultaneously seeing Carole and Stephanie without either woman knowing that until the night Charlie took Carole into the city to see Danny and James play at the Night Owl.

Charlie's relationship with Stephanie would torture Carole until eventually after Carole, Danny and Joyce, and

Stephanie all migrated to Los Angeles (early in 1968 sans Charlie), Stephanie and Carole actually became friends. Carole generously extended her home to Stephanie when she had nowhere to live in LA.

* * *

In April 1967, Carole wrote to tell me the guys had been practicing at the Scene, the uptown hot spot where groups could perform for journalists and record label gurus. In return for a few practice nights, the group was playing a set a night for a week for free. They had a gig coming up the next week in Philly, and their next plan was to go back into a studio to record one of their own songs. Carole and Gerry were invited by them to go to the practice, and Gerry went alone. After he heard a few things, he told Carole the group should have a stab at recording on their own.

Rick wrote me in April '67 with a funny story to report:

> Two and a half guesses where I am. Yep, that's right . . . home of Chubby Checker, Dick Clark, etc. Actually (a small part) of Philly is pretty nice . . . it's not hard to imagine colonial clothes and high carriages. We are trying to save money [so] we are staying in this flea-bag hotel . . . Myke keeps yelling out the window "OK, where are the whores!" [I] saw Alex [Kaye] the other night . . . we sat in the "Tin Angel" and talked to Emmaretta Marks

(she's working there . . . she says hello, by the way) How's that for a nice newsy letter . . . . Myke's throwing up in the bathroom . . . Miss you (a lot!) Rick

Rick's humor was back in his writing, and it made me laugh and pity them at the same time as I read this, just picturing Myke screaming for whores out the window down to the grimy streets of Philadelphia. I could see red neon lights flickering due to age and wear, casting a silhouette over the ladies of the night to hide the similar decay in their faces. I would later come to learn that Philly was a depressing place that only ever felt like a large town rather than the important city it wanted to be called. Except for the Liberty Bell, there was little to draw visitors, other than the suburban, parochial, conservative patrons who ventured out to the few good waterfront restaurants only to return to their quaintness, leaving the city streets empty after around 10:00 p.m. Yet any paying gig in 1967 was worth a night or two of funmaking at the home of our Declaration of Independence, national anthem, and country flag.

By early May of that year, Carole wrote with the latest unrest stirring the group. She was telling me:

Dear Kathy, . . . the latest news: Dave has left Sue—he is with some girl in Philly. [Sue] is coping as best as can be expected. My next news: is about Rick—yesterday his guitar was stolen . . . the best I can do (and you)

is to hope it is recovered unharmed. What a crummy thing to happen! I'll see you the end of May. Stay well, Love, Carole

I was freaked by all this news. First, I was sad to hear that Dave was leaving Sue, although it was expected. But somehow, I didn't think Sue would be quite as devastated as I would have been if it were happening to me. But I really was saddened to hear that Rick had lost his guitar—I just knew he was up there, crushed as much as if someone had taken a knife to his heart.

A week later, Carole wrote me with an update that was intended to relieve any worries I might have had about Rick following in Dave's path. She said:

> Dave rolled back home to Sue like nothing happened . . . apparently he saw the light . . . . From bits and snatches I hear, you don't have to worry about Rick . . . he's certainly not going to build up to what he has with you with any other chick. We've established that there must be something there with you and only you.

Carole just had a way of comforting me, and she knew that the news of Dave breaking away from Sue was making me nervous, if not crazy. It made me feel good to know that, although I was just a girlfriend, this whole group of friends acknowledged that the love Rick and I had between us was genuine and unique in the midst of all the temptations these guys dealt with every day. That eased my mind.

In late spring of 1967, Carole wrote to say, since she spoke to me last, Rick called Gerry and asked him to come down to hear the guys recording. She said Rick didn't do it as any favor but because they really wanted Gerry there and it really brought him up a lot. Gerry was going to help the guys mix the tracks they were producing.

At this point, Carole was deciding to stay out of the way of Gerry and The Myddle Class, and she told me she bought a sewing machine; she had made dresses for the kids and a blouse for herself. Carole's focus on sewing to redirect her energies only made me think of the old adage that when you head is full of conflict, it is time to do something with your hands.

I sensed that she was subtly telling me that Gerry needed to feel more in charge of the work with The Myddle Class and wanted Carole to step back. That was the struggle she dealt with throughout her marriage to Gerry—and likely through those that followed—that her being strong and capable at her trade was often threatening, even in the wake of apparent talents of the men in her life. Somehow, the talents these men should have been independently proud of just seemed to be overshadowed by Carole's. I never sensed that she wanted to impose that kind of intimidation, and in fact, I felt she more typically downplayed her strengths. Maybe she just knew she needed to, particularly back in those times of Ozzie and Harriet. But wasn't that quite unfair? In her heart and mind, she felt dwarfed by Gerry's remarkable competencies; after all, he was the man who could write lyrics that clearly echoed a woman's perspective. But without him believing in himself sufficiently, Carole had to walk a thin line.

As it turned out, while I was home for the summer, I joined Carole in a project we both undertook to make Nehru shirts for Gerry and Rick to mimic the style the Beatles wore when they got caught up in the Maharishi culture that influenced the release of *Sgt. Pepper's Lonely Hearts Club Band*. I think the guys wore the shirts once, and that was the end of that.

When we were tired of sewing, we retreated to where Carole was most comfortable, in the red, black, and white piano room where Carole would write. It was always in this tiny room that Carole would reveal to us her developing melodies she was matching with Gerry's latest deeply sensitive lyrics. I remember being among the first to hear so many of their songs written during those few years that marked a lull in the rapid releases of their product.

The ones I remember as my most favorites were Carole's original introductions of "Goin' Back," which is a sweet, mindful man's memories back to his boyhood, younger days of innocence; and her sultry performance of "Snow Queen*," a jazzy tempo put to the tale of the

---

* One can find this song among many of Carole King's best on YouTube. This one is accompanied by an outstanding video of the streets of New York City—mostly Brooklyn from the '60s decade. Watching it gave me thrills and chills.

legendary tease of a discotheque caged go-go dancer of the day who men could only look up to and "come on with their eyes", knowing she was beyond their reach.

By the end of spring we were sunbathing in the south. I remember getting home in May and going to see Carole at home. She greeted me at the door with a loud scream. I looked great with my tanned skin, long hair, and my bright orange sleeveless top with a matching printed orange miniskirt. We were so happy to be together again; we hugged each other in anticipation of another sizzling summer.

Chapter Eleven

SUMMER OF '67

Love Is In The Air

AFTER PLAYING ROUTINELY at the Café Wha? and Café Au Go Go during the summer of 1967, The Myddle Class moved over to play at the Night Owl Café in the Village and continued recording demos for Carole and Gerry.

Rick was still living with Charlie at his parents' home in Mountainside. I lived at home in Stirling about fifteen miles away. I could go to Mountainside by way of the Route 22 highway, but the shortcut was to go from Stirling to New Providence and drive through the Watchung Reservation—a forest preserve of wooded camp grounds and parks. It was surrounded by residential towns and neighborhoods, but it was about five miles wide on all sides with long winding roads and multiple circles that

could take you east, west, north, or south. I learned to
drive to Charlie's house through these roads, but it was a
tricky route, and you could take one wrong turn and be
headed for a north rather than an east exit pretty easily.

When Rick's dad was getting remarried to his friend Carol
on a Saturday afternoon in July, he asked Rick to be his best
man. The wedding was in Scarsdale, New York, and I was
responsible to pick up Rick at Charlie's house and get us to
the wedding. Well, needless to say, I was running a little late,
and being in a hurry driving through the reservation, at some
point, I knew I had taken a wrong turn in the middle of the
woods. There were three or four turns off one of the circles,
and I missed the turn I needed to take me to Charlie's house.
Before I knew it, I was circling back and forth to get where
I was going. I finally figured it out, but not until I was nearly
an hour late to pick up Rick for the drive to Scarsdale.

He never spoke an angry word; he never said he
was mad at me, but I knew I had put him in a very bad
position. We must have talked about something on the
hour drive north, but all I remember is feeling just terrible
that the day was very important for him, and I blew it.

We arrived at the place of the wedding. It was being
held in a room in a restaurant decorated for a reception
with buffet tables of food and flowers with rows of white
chairs that reflected the bright sunlight. The ceremony
had already started. I stayed to the back of the seating
while Rick went up to his dad and Carol and the wedding
party. I don't know what he tried to explain, but it seemed
like, although disappointed, this was not going to spoil
that day for his dad.

After the ceremony, we stayed a short while for something to eat and drink. I know we didn't mingle much with the invited. It was mostly people Rick's dad and Carol worked with in New York City at Hanes. Bonnie and Steve were there, of course. I don't know what I had to say to anyone. I just remember feeling like I stuck out in this crowd like the proverbial sore thumb. I was wearing a sleeveless dress that was white with blue dots, with white shoes, and my hair tied back in a ponytail. It was the closest I got to being dressed up, but it was a summer daytime wedding, and I guess I looked all right. I just remember seeing Carol look very happy and pretty. The day was hers.

When we left the wedding, we drove into the city. We just walked around the Village for a while. Now I really stuck out among the Village crowd. Rick just seemed to want to walk and walk with no real purpose and no real place to go in mind. It was a hot summer day, and I remember I just tried to keep up with his quick pace of wandering. He didn't have much to say but he never told me I had caused him any problem. I could tell he was very upset that, once again, he felt he let his father down. There must have been a comment or two when he greeted his dad that day, however he never told me what words they had between them. The pain was in his face, but he would never let on that he was hurting.

Finally, we ran into Emmaretta Marks on the street. She was a fan of the band as a friend who had worked at the Cafe Au Go Go (and later briefly went on the road to the West Coast with the Blues Project). After we had a few laughs with Emmaretta, Rick finally opened up, and the day seemed to be behind us.

Café Au Go Go poster: circa 1966; Used with permission.

Demo disc—"I Happen To Love You"—1966 B-side of single "Don't Let Me Sleep Too Long," Recorded at Dick Charles studio, New York City.

The Myddle Class performance, 1966: left to right—Myke Rosa, Rick Philp, Dave Palmer (front); Danny Mansolino (back); Charlie Larkey (source unknown).

DJ Lineup – August, 1966
WPTR Radio – Albany, NY

THE SEVEN

DYNAMIC

DEJAYS

DON De ROSA
6-9 AM Daily
6-10 AM Saturday

IT'S A

MUSIC

EXPLOSION

ON

WPTR
1540

CHARLIE BROWN
9 AM-Noon Daily
10 AM-2 PM Saturday

"BOOM BOOM" BRANNIGAN
Noon-4 PM Daily
2-7 Saturday

JOHNNY WALKER
4-8 PM Daily
2-7 PM Sunday

ROGER SCOTT
8 PM-Midnight Daily
7 PM-Midnight Sunday

LYLE WOOD
Midnight-6 AM

BRUCE WAYNE
Weekends

50,000 WATTS OF

MUSIC — 24 HOURS EVERY DAY

FOR THE GREAT NORTHEAST

Albany radio station promotion. August, 1966. Used by permission WPTR Radio.

TOP 40 TUNEDEX

WEEK OF AUGUST 13 - 19, 1966

1. *DON'T LET ME SLEEP TOO LONG. . .Myddle Class
2. *LI'L RED RIDING HOOD. . . . .
   Sam The Sham & The Pharaohs
3. *SEE YOU IN SEPTEMBER. . . . . . The Happenings
4. **YELLOW SUBMARINE/ELEANOR RIGBY· · · · · · ·
   The Beatles
5. *SUNSHINE SUPERMAN. . . . . Donovan
6. **BUS STOP . . . . The Hollies
7. *SUMMER IN THE CITY. . . . . Lovin' Spoonful
8. *MAKE ME BELONG TO YOU. . . . . . Barbara Lewis
9. *WOULDN'T IT BE NICE. . . . . Beach Boys
10. HEY JOE. Tim Rose
11. *YOU CAN'T HURRY LOVE. . . . . . . The Supremes
12. *AIN'T TOO PROUD TO BEG. . . . .The Temptations
13. *WARM AND TENDER LOVE. . . . . . .Percy Sledge
14. *LAND OF 1000 DANCES. . . . . Wilson Pickett
15. *I SAW HER AGAIN. . . . . Mamas & Papas
16. **DISTANT SHORES. . . . . Chad & Jeremy
17. *I COULDN'T LIVE WITHOUT YOUR LOVE. . . . . .
    Petula Clark
18. *THE JOKER WENT WILD. . . . . Brian Hyland
19. *SUNNY. . . . . Bobby Hebb
20. *SWEET DREAMS . . . . Tommy McLain
21. *HUNGRY. . . . . .Paul Revere & The Raiders
22. *DOUBLE SHOT . . . . Swingin' Medallions
23. *WIPE OUT . . . . The Surfaris
24. *WE CAN'T GO ON THIS WAY. . .Teddy & The Pandas
25. *HANKY PANKY . . . . The Shondells
26. *SWEET PEA . . . . Tommy Roe
27. *ALONG COMES MARY . . . . .The Association
28. *I LOVE YOU 1000 TIMES. . . . . . . .The Platters
29. *TURN-DOWN DAY . . . . The Cyrkle
30. *MY HEART'S SYMPHONY . . . .
    Gary Lewis & The Playboys
31. *THEY'RE COMING TO TAKE ME AWAY HA-HAA. . .
    Napoleon XIV
32. *HOLD ON! . . . . Sam & Dave
33. **SUNNY AFTERNOON. . . . . .a. . . . . . The Kinks
34. *RAIN/PAPERBACK WRITER. . . . . . .The Beatles
35. **WITH A GIRL LIKE YOU. . . . . The Troggs
36. *LIVIN' ABOVE YOUR HEAD. . Jay & The Americans
37. *COUNTING. . . . . .The Deep Six
38. *WORLD OF FANTASY. . . . . Five Stairsteps
39. *THERE WILL NEVER BE ANOTHER YOU . . . . . .
    Chris Montez
40. *SHE DRIVES ME OUT OF MY MIND. . . . .
    Swingin' Medallions

Underlined tunes showed greatest advances during the past week.

** indicates former WPTR British Exclusives - heard ONLY on WPTR until released in the U. S.

* Indicates former Picks Au Go Go heard FIRST on WPTR the No. 1 hit-making station in the nation.

TOP 15 ALBUMS

1. BLONDE ON BLONDE . . . . Bob Dylan
2. BEST OF THE BEACH BOYS. . . . . Beach Boys
3. AFTERMATH . . . . Rolling Stones
4. YESTERDAY AND TODAY! . . . . The Beatles
5. WILD THING . . . . .The Troggs
6. WHEN A MAN LOVES A WOMAN . . . . . . Percy Sledge
7. GETTIN' READY. . . . . The Temptations
8. BEST OF THE ANIMALS . . . . The Animals
9. BEST OF PETER AND GORDON . . . . . . Peter & Gordon
10. HOLD ON' . . . . Sam & Dave
11. ANIMALIZATIONS . . . . The Animals
12. HANKY PANKY. . . . . .The Shondells
13. WONDERFULNESS . . . . Bill Cosby
14. I LOVE YOU 1000 TIMES . . . . The Platters
15. STRANGERS IN THE NIGHT . . . . Frank Sinatra

WPTR EXCLUSIVES

DAVE DEE, DOZY, BEAKY, MICK & TICH . . . . L P
I CAN MAKE IT WITH YOU BABY . . . . Pozo Seco Singers
FROM NOWHERE THE TROGGS . . - - - - - - - - - - - - L.P

PICKS AU GO GO

GOOD TIME CAR. . . . . New Tweedy Brothers
RAINING IN MY HEART. . . . . The Legend
IT'S BETTER TO HAVE LOVED A LITTLE/HOLDING ON. . . .
The Tams
THE LONG CIGARETTE. . . . . .The Reflections
A WOMAN OF THE WORLD. . . . . The Gentrys
I GOT TO HANDLE IT . . . . The Capitols
BORN A WOMAN . . . . .Sandy Posey
A SURFER'S DREAM . . . . Jan & Dean
PSYCHOTIC REACTION . . . . Count Five
JUST LIKE A WOMAN . . . . Manfred Mann
SUMMER SAMBA . . . . .Walter Wanderly
GREEN BACK DOLLAR . . . . Jamie Coe
UNDER MY THUMB . . . . Del Shannon
THE KIDS ARE ALRIGHT. . . . . The Who
WALK AWAY RENEE . . . . The Left Banke
MAMA'S LITTLE GIRL . . . . Reparata & The Delrons
IT HURTS ME . . . . Bobby Goldsboro
YOU'LL NEVER KNOW WHAT'S IN MY HEART. . .The Hi-Five
BABY NOT NOW. . . . . CL & The Pictures
BABY TOYS . . . . The Toys

LOOKING AHEAD

BABY'S GONE . . . . Graham Bonney (Mike)
OUT OF TIME . . . . Chris Farlowe (MGM)
KEEP LOOKING. . . . . Solomon Burke
BORN TO BE WITH YOU J . . . . : : . . . . . The Silkie
OUTSIDE CHANCE. . . . . The Turtles
CHERRY CHERRY. . . . . Neil Diamond
POOR DOG. . . . . Little Richard
CHERYL ANN. . . . . Tim Tam & The Turn Ons
MR. DIEINGLY SAD. . . . . The Critters
SEARCHING FOR MY LOVE . . . . Bobby Moore
PHILLY FREEZE. . . . . .Alvin Cash
SUMMERTIME . . . . Billy Stewart
SATISFIED WITH YOU. . . . . Dave Clark Five

Courtesy: It's A Music Explosion On WPTR-1540: Albany, NY Publication : August 13-19, 1966

Albany radio station promotion. August 13, 1966. The Myddle Class single, "Don't Let Me Slelep Too Long" as #1; The Beatles, "Yellow Submarine/ Eleanor Rigby, #4. Used by permission from WPTR Radio.

(Top) Beacon Street, Boston Row Home; Basement Apartment at 233 Beacon St. (access blocked). (Bottom) Boston Common Park, between Beacon Street and Emerson College campus.

(Top) Paramount Theatre of Emerson College-School of Performing Arts (renovated in new millennium); Emerson College dormitory/classroom buildings, Boylston St. marked by school flags. (Bottom) Boston Trinity Church, Copley Square, Boston-Site of Memorial Service for Rick Philp, May, 1969; Inside Trinity Church.

Chapter Twelve

HE LOVES ME, HE LOVES ME NOT, HE LOVES ME

Back To The Future

NOW LATE IN the day, my son, having absorbed the sorted details about Rick's struggles had listened to many more stories than he had expected to hear. From all that I had shared he was now interested in learning when and why Rick decided to go back to school. We were coming full circle around to the episodes of the history that would be the most painful to recall let alone explain. It actually took me a short while to find the courage to look back at the pictures of The Myddle Class at the height of their success and early innocence and to look again at the newspaper articles about the tragic ending to what Rick had hoped would be a new beginning.

I explained that it was somewhat prompted by Carole and Gerry's relationship showing final decay. With Dave and Rick's opportunity to have a writing contract separate from the group's recordings developing slowly, Rick chose to revert to his ultimate desire to finish school through whatever means and amount of time it might take.

By fall of 1967 Rick was enrolled at Emerson College and happily entrenched in Boston. With Rick away, Charlie moved from his parents' home to live with Stephanie in her apartment on the city's upper west side.

Once again, I did not return to school in Virginia for the fall semester of '67. Instead, I got a new job-this time working for a pharmaceutical company in New Providence. I worked for six months and later I arranged to get back down to Virginia for the spring semester, starting in February 1968. Throughout the school year of '67-'68 Rick returned home to NY/NJ often to join the group for performances and recording sessions but I first had to be happy with only more letters.

Rick's first letter from Boston came in late September with a little humor saying:

> . . . High, actually I'm not . . . I just woke
> up . . . Therefore, good morning!

Rick described Boston's first "smoke-in". He was amazed that everyone was really smoking right in Boston Common. There were TV cameras . . . hippies (Boston variety) singing and a bunch of old people trying to see

what was going on. He said, by far his best class was a
psych course, telling me:

> I may even switch majors . . . it is really great
> to watch how hard I'm working in all these
> classes . . . wonder how long it will last . . .
> Call ya' this week . . . Rick

Amazingly, Rick had found Myke Rosa the night
before wandering around Boston. Rick said Myke looked
great, but different with his hair cut off after starting to
work part-time in a New York restaurant kitchen.

I was happy to hear that Rick seemed to be comfortable
with his decision to go back to school and that he liked
Boston. I decided to make another visit to see Rick in
his new college town.

Rick called me about the plans he had for me to come
to Boston. He said he and his new roommate were looking
forward to making a nice Italian dinner for the first night
I was to arrive. Rick was enjoying the lighthearted sense
of relief this new environment and a return to school was
giving him. Over the phone he told me he wanted this
visit to be special and how his roommate had spent hours
talking to the little Italian guy who ran the grocery store
to get the right way to make pasta sauce. Rick corrected
himself to call it gravy! He started poking a little fun at
how my family's traditional chore for every Sunday dinner
was to make pasta with gravy and meatballs. He had seen
plenty of pasta and gravy (sans meatballs) served at my
mother's Christmas Eve dinners. Even at what was meant

to be a meatless, mostly fish dinner, there was always spaghetti on the menu.

He went on about how his roommate had a passion for cooking elaborate meals and that he was going after this menu like a pit bull. So when I arrived in Boston for my first visit there, as soon as I met Rick's new roommate, I called him "Dog". After we did have a great meal and a lot of fun together that night, that nickname stuck.

This time, meeting Rick at school was very different. I was not visiting a sprawling, serene campus of colonial brick buildings reeking with stature and heritage. This was a large-city school with little feel of a campus. The apparent obleisk of Boston University was a dormitory that was one of the tallest buildings along the Charles River that separated the city from the town of Cambridge on the other side.

Emerson College bordered the lush Boston Common public parks as an inner-city school where facilities, classrooms, and dormitories were embedded in converted old buildings. There were many similar, small schools that covered the Boston landscape, leaving the Back Bay a haven for college students to wander the city streets among the suits of a hustling-bustling downtown business district.

Boston did have its unique colonialism that spectacularly glistened in its cobblestoned streets and charming row homes that were beautifully maintained as they historically existed two hundred years before. This city was compact and its narrow streets were typically snarled with commuters.

Rick and Dog lived in a Beacon Street basement apartment where with just a few steps to climb and a couple of blocks to walk you could reach Starrow Drive to approach a new day with a gorgeous view of the Charles River and get a glimpse of the top of the domed building that centered the Cambridge campus of MIT. You really felt the tradition of old Boston when, as an early fall chill combined with a warm morning sun reflecting off the river's water, you could watch the Harvard rowing teams stretched across the horizon practicing their synchronous strides in silence like in a motion picture.

A walk through the east side of the Boston Public Garden led you toward the Capital Building with its gold dome reflecting the richness of this beautiful city. The nearby landmark section of Beacon Hill spilled over with all the character and appeal of early American gas lantern lamp posts lining more cobble stoned streets and sidewalks and the best of the best row homes, quaint restaurants and bars.

In spite of the alluring environment, the weekend we spent in Boston didn't go so well. I was feeling a little abandoned and thought that Rick was settling himself into a new place he found more comfortable than being at home near me. He was actually enjoying school and I began to feel I was missing out on something by not having gone back to college myself. When I returned home from that first visit, I began to feel a strain on our connection; maybe it was due to my increasing sense that distance would finally cause a total collapse of this house of cards. After getting almost weekly letters, nearly a month passed until Rick's next letter. At this point with Rick loving Boston, our relationship was not all roses.

I recall a distressing phone call one October night when I decided to be less than forgiving that I had not heard from Rick since our visit. I got a reaction which included some unprecedented push-back. The conversation began with Rick saying: "Well, remember all that work and studying I've been into . . . it just stopped. All day I hassled myself alternately feeling sorry for you and for myself . . . for us." I said, "It's just a little thing I want from you". He replied, "Yeah, but I said I was sorry, what do you want?" I told him "You know, I just wanted to get a letter from you if you couldn't get home. How can you say you have no time?" He came back with an apologetic "I know . . . you've taken a lot more shit from me than I could ever take from you . . . OK . . . Enough!"

I felt I could continue to make a strong point by saying, "You think it's OK because you went the tiniest bit out of your way . . . for someone you supposedly love . . . that's a pretty strong word ya' know." He replied in a patient voice "I know, I know . . . and I do love you . . . honey, I feel bad . . . and . . . well I couldn't just write you a letter saying 'Hi there, how are ya' . . . things are fine here . . . nonsense . . . crap . . .'"

I finally heard enough and I said, "I'm happy we can talk about this." He remarked, "I just hope you understand; to top it—I won't be home this weekend. I'm playing Saturday . . . Try to understand. I love you."

A SONG FOR YOU 181

When we ended that call, I started to worry that maybe I pushed too far. Had I crossed the line with one-too-many complaints about feeling left out? But didn't I have a right to make my needs be known? Was I always going to be the one who compromised and accepted taking a backseat to so many other priorities? Maybe this was the deal and what came with the territory of wanting someone who so many others also wanted. Did I need to just feel lucky to have him at all? Maybe I just didn't know how to feel entitled and when I wanted to test those waters, the strategy would always backfire.

By Rick's next letter our earlier setback seemed to be over. He wrote:

> Kath' . . . Nice to see your letter when I came in . . . . I'm excited . . . got an A+ on my history paper, quote: (Dr. John Coffee) . . . "no one else in the class has ever approached this kind of work" . . . he was pretty happy with it. Guess you know I'll be flying in Tuesday morning for that session . . . [it] was nice to hear from Gerry . . . Love, Rick

Our short spat that fall had resolved itself into me feeling like nothing had actually happened to threaten our bond. I started to realize that Rick had his good days and bad days; when he was feeling good about what was going on around him, he wanted me to know he was still sharing everything with me. That was good and maybe the way it should be.

* * *

It was late in the year when Carole helped me to get a
$900.00 car loan for me to buy a '62, mint-green, Buick
Skylark for my commute to work. My father came with
me to pick up the car. It was during an early snowfall while
driving home when I skidded on an icy slick, slipping off
the road. My father could only think about the cars of his
that I had ruined with my three accidents, all before I was
nineteen. He didn't say a word, but I could tell what he
was thinking. Rick was a lot like my dad; they both dealt
with me in their quiet, tender ways, seldom finding fault
with me, and if they did, it was with few critical words
and always a gentle touch.

Sometime late in 1967, The Myddle Class had a chance
to do a gig in Montreal, Quebec, Canada. I got a postcard
from Rick written in the French he was still learning; he
wrote a sweet sentiment, telling me:

> je ne fais qu'arrive . . . Je m'ennuie déjà . . .
> nous devrions rendezvous . . . ensemble un
> de jours . . . oi ma chere . . . je suis en amour
> avec to . . . ah oui . . . amities, Richard

It translated roughly into: I just arrived . . . I am bored
already . . . we should arrange to meet here together one
of these days . . . my dear . . . I am in love with you . . .
ah yes. All my best, Richard

Near the end of the year was about the time when
Gerry had given Jerry Wexler their newest song, "(You

Make Me Feel Like) A Natural Woman" for Aretha Franklin to record.

During those few fall months while I was living at home and Rick was the one away at school, Carole and I became even closer friends. I spent a lot of weekends at her house just hanging out with Carole, her housekeeper and live-in babysitter, Willa-Mae, and the two girls along with their pets*—the Alaskan husky, Lika, and Carole's cat, Telemicus.

I vividly recall spending one entire afternoon with Carole in her bedroom where they had a wall of ceiling to floor, teak built-in cabinets that served not only as dressers, but as filing space for all their demo discs and records they had collected. It also held the sophisticated stereo equipment that pounded sound through speakers in the ceiling and in the utilitarian headboard on the other side of the room. We sat on the bed with the demos spread all around us and Carole played them one by one for my mouth-dropping awe.

I heard all the old stuff from the early sixties and Carole proudly told me the stories behind writing "Will You Love Me Tomorrow?" "Take Good Care of My Baby," "Hey Girl," and even her own release of "It Might As Well Rain Until September," which she described as a minor hit in England.

---

* Both of the house pets made the move from New Jersey to Los Angeles and each is featured on Carole's album covers; particularly her cat is seen on *Tapestry* sitting with Carole on the window seat of her first home on Wonderland Avenue in Laurel Canyon.

Carole explained to me how the record business royalties worked and how her and Gerry's songs were managed by BMI, which provided them with healthy quarterly checks to reflect the tally of three cents each time a song was played on the radio or purchased from a record store. She described how some writers like Burt Bacharach and Hal David commanded from ASCAP as much as ten cents a play for the songs they were releasing by then very popular Dionne Warwick.

We loved listening repeatedly to some of the newer demos that Carole alone or with backup by part or all of The Myddle Class had recorded: "I Can't Make It Alone," "No Easy Way Down," and "Don't Forget About Me" (all recorded by Dusty Springfield). Among these demos I witnessed in the making was the heady "Wasn't Born to Follow," later released by The Byrds and featured in the soundtrack ear-marking the highly envied freedom of a few lost souls in the counter-cultural '60s movie *Easy Rider,* which catapulted the film acting careers of Peter Fonda, Dennis Hopper, and Jack Nicholson.

I suspected some kind of omen in Carole's desire to play the old demo discs for me and to think back over the early days of her and Gerry's success as young songwriters. I would soon come to realize that at the time Carole and Gerry were again considering ending their marriage. They were planning to split and separately go out to live in Los Angeles.

She saved this news for a November day when she asked me if I would like to make a trip to Los Angeles with her and Gerry. It was about the time when Aretha

Franklin's recording of "A Natural Woman" was about to be finished that I came to realize it was to become the last Goffin and King successful collaboration for a long while.

Carole and I made an early winter trip to the West Coast and Gerry followed us. We checked into a swank downtown hotel where a room on around the twentieth floor had been booked for us. I remember Carole and I arrived at the hotel late into the evening and as we opened the floor-to-ceiling draperies of the wide picture window, all we saw was an array of colorful lights painting the blackness of the night as far as the eye could see, mostly coming from the tiny white street lights that spanned the valley of homes and commerce that made up the city of Los Angeles.

Gerry arrived very late that night and in the morning when Carole and I were up and ready to go to the Screen-Gems/Columbia Music studios, Gerry was fast asleep in the bed and couldn't be aroused. Carole said it was jet lag. We took off for the day, and I know I met some important people at the plush offices at 77 Sunset Strip. I mostly remember how beautifully the Los Angeles tall palm trees that lined the busy street swayed in the soft breeze and sparkled in the summery bright sunshine.

I don't recall exactly what the last straw was, but by early winter of 1968 Carole and Gerry had sold their West Orange home and were moving on. They had just recently decorated the lower-level family room in blue and yellow chairs and accessories that faced a fireplace surrounded by a new built-in sound-system. It was quite comfortable. But shortly thereafter they sold the house "turn-key" with practically everything in it except for their clothes. The lady who bought the home wanted not only the furniture they were willing to leave behind, but she wanted them to throw in the Kirby canister vacuum cleaner. I guess when the time came to simply look forward to the changes that would be quite drastic they didn't seem to care much about a stupid vacuum. It stayed with the house and Carole and Gerry made their exodus to the West Coast early in 1968.

* * *

Rick next wrote me in mid-January 1968 to say,

> Kathy, Hey! It's been a long time since I've written you a letter . . . hmmm! Got a letter from Stephanie (Margino) . . . she's pretty messed up . . . (over Charlie leaving her). I guess I feel sorry for her. I think she's really scared, like this is the first time she's ever run up against a situation like this (not knowing where you're going . . . or who you're going with) Enough!

Stephanie had deeply loved Charlie and she had to deal with the fact that he was torn by his love for Carole and he chose to move back home to sort out who he wanted to be with. Soon after this Stephanie decided to make a visit to her friends, Danny and Joyce, who had made the permanent move to live married in Los Angeles as did Carole and Gerry, although separated and alone at first.

Carole actually had Stephanie live with her in her new LA home for six months until Stephanie reconnected with another old New York boyfriend, John Fishbach, and Carole finally had Charlie convinced he would move west to live with her. Sue Palmer, after divorcing Dave, would later hook up with Gerry and move in with him where he found a home in Bel Air.

Rick seemed to honestly be touched by Stephanie's letter. He was expressing to me some of his own fears about how to keep a relationship like ours together in the midst of so much uncertainty about what the future might bring to bear for him and our friends.

Somehow, everyone seemed to turn to Rick for advice on their love skirmishes. He was either seen to be the most sympathetic or the most content in his own labor of love that Carole, Bonnie, now Stephanie and soon Dog's girlfriend, Jane, all found it easy to pour out their despair over the noncommittal men in their lives to Rick. He didn't really like to give anyone advice, but he was a good listener and they all knew he would be gentle with their feelings; if he couldn't say something encouraging about their situation, he wouldn't say anything at all. However, he would never make them feel foolish to have spewed their pain-filled guts.

* * *

By February of 1968, my boyfriend was living in Boston and enjoying a new effort at restructuring his college education, my best friend was heading to live in California, and I suddenly decided to take off to Virginia to return to school myself. The inquiry I made to my school prompted a phone call to me saying, "If you want to come back down, we'll find you a room."

After I had written to Rick to tell him I had quite quickly decided to go back to Virginia, he wrote me to say:

> . . . I don't know if you realize how surprised I was at your announcement that you are going back to Virginia . . . it really . . . uh . . . shocked me . . . I think I'll save my reaction for another time.

Rick filled the letter with talk about his classes and he ended it saying:

> . . . I Miss you and I Love You, Rick

In the first letter I received from Rick when I was back at school he wrote the following:

> Kath' Nice to hear from you my dear . . . I was frankly worried . . . glad you're making out well (??) I mean good that you're doing . . . It's not that writing a letter is difficult for me, it's using words that causes problems . . . Uh . . . I worked this weekend with a group called the Barbarians. Actually it was fun . . . I got to f___ around a little . . . you know . . . played

Jimi Hendrix for the little Jr. High School girls—and I made $75 for one night.

Rick was trying to make his letter sound as if he was happy for me that I was also back in school and that he would keep writing about what was going on with him. He knew he could no longer keep me informed about Carole and Gerry because he was equally confused and surprised by their move as he was mine. It took a while before there would be news from Los Angeles.

Rick's next letter was all about Boston. He wrote to say that Dog's girlfriend, Jane, was all excited about getting a letter from me. He wrote:

> Jane really likes you . . . we talked about you for a long time the day we went drinking for my birthday. In many ways she reminds me of you . . . . I hope she and Dog straighten things out . . . she comes to me for advice and I'm not sure what to say at times. Love, Rick

Rick was now in the middle of the trials and tribulations of Dog and Jane's tentative relationship. Maybe he was simply seen by all as the one who had his own love relationship all figured out.

Myke Rosa had gone to spend some time in California early in 1968. His girlfriend at the time had the chance to join him there but she decided not to go; that was a choice she regretted.

Back in school in Virginia in the winter of 1968 I got a letter from Myke's girlfriend telling me she was distressed over whether or not she was foolish to leave Myke alone in Los Angeles, but she couldn't be sure what Myke wanted from her. She wanted me to know that Alice, a friend from Berkeley Heights who was also in school in Boston, had been home for a visit after seeing Rick there. Her letter told me, "Alice said Rick told her he really loves you," and that Alice said she was really surprised because Rick did not seem like the type of guy who would just come out and say something like that. She was really glad for me to hear that and she hoped I was too; it was something she was hoping to hear.

I know that for years I remembered someone had written me about this. Now I recalled how wonderful it was to hear that at the time and especially coming from someone I wasn't all that close to. It made me think that just about everyone who knew Rick and me had a concern or interest in how we felt about one and other. Maybe Rick actually expressed his feelings for me to some of these girls as they sought his love advice. That just amazed me.

* * *

Around this time, Rick had talked to Al who hadn't talked to anyone in a long time. Al didn't know about the new agreement Carole and Gerry had arranged to get Rick and Dave a new contract for the songs they were writing. Rick told him the bare essentials and he explained to me,

[Al's] pretty much apart from the group now . . . just sort of an interested friend. No matter how much shit he's put anyone through, I still like him for some reason.

Rick didn't have the relationship with Al Aronowitz that Dave had developed, but he still respected the man for his zest for the music business and Al's beliefs that The Myddle Class deserved to reach greatness. Unfortunately, Al's efforts had often been disruptive and now all that no longer mattered.

By March, Rick wrote to tell me:

Kath' Mr. Corbette, my English teacher, was talking about how people have lost their sensuality . . . how when people need to get on a subway their most important objective is getting on a particular subway . . . and how people's frustrations are erected on their failures . . . there will always be another subway . . . I wonder if Dad has to get that one subway!

Rick seemed to continue to struggle with the chasm he felt he and his father had developed in their relationship. He knew his dad could not understand how patient Rick was with the long quest for a career in music and that he would never understand how an everyday commute on a particular set of trains or subways would never be a priority in Rick's life. Even though Rick was back in school, he just knew his father would never approve of the outcome, even if he ever finished.

* * *

Dave was on his way to Boston in April planning to enroll at Emerson in the fall of '68. Dave would get a job since he had no money, but Rick needed to find him a place to live. Rick said, if Dave was at all upset that Sue was leaving to go live in LA with Gerry, he showed no signs of caring.

Rick expressed his reaction to Dave coming to Boston as similar to when one feels that the world he had sought out for such a long time was being invaded by someone from a past world. He hoped it would work out and that they would reconnect to write together again. Rick's sounding disappointed that he was going to need to share Boston with Dave bothered me a little, but at the same time, he was inviting me to come back up to see him, so I didn't put myself in the same category as Dave—one seen as an intruder.

I just figured Rick was concerned with having to be responsible for Dave once he arrived there and that perhaps he worried it could become a new burden on him to help Dave get over the loneliness he would likely start out with in a new city.

Luckily, Dave soon convinced his new woman from Philly to move her career to Boston and to share an apartment with him. It was later in Boston that I met Dave's girlfriend, Nancy; she was an advertising graphic artist and a beautiful, slightly older woman. Nancy helped

Dave realize he could love again, but she could not thwart his indulgences when he felt at a loss for motivation and wasn't in the mood to be productive or reliable. Dave enrolled at Emerson, but he never made much of a go at school once again. Boston was only a temporary placeholder for his life while he wasn't sure what he really wanted after stardom didn't materialize.

* * *

By early in 1968 Carole was now settling into her new LA lifestyle and she was looking to form a group for her first album production independent from Gerry. She had started to write some new songs with a young lyricist, Toni Stern. Carole invited Rick to come out to play on the album she was planning to record in the summer of '68.

Carole was still trying to convince Charlie to come live with her in Los Angeles and to be a part of her group with Rick. Rick called me, all excited about this new opportunity, and asked me to plan to go with him to spend the summer in Los Angeles. He wrote saying the following:

> Kath' I talked to Carole . . . she's trying to get Lou Adler to produce her album . . . that could be nice . . . she's got a possible house [she would rent for us to stay in for the summer] . . . it's being looked into . . . . Jane and Dog want to join us for the summer, but . . . well . . . they're not seeing each other

for a while, at the moment (Dog's idea) but they're fine anyway . . . confusing-huh? . . . it's like a game . . . anyway . . . our plans [to go to LA] are still going ahead on schedule . . . so don't worry . . . . Whew! I Miss you, Baby, Take care, Love Rick

While I tried to be interested in all the news Rick was sending about Dave, Sue, Carole, Stephanie and also Dog and Jane, all I could think of was how excited I was that Rick was invited by Carole to go spend the summer in Los Angeles to record with her on a new album and that as excited as he was by the opportunity, he wanted me there with him. I was excited for him for his chance to record with Carole and Charlie, but I was thrilled for the chance we were going to have to spend the entire summer together—in California. WOW! I couldn't wait.

Chapter Thirteen

CALIFORNIA DREAMIN'

Summer Of '68 In Los Angeles

AFTER I HAD done two stints at school in Virginia while Rick had been in Pennsylvania, New York, and now Boston, Massachusetts, we were going to take Carole up on her invitation to spend the summer of 1968 in Los Angeles. Rick was going to join Carole and Charlie and Danny Kootch in recording an album of new songs Carole was writing both on her own and with her new lyricist, Toni Stern. Carole had

Lou Adler* of the Mamas and the Papas to produce the project. I was going to need to work once I got out there. Dog and Jane were supposed to go with us just to be a part of it all. As it turned out, either Dog, Jane herself, or her parents decided she would not be making that trip.

So as I planned to fly out to LA, I got home from school and took a job for a few weeks to earn enough money for a round-trip plane ticket and to keep $100 in my pocket until I could get a LA job. Just shortly before I left for Los Angeles, Bobby Kennedy had been shot and killed in the Ambassador Hotel there while he was campaigning to become a presidential candidate.

When I arrived, Carole had rented us a house near by Laurel Canyon where she was living. The house was just blocks above the intersection of Hollywood Boulevard and Vine Street. A nice walk along Hollywood Boulevard would take you to the famous Grauman's Chinese

---

* Lou Adler was a well-established Hollywood record producer of successful artists like Jan and Dean, Sam Cooke, Barry McGuire ("Eve of Destruction") and the Mamas and the Papas by the time Carole moved to LA and engaged Adler to produce the album she planned to record (as The City) with Charlie and Rick in 1968. Adler had recently sold his Dunhill Records label to ABC Records, and through their associations with Screen-Gems Music, Lou signed Carole to his newly founded label, Ode Records, which would release Carole's The City album, *Now That Everything's Been Said*, in late 1969 and the later solo blockbuster, *Tapestry*, in 1971 and more. Meeting Adler in 1968, I remember him as a handsome, always-wearing-a-hat dapper, confident man who apparently lived up to his reputation for being a ladies' man as he fathered seven sons by various women. Along with being known for his creativity in music and film, Lou Adler is credited with his focus on charities, particularly those for life-threatening childhood illnesses. (Wikipedia, Lou Adler 2010); (Wikipedia, The Mamas & the Papas 2010)

Theatre and the Hollywood Walk of Fame, where you could browse the star-studded inlays to the sidewalk that donned the names and handprints of Hollywood's most famous. The house was a cute two-bedroom, sparsely furnished, and I gave it a bit of a personal touch by hanging curtains in the kitchen window.

In spite of the nerve-racking social climate in Los Angeles after the RFK assassination, Charlie had moved in with Carole just days before I arrived. Charlie seemed pleased to be there, although it had taken him about nine months to decide he would actually go; that is, go to live with Carole.

One day Charlie offered to take me for a ride on his new motorcycle. I was game. He took me along the winding terrain of the Santa Monica mountains up Laurel Canyon Boulevard all the way to the top of Mulholland Drive and back down the hills from which we could overlook the valley of Studio City, Griffith Park with its Hollywood sign and the southern vista of downtown Los Angeles. That was pretty cool, not only for the view but also for the fact that Charlie chose to show it to me. He was a quiet guy, but I think he knew how important it was to me that I was going to be in LA with Rick. He and Rick had lived together for over a year, and I think Charlie understood more than anyone what Rick and I had between us.

Dog and Rick were driving from Boston to Los Angeles in Dog's car. Several days into the cross-country trip and just after reaching the Nevada border with California, the extreme heat of the Death Valley desert caused the transmission of the car to crap out. The guys spent an entire day and half the money they were traveling with to get the car fixed. When they finally arrived in Los Angeles, they were wasted. I can speak to the fact that Rick was hot, tired, and horny because by the time they found the house, it was around ten at night as we just headed for bed.

The next morning, Dog came into the room Rick and I stayed in, and he wanted to talk. They told me some funny stories about their travels, particularly about the snaggletoothed, beer-bellied, long-bearded cowboy with a ponytail who ran the only fill-up garage in the desert who had to fix the car for them. Then Dog said to us, "Listen, you can't close the door so tight." We didn't (or at least I didn't) understand the comment at first, taking it very literally. He went further to explain that he needed to not feel shut out from us, and he feared that he might, maybe because he was there without Jane. We had to reassure Dog that he would be welcome in Los Angeles as much as we were, and it would all be OK.

I landed a job at the IHOP across the street from the 77 Sunset Strip building that housed the Screen Gems/Columbia Music offices. I knew I was not going to get assigned to a 10:00 a.m. to 3:00 p.m. shift, which would have been ideal. I ended up having to work from 9:00 p.m. to 4:00 a.m. It sounds brutal, but it did allow me to have the days free, which was good because most of the group's recording sessions that Rick was there for would be at night, and sometimes those sessions would go 'til 2:00 a.m. or later. We had a chance to spend daytime hours doing fun things.

Carole and I would go shopping or, some days, we would just sit in the sun. I could hang out while the group practiced sometimes at Carole's house or when she was playing around with writing. A couple of times, I joined Carole in going to the Screen Gems offices when she needed to play for the bosses to show she was being productive. On one visit there with Carole, I had the chance to hear Neil Sedaka play some new stuff for Donny Kirshner.

At the time, Carole was still writing sometimes with Gerry, who was living in his own home in Bel Air with Sue Palmer. Rick and I went to Gerry's house a couple of times to visit with Gerry and Sue. They apparently were very happy out there together. It seemed a little strange, but by then, no interchange of relationships was a surprise.

As Carole was writing with Toni Stern, she would visit at Carole's house from time to time to make some changes to lyrics. The plan was to record these new songs by Carole and Toni as well as others by Carole and Gerry and form a group to be called The City. They had studio musicians to fill in drums and other background, including Danny Kortchmar on rhythm guitar. They were to have the songs produced by Lou Adler, and the plans were for an album to be released on Lou's own new record label, Ode Records. In the summer of '68, while separated but not yet divorced from Shelley Fabres, Lou Adler lived with Peggy Lipton, who was best known for the then soon-to-be hit TV show *The Mod Squad*. He had produced an album by Peggy. There was something about these relationships between music producers and their performers that seemed often to literally wind them up in bed together. Lou Adler was mostly known for having produced the Mamas and the Papas on their work "California Dreamin'."

Now Danny Kootch and his wife, Joyce, who we knew from New York, were in Los Angeles, primarily to pursue his career in music. But as it turned out, Joyce also wanted to pursue a career of her own as an actress. They later split, and as much as Danny loved Joyce, he realized that such a strong desire to be somebody in this world of show business was stronger than any bond they once had.

Then there was Stephanie. She had lived in New York for years, once the girlfriend of James Taylor, whom she met through Danny Kootch. Then Stephanie had her fling with Charlie, whom she lost to his love for Carole. Once Stephanie followed the crowd to LA, she and Carole both knew of each other's history with Charlie and although uncomfortable at first, they all ended up good friends for a long time thereafter.

I remember visiting Stephanie in her own new place that summer of '68. She talked about how James planned to return to LA in the fall after his long recording stay in London. She was planning to have James live with her, likely hoping to resurrect their relationship. It may have lasted a short time, but way too much had happened to James since their times together, and that reunion was not to be. He had been signed to Apple Records to record his music under the production of none other than Peter Asher of Peter and Gordon and the brother of Paul McCartney's first girlfriend, Jane Asher. Actually, that album featured James's early greats: "Carolina In My Mind," and "Something In The Way She Moves." In later "Fire and Rain," James tells the story about learning of a close friend's suicide and he admits that after writing this song, he didn't know who to send it to. It was pretty well known that James had fried his brains on drugs, but that seemed to bring out the best in him. As long as some of his type could write and sing the way they did, no one was too concerned about how many drugs they induced.

Stephanie was determined she would land one of these guys or at least one of these types. She was a pretty little girl, and I thought she must have had some bread coming in from the rich parents of Larchmont, New York, because she lived a nice lifestyle both in New York and LA Stephanie was very likeable. She knew what she wanted, if not with whom, and I gave her credit for hanging in.

OMG! This was all pretty exciting, but it made me wonder. How could any simplistic relationship I envisioned survive the manic, capricious turmoil of this lifestyle? How could these incredibly talented, near-genius people be so egotistical and self-serving on one hand, yet be so insecure, indecisive, and confused in their interpersonal relationships with people they thought they loved? I wondered how my immaterial self, with no talent to contribute and only a work ethic and perhaps some sense of humor could hold the interest of one tempted by this freewheeling environment. What was to become of me and Rick and us as a couple? At least spending the summer of 1968 in Los Angeles, watching these greats manage to tolerate the unforgivable, told me I should go for it, hang in there like Stephanie, and test the levels of endurance that would be required to keep me in the game.

In fact, Rick and I started talking about how I should apply to the University of Massachusetts to return to school and have the chance to be near him in Boston. I sent for the paperwork and did exactly that.

One day when none of us had to go to work, we decide to go visit a guy we knew from back east who had followed the band a long time, who was now living at Venice Beach. Dog, Rick, and I took the ride out Sunset Boulevard past UCLA, through Santa Monica, and down the coast a bit to Venice. The Pacific Ocean beaches were nothing like the Jersey Shore. The ocean had some high waves, but they were out deep where you couldn't just wade to them and ride them into shore unless you were on a surfboard. The beaches were not deep with white sand; they were shallow and full of pebbles. Houses were built along the shore with some up on cliffs.

It was different, but we were there in our bathing suits, and we sat on the beach to soak in the sun. I remember going into the water for a short swim. I came out all wet, including having my hair soaked like I had just washed it. I was tan and wearing a white bathing suit and I remember Dog saying to me when I returned to sit down on our blanket, "Now I know why he loves you."

He proceeded to bring up Elayne, Jane's friend from New York, who attended Emerson with them all. He said, "Elayne thinks she is Rick's girlfriend in Boston, but I've told her Rick loves you." I guessed he meant it as a compliment, but I didn't realize then that he was sort of telling himself something more than telling me anything. In hindsight, I had to think back to how manipulative Dog was being, trying to imprint in my mind an image of Rick sharing enough of a closeness with Elayne that she could believe that she was his girlfriend while trying to make his point seem to me to be a validation of Rick's love for me.

I should have worried more about the implication of what Rick might face going back to Boston with me in tow while Elayne was waiting there, expecting to renew the union she must have attached real importance to. I didn't realize the shrewdness in which Dog was planting skepticism in my subconscious; I was being fooled into thinking he was paying homage to the relationship Rick and I shared, but he was purposefully causing me doubts.

Dog had found a job at a restaurant working in the kitchen. He worked a dinner shift which stretched from early afternoons into late evenings. One night, Rick and I were at the house when Dog came back from work. He came into the bedroom wanting to tell us about this terrible thing that had happened at the restaurant. He said this young guy he worked with in the kitchen was using a meat slicer, and the blade separated from the machine and cut the guy's head off right there in front of him. We were stunned. It sounded like an awful thing, let alone something Dog had to witness. But he told the story with a weird smile on his face and gleam in his eye as if it didn't bother him. It was stranger to me, though, when we didn't hear anything about it in the news. We certainly didn't dwell on it, but when I think back, I remember asking myself whether or not that was actually a true story or was it just something Dog lied about because he wanted some attention. I know I started to wonder about his motives and started to find him to be a quite dishonest, almost creepy sort of guy.

I kept thinking about the way he brought up Elayne's feelings for Rick, and I began to wonder if I was being set up to cause some sort of conflicting situation in Boston that would make Rick uncomfortable with his two worlds converging in the same place. Dog somehow knew I would back down from anything that would make me feel I was putting Rick in an awkward position and that I would never allow that to happen.

The summer was flying by with all the work and play. It was soon coming to an end. Rick and I had talked a lot about needing to go back to school. Although he was very much into the recording with Carole and the guys, he never said he didn't want to go back east. I guess I didn't know at the time how closely they had come to completing half the songs for an album. It was like the summer of 1966 all over again. It was all there, right in his hands. Maybe he was walking away from the very opportunity he always wanted, but it could wait, and he was committed to finishing school. It was like Mr. Corbette saying, "There will be another subway."

I had applied to go to the University of Massachusetts campus in Boston so that we could finally both be attending school but not be thirteen hours apart. My sister Linda had written me a letter to tell me I had papers from U-Mass waiting for me and I should call her at home. She later told me that my mother had received a collect call from someone claiming to be me. Then a girl on the phone asked my mother if she knew her daughter was living in Los Angeles with two guys. Linda said my mother was furious about the call. Later, my mother felt someone wanted to get me in trouble, and she couldn't understand that. I had always believed that my parents trusted me, especially because they liked Rick so much and they trusted him. Even though we did have this crazy life in and around New York City, they seemed to be OK with it all.

I was surprised to hear that my mother was upset to think that Rick and I would be staying together in LA I guess I just assumed that my parents figured that would be the case. Anyway, I could only think that, especially since the call came from New York, the person calling my house was either Dog's girlfriend Jane or Elayne, who wanted to be Rick's steady girl. I wondered and worried whether somehow Dog had set up the girls to make that call to my parents to make sure that I was going to get into trouble for wanting to go to Boston to be living near or perhaps even with Rick, and maybe my parents would forbid it.

I talked to Rick about the conversation I had with my sister and I asked him if he thought his friends in Boston, especially Dog might not want to see me come there. He said that was nonsense. I told him my sister said my parents thought we were getting married in LA. He just smiled at me and said, "We will one day, babe." That was all that needed to be said. I know the idea of marriage didn't cross my mind or my lips for a very long time to come.

When I got home from Los Angeles, nothing was ever said about the odd phone call. I made my plans to go to Boston to live with my high school friend Barb who was attending Boston University. All indications were that Rick and I both looked forward to this opportunity for us to share more time together, and he didn't show any signs of expecting trouble.

Chapter Fourteen

ALTERED STATES

I Will Bring You Sorrow

W HEN I RETURNED to New Jersey from the summer of 1968 in Los Angeles, I had been accepted to enroll at U-Mass in Boston. I was going to share a place with a high school friend, Barbara, in Cambridge across the Charles River west of the Back Bay row homes of Beacon Street in Boston, where Rick and Dog would share an apartment. Cambridge was a walk or short drive across the bridge to get to the Boston side. U-Mass was on the southeast side of Boston Common. It seemed like a good choice to be able to stay closer to Rick finally after several years of being so far away in school in Virginia.

When I got to Stirling with a week before school started, I bought a car to take to Boston. It was a two-toned green

'56 Chevy. For $100, I had not only bought a car, but I
had also invested further in my independence. Rick and
I drove up to Boston together, and I settled in at the
basement apartment with Barb and her artist boyfriend,
Chris. I got set up for classes at U-Mass with my $1,100
payment for tuition. After all, I could spend a month there,
and if I didn't like it and wanted to withdraw, I could get
my tuition payment refunded. What did I have to lose?

I needed to work for rent and spending money. So I
walked into the Pall's Mall*, a jazz nightclub on Boylston
Street, and I asked for a job as a cocktail waitress. With
help from the bartender, I learned enough about how to
garnish mixed drinks to get by. It was in this club that
Rick and I met Lloyd Baskin playing piano and singing
some original songs he had written. Lloyd had a wife,
Melanie, and a child. Lloyd became a good friend, and
he eventually played piano at studio sessions Rick and
Dave booked to record more of their own writings. The
job was pretty cool, but I had little time for just hanging
out. I went to classes and sometimes saw Rick during the
day, and some nights Rick joined me for dinner before
I would go to work. Some nights I went to be with him
after I got off work instead of going to Cambridge.
Things were going along OK.

Shortly after arriving in Boston that September of
1968 to celebrate my twenty-first birthday, Rick and
I went out for dinner and planned to return to the

---

* Pall's Mall featured 1970s early performances by Aerosmith with Steven
Tyler; in 2010, the original site of the club is now a fast-food restaurant.

apartment where I was living. Barb and Chris were out for the night, and we had the apartment to ourselves. I remember us lying down on my bed, and we started to talk about me being in Boston. I thought it was a decision we made together, to be closer after all the changes we went through between 1965, '66, and '67, being in separate schools miles apart. Rick seemed to enjoy having me nearby, although he wanted to maintain his school life and his studio recording work and all the freedom required for all that while also having his girlfriend there when spending time together was comfortable and convenient. I knew that was what I should expect.

While we were laying down together, I thought we were sharing a very intimate evening, and I decided to bring up a subject I thought might make our scarce time together more fun and exciting. I said, "You know, I have always felt fine with not joining in whenever the LA crowd would share a joint, but now it's just us here." I was comfortable that it was accepted that if I didn't want to smoke, I could just say no thanks. I had decided it was time that I tried some grass, and I wanted my first time to be with just Rick. He happened to have a joint on him. He said he would take me through it and I could trust him that it was not going to be scary. So I decided if I was going to stick through this relationship for the long run and try to become closer to Rick than ever before, I needed to get past this milestone. I said, "I'm ready now." He lit up the small joint that was freshly rolled, and he took a long drag. He passed me the joint, and he told me to just take a deep breath and hold it. And so I did.

It reminded me of the time when I was thirteen, and I took one of my mother's unfiltered cigarettes into the bathroom, and I decided to try to smoke it. After all, my sister smoked, and all my cousins smoked, and I felt like I was missing out on something good. I remembered how I sat on the toilet, lit a match, and started to smoke that cigarette. As I inhaled, I felt my lungs fill with a deep, burning pain. My heart stopped for what felt like a lifetime, and I thought I was going to die. As I sat in the bathroom with smoke burning the inside of my chest, the room just spun in a circle like the house in the cyclone in *The Wizard of Oz*. After getting totally sick to my stomach on one puff on that cigarette, I never tried to smoke again.

It reminded me of when I was just three years old, and I was in a hospital room with my two older sisters to have our tonsils removed. We were each less than two years apart in age. My oldest sister, Mary Lou was seven, and she was taken from the room first. I remember becoming afraid that she was not coming back. When they wheeled her bed back into the room and took my five-year-old sister, Linda, out of the room, they gave Mary Lou a bowl of ice cream. When Linda came back into the room, they were coming to take me away. I was three years old, and I vividly remember, like it was yesterday, holding on to the post of my crib, yelling because I didn't want to leave my sisters. They took me into a room and laid me down on a table, holding down my arms and legs, and all I saw was this mask being placed over my nose and mouth. The next thing I saw was a set of dark concentric circles spinning like a pinwheel fading from black to a bright white light, and I was out.

I remembered this when at age eight in the third grade on a Friday afternoon when, after I returned to school from going home for lunch, I began to get a stomachache. I didn't want to go back home because it was the last day of school before Easter Sunday, and I wanted to dye Easter eggs. The pain in my stomach got so bad I had to tell my teacher. She sent me to the nurse's room, and they tried to call my mother, but she was not at home. Finally, at the end of the school day, they called my grandmother, and my uncle Vinnie came to get me from school. He took me to my grandmother's house where I fell asleep on the sofa until my mother came home around five o'clock. When she called the family doctor, she was told to bring me immediately to Summit Hospital. That was about a half-hour ride. They determined I had a ruptured appendix, and I needed emergency surgery.

My dad had been called at work, and he just got to my hospital bed when they were ready to take me to an OR. I was very much aware that they were going to give me that mask again with ether. I told my dad I didn't want that mask. He said, "They are not going to give you ether, they will give you a little shot in your arm to put you to sleep." So I went into the OR, half asleep already. The next thing I saw was the mask coming over my nose and mouth again, and I started to kick and scream. I remember the doctor telling me, "If you don't like it, just blow it away." So I took a very deep breath to blow away the mask. The next thing I knew, it was all over.

Here I was with this drag on a joint filling my lungs, waiting for the room to start spinning. My chest didn't burn like it did from the smoke of a cigarette; it didn't make my heart stop. The room wasn't spinning; in fact, everything I was seeing and doing was moving in slow motion. I remember Rick and I just laughed out loud and enjoyed feeling very silly. I don't know what else we talked about, but I know I felt I had pleased Rick that night.

A couple of weeks passed, and every time I would go to see Rick at the apartment to try to spend time with the guys, I was being made to feel less and less welcome by Dog. I felt like I was intruding and that I was not in on the jokes he wanted to only share with Rick. He would brag about a dinner he had cooked a night before I was there or a place they had gone without me while I worked enhancing my feelings of being left out.

I remember one night, Dog and I were alone in the apartment for a short time. He started telling me how much time Rick was spending with Elayne like he had before I came to Boston. Dog went so far as to tell me that Rick had strong feelings for Elayne, and it was becoming difficult for him to decide who he wanted to be with. I was taken aback to say the least.

I started to doubt myself and my choice to move to Boston to try to fit into the life Rick had there. I began to doubt Rick's feelings for me; especially whether he was sure it was a good idea for me to be in Boston. After all, he was not living with me; he was living with Dog and going to classes with Elayne. I remembered his letter about Dave coming up to Boston, how Rick felt the world he wanted for such a long time was being invaded by someone from a past world and only maybe it would work out.

I was not very happy with the classes I was taking at U-Mass—I didn't even have a psych course, and I was feeling like maybe I was going to waste a semester taking classes that didn't count for much. I started to worry a lot. I agonized about the money spent on a school that wasn't a good fit. I started to be uncomfortable in my living arrangement—Barb had Chris living at our (actually her) apartment. I was the guest roommate. Rick was comfortable with sharing an apartment with Dog—that was what he had committed to when we all returned from Los Angeles.

I began to fear that maybe I just didn't fit in there, and I would only cause Rick heartache to put the pressure on him to prove his love for me when he had so many other expectations to fulfill and so many other things, like his music, that should be his priority. A girlfriend breathing down his neck to make choices was not what he needed.

* * *

At this point of talking, I felt pangs in my stomach as I was revealing the most intimate details of the most threatening time of my life and I was getting a bit uneasy. My son stopped me and touched my hand as if to say it was OK to slow down. He decided to intervene to let me calm my nervous speech and he said: "You must have been angry about the situation you and Rick were put in. It sounds like you felt a need to avoid being hurt by someone you loved very much—even if that was not Rick's intent."

I immediately felt a warm comfort, sensing that even at his young age, my son could actually get the anxiety I was feeling and I found the strength to simply say: "My past never allowed me to feel entitled to much of anything, and I always told myself I'd never stay where I was not wanted."

* * *

I went on to explain that in spite of all my self-doubt and the pressure I felt to not lose the scarce money I had paid to enroll at U-Mass, I was not sure that Dog was telling me the truth. I had my distrustful impression of something being terribly wrong with his words and actions. I felt a strange sense of irritation about the way Dog had an odd control on Rick with his devious attempts to dominate his time and attention. Rick never seemed to notice the peculiarity that I asserted was present in Dog's behavior. At least he would never admit—even if he felt something—that I might be right that there was an intentional exertion in the way Dog tried to wedge himself between us and endeavor to manipulate Rick and intimidate me.

One night, I tried to discuss with Rick my feelings and my suspicions about Dog wanting something more from him than just a friendship. I said it appeared to me to be unhealthy. He would not hear of it. He told me I was wrong about Dog. He said Dog was the only person he could rely on when he first went to Boston, and he would not abandon him. I thought Rick believed Dog understood the conflicts he had with his father. It was as if Dog was giving Rick ways to deal with his father's chastising so that Rick did not need to own the problems of his insecurities nor the solutions himself. This created a powerful hold on Rick. He expressed feelings of closeness with this friend that I felt I could not rival.

I feared I was running out of time to figure this whole thing out. If I would withdraw from school in time to get back the money I could not afford to lose and were to leave Boston to return to school in Virginia, I might lose Rick forever. If I stayed, I might stress our relationship to a point of driving him away anyway. It was a no-win situation, and my back was against a wall. I decided to call my school in Virginia to ask if I could enroll in classes although the semester was already several weeks in progress. They said, "Come on down, we will find you a dorm room." I knew I had to go.

I spent the next morning going to the offices at U-Mass to do what it took to drop out of my classes and get back the money I had paid for school and now needed to take down to Virginia. Withdrawal went quickly.

As I was walking back across Boston Common out toward Beacon Street, I saw Rick approaching me on the sidewalk. He met me with a smile and tears in his eyes. We sat down on a park bench to try to comprehend what had just happened. He said he didn't want me to go. All I could do was explain that I had received the money refund from U-Mass, and I needed to go back to my apartment to get my things together and pack the car.

He cried and hugged me tight. He had a sad sort of fear in his voice as he said, "I wish you would stay, but I understand. I never wanted to hurt you." He said he wanted to drive home with me and spend a little more time with me before I left for Virginia. I said that would be nice. I didn't cry after I had made my decision to get back to school.

I just went through the paces of packing and saying good-bye to Barb and Chris. I went to the jazz club to get my last paycheck. I even went to spend the night with Rick and say good-bye to Dog who was as sweet as he could be to me that night. He seemed to be taking pleasure in my leaving and displayed no sense of blame or awareness that he had contributed to my decision. We didn't really talk about what was happening; we just had a nice meal together and shared some laughs. There was nothing more to say. There was not going to be any hard feelings. I would just slip away without much fanfare and leave no guilt to be felt. I had a feeling of calm in the midst of my sadness.

There was just the trip to make to New Jersey and then the trip to Virginia. I would keep my thoughts and feelings to myself and place no fault with anyone. It would be as if the past month had never happened. I would just grin and bear it all alone. When Rick and I finally decided to get some sleep, we turned out the lights and mostly just held each other as tight as a couple might feel a need to when threatened by a lightning storm. I wanted the darkness to last forever and feel how we did during the NYC recording sessions: it's not tomorrow until the sun comes up.

So the next day, we drove home to New Jersey. The trip seemed to go quickly. It was about a four-and-a-half-hour ride. We listened to a lot of music and talked as if this trip would change nothing about our relationship. I still loved Rick, and he still loved me. The love songs I heard on the radio only reinforced my understanding that the most important thing to him was his love for his music and his passion for writing and playing.

When we arrived in New Jersey, we went to Rick's house for a while. Rick played the piano in the living room for a while. Then we sat downstairs in the small basement den finished in knotty pine paneling where Rick's dad had built a bar and that still had touches of his mother's early American decorating making it cozy and charming. Rick pulled out his guitar and began to play for me more of the melody he was writing. It was a mix of the R & B and chinky riffs he was known to play, throwing in those hard-to-reach harmonics that just sent chills down my spine.

As much as I knew I was headed toward putting a new thirteen-hour distance between us, I knew this was someone who could do no wrong, and I would lay down my heart for him forever. We would still write letters back and forth. I would go back to school and tell the girls about my summer in Los Angeles and all the excitement that was still ahead for Rick and Carole. I would stay as involved as ever in all that would later become plans for

Rick, Dave, and even Danny Mansolino and Myke Rosa to go to Los Angeles during the next summer to work with Gerry or also with Carole, or perhaps with them both together again.

A school year would go by as quickly as ever. We would be home for Thanksgiving and then Christmas in a few short weeks, and before we knew it, we would be on winter break. The spring semesters always went the fastest. I would be sunbathing on the roof of the dorm in April and going home in May with a tan. It was as if we were committed to each other more than ever before. Although I was walking away from the life I told myself I would never give up for anything, I felt we still shared our unspoken promises. But I was sending him back to Boston alone and going off in a different direction from the most important person to me. Was I crazy?

As much as I wanted to share every day with this love of my life, I was not going to stand in the way of his freedom to feel entitled to make all his sacrifices worthwhile. Rick needed his space. He needed to experience the accomplishments that he plotted in his head, knowing they had cost him dearly to this point. He had sacrificed much more than anyone could imagine through their perspectives of limited aspirations. He had already made the ultimate sacrifice having disappointed his dad by choosing to follow his own dreams rather than those his father had for him as an adult. That cut was the deepest. Major obstacles had been overcome, and he didn't need new ones, like an unhappy girlfriend, to clutter his path to life's fulfillment. Now it was his turn to pursue his desires and make his dreams a reality. Maybe later, only when he could totally be happy with his own choices, he could fully love another. Rick needed to complete the journey he selected for himself before he could decide who he wanted to find at the end of the road.

Book Three: You Gave Me The Best Of Your Love

Chapter Fifteen

I STILL BELIEVE IN YOU

Nothin' But Heartache And Danger Lurking

I WAS ONLY one week back at school in Virginia when I received my first letter from Rick after leaving Boston. It sounded a bit ominous, but it was Rick's way of trying to give me news as if he knew I needed to feel like I was still there living through the days' events with him. I read some regret in his words that said:

> Kath' I've started this letter a couple of times . . . seems silly to say . . . 'Hi how are you, OK, general bullshit' . . . Everything's fairly calm around here . . . . I've been painting the other apartment . . . it's messy, but it keeps me busy . . . . Dave and I are close to finishing a couple of songs . . . trying to get

some studio time next week . . . . Enough . . .
I miss you . . . I've really felt sort of strange
since you've gone . . . especially at night (!?!)
Love, Rick.

Rick was subtly telling me he was perhaps conceding
to some of my reasons for leaving Boston as he had
decided to take the quasi-separate apartment that was
hidden behind the front rooms of the basement place
he shared with Dog. I was glad to hear that he was taking
meaningful steps toward finding some independence
from Dog's control over him. There must have been some
discussion of why Rick needed his own space, but he was
sparing me of those details. In any case, I was happy to
think that maybe my words of caution had seeped into
Rick's thoughts, and he was heeding my advice.

By the end of that month of October that we were
apart, Rick was writing about some frustrations amidst
some encouraging activities. He wrote saying:

Hi Hon . . . I was a little confused but obviously
you got my letter . . . it took a while . . . just to
check: you sent one letter, right? I'm having
trouble getting mail . . . and Carole still hasn't
gotten any of the letters I sent her! . . . . Let's
see, the weekend Gerry and Sue were here
was really nice . . . Myke came up with them
and I found Danny Mansolino has been
living over in Charlestown . . . . The outcome
was . . . well, maybe a group. Gerry heard the

songs Dave and I have written ["Keys To The Kingdom" and "Redbeard"]—we heard the one he and Carole had written ["Mr. Charlie"] (which was great!). So right now we're (Dave, Danny, Lloyd and myself) getting together and working out vocal parts . . . we sound pretty well together.

Rick's next letter sounded like he was truly worried about menacing events that he was enduring in the last few weeks. I was getting very apprehensive and concerned for him and wondered if he was coping or just naively trying to ignore the real horror he was living through as I read his message:

I still haven't gotten my check from California . . . we had two fires here . . . the arson squad was here today; there seems to be some evidence that they were set (both in my apartment) I lost a lot of clothes and books but the guitars are all right . . . Sorry all the news is sort of depressing.

I could not stand to hear Rick sound so obviously sad that he was no longer trying so much to hide his fear and his feelings from me. I needed to speak with him, so I gave him a call that day. Over the phone, he tried to reassure me that while Dog was trying to make him feel guilty and uncomfortable about wanting to leave school to again go to Los Angeles, he was sure he could make it through just a couple of more weeks to the end of exams, and he would be getting a break from there.

To change the subject, Rick told me Charlie found out that Gerry had played their new song for him and Dave and Charlie got mad. Now Carole was refusing to write any songs with Gerry. Rick figured Carole was sort of mad at him because she and Charlie started thinking this whole thing (about the old band members returning to Los Angeles) was as a group, and Charlie was feeling left out. As usual, he told me that none of that was important, really. He told me he missed me very much, and we both said "I love you" as we said goodbye.

I was thrilled for Rick that he was looking forward to another opportunity to renew his professional relationship with Gerry and that it would include all the guys Rick felt loyalty to, even if it might not include Charlie, who was finally showing his allegiance to Carole. While it was very disturbing to hear that Rick had endured fires in the back apartment he had moved into and a loss of other personal belongings, it seemed that he was dealing with all the unrelenting events. The loss of both inbound and outbound mail, especially letters from me and to Carole and perhaps money from Screen Gems seemed odd, but Rick was minimizing his concern for all this. What mostly made me feel good was that Rick was no longer digging his heels into Boston and the secondarily important people there.

By January, 1969 Rick wrote the following:

Kath' Well . . . I thought I had a chance to pull through this semester . . . but somehow

I managed to get stuck with three exams on one day . . . . For intercession, I'll likely stay here for a few days and maybe write some songs (if I have a chance to be completely alone) [then] Fly to New York—wander on home . . . see you if you can get home too . . . Let me know when you're getting off . . . (sounds like a proposition) . . . I expect something terrible to happen soon . . . . Lloyd and Melanie say hello! . . . . I love you, Rick.

Rick had a strange way in his letters of giving me pieces of his thoughts in a mixture of his up and down feelings. His life now was such a constant twist of highs and lows, I worried about him as I remembered one of his first letters saying, "Strong I am not."

I was pleased to hear that Rick believed I had the strength to handle him telling me how painful each day was even if there were some things to be optimistic about. But that comfort level we shared was at the core of our union, and it was what allowed us to maintain our reliance on one another to always get it. In spite of warning signals, I was not ready to think anything terribly menacing could be on the horizon. Who would have thought that?

Again, we only had our own experiences as a point of reference to design our thoughts and expectations, and danger was not what I envisioned. It just sounded like all Rick needed to do was manage a few remaining months

in his shaky living arrangement, and he could escape all
the hassles. Maybe I think that now after knowing the
outcome, but at the time, while I feared all the horrifying
mishaps were Dog's doings, I am sure I never expected
that he might take desperate measures to express his
frustration that he might be reduced to insignificant
importance in Rick's future plans.

Rick's next note came in a card when he wrote:

> Did you ever get one of those dumb cards
> that don't say anything, and the person had
> no real reason to send it? Actually . . . this is
> a general wish-you-were-here card . . . . We'll
> finish demos on "Keys" and "Redbeard" this
> week (both need mixes) . . . . I hope Screen
> Gems will be impressed because I think they
> cut me off . . . haven't received a check in
> two weeks. More details to follow.
> I love you, Rick.

Once again, Rick's emotional roller coaster was
racing through his words as he tried to be jovial in
the midst of some angst. However, now my worry
intensified as I read his words. It was only February,
and Rick had to make it through several more months
of what started to sound like terror. I felt a kind of
symbiotic moroseness in my gut with concern and
anger that I had to wait for a visit over winter break
before Rick and I could see each other and I could
try to ease his pain. I wanted to hear more details so

I could somehow offer my words of encouragement and support that he was headed for better times. Maybe I was able to convey my support in my next letter to him, but I knew I could not impact events if there was something destructive in motion in Boston. It never dawned on me to tell him to leave there.

* * *

In early spring of 1969, Rick wrote telling me that he had made a trip home to see his dad, who was in the hospital for kidney stones. Dog had gone home with him on that trip also to see his own mother. During this visit home, the two guys were in a car accident in Rick's father's car. There was significant damage to the car. Dog had sustained some injuries. Rick seemed to escape the accident with only a minor neck sprain. Ruining his dad's car did not sit well with his father, and there was some discourse that followed after that incident.

From Rick's accounts of his dad's reaction to the car accident, I suspected that part of his dad's increased frustrations with Rick following this incident and visit may have had something to do with his newly developed distrust, if not also dislike, for Dog. Parents just sometimes have a sixth sense about how their children are treated by friends that doesn't always settle well within them. Maybe Rick's dad saw something he didn't like and thought he should address in a similar way to how he always reacted to his distaste for the music business that he had hoped Rick would one day turn away from. He soon began to tell Rick he wanted him to leave Boston, come home, and get a real job. In March, Rick wrote saying:

> Kath' I'm having a lot of mail stolen, including checks but I finally got both of your letters. I can't figure out what they do with mail around here . . . . I called Screen Gems and had them stop payment of the checks . . . I'm afraid the new checks were stolen too.

Rick continued to let me know he was enduring what sounded like real fear, but he also kept trying to focus on the positive things that he was looking forward to as he approached leaving Boston. He soon wrote saying:

> . . . Lots to tell you . . . Dave, Lloyd and I worked on the two demos at the new studio ("Redbeard" and "Keys to the Kingdom"). I think I'm improving as a producer . . . .

Rick told me that Charlie had called up Gerry to say he would be grateful to be allowed to play as part of the yet un-named new group he planned to record that summer.

Rick told Gerry he'd like to have Charlie rejoin the group. Gerry said he liked Charlie's part on "Can't Make

It Alone" and would actually enjoy having Charlie on the
album—as long as he didn't need to be his buddy. Rick
wrote to let me know:

> . . . . So it looks funny . . . but the [new group]
> line-up could read: Dave Palmer—vocals,
> cow bell; Rick Phillip (they'll spell it wrong
> anyway)-guitar; Myke Rosa—drums; Danny
> Mansolino—organ; Charlie Larkey—bass;
> Lloyd Baskin—piano. Well, it's 5:30 a.m . . . .
> I'll continue this tomorrow . . . .

This was the happiest I had heard Rick sound in a
very long time, and I even laughed a little as I read his
funmaking of the way Gerry and Charlie maintained a
semblance of respect for each other. That was a good
thing because I was sure that if Carole sensed some
sort of truce between these two most important men
in her life, she would be happy and maybe even find
a way to participate in the vision of a reunion among
them all.

Regardless, I was feeling more relaxed with Rick's
hopefulness even though the stuff about still missing
mail and money sounded like a terrible thing that he
was trying to put in the back of his mind. I could only
think that Dog was behind all this intimidating nonsense
that Rick felt obligated to report, but it sounded like
Rick was handling it. Maybe I didn't need to think the
worst.

Rick sent me a reel-to-reel tape* of the songs they had recorded in those 1969 Boston studio sessions. It included a version of "I Can't Make It Alone" the group was going to try to rerecord again under Gerry's re-production. A later, finally released version by Dusty Springfield reflected a soulful woman's perspective backed by a full-string orchestra's R & B arrangement. Rick's performance on this demo is quite impressive as is Dave's efforts to get his voice to reach the highs intended for Bobby Hatfield and the low baritone range of Bill Medley for whom the song had been written. It was pretty good but it could likely be improved upon by Gerry's touches.

Rick was very proud of the capabilities he was developing as a producer. Lloyd Baskin's talents as a singer on lead and harmonies and as a piano artist were actually in Rick's league, and Rick was happy to have Lloyd working with them. Lloyd solidly sang lead on

---

* During the writing of this book, I took this forty year-old tape to the City Lights Recording Studio in central New Jersey to have the four songs on it digitally converted and copied onto CDs. It was the first time I had heard the recordings in all these years, and I was amazed at how timeless these songs were. It held demos performed in the winter of 1968–69 by Rick and Dave and other friends in Boston of Carole and Gerry's song "Mr. Charlie" and Dave and Rick's songs "Redbeard" and "Keys to the Kingdom," a song that highlights Rick's marked ability to play harmonic notes. The tape included a demo recording of Carole and Gerry's "I Can't Make It Alone" performed earlier by The Myddle Class, featuring Carole on piano. I added to the CD a Myddle Class demo recording I held on to from earlier years of Bob Dylan's "I Shall Be Released" on which the lead female singer is unidentified.

their version of "Mr. Charlie," which is a takeoff on the competitive nature of the relationship between Charlie and Gerry and aptly portrays Charlie's later request to be part of the reunion being planned for the summer of 1969.

The best of these recording sessions is the performances and production of Dave and Rick's song, "Keys to the Kingdom." To me, this jewel epitomizes how, like watercolors to a canvas, music and lyrics can paint a picture of emotion at a point in time. I've always thought this song was written with me in mind. The melody and the harmonics were the same that Rick had played for me that October day in his dad's basement when we had driven home together for me to return to Virginia.

The verse, bridge and chorus tell the story of a revelation followed by a decision for two anguished lovers to part ways, but not forget each other:

> What am I gonna do now . . . .
> Leave me the keys to the kingdom
> Let me believe in your wisdom, child
> If only for a little while . . . .
> (Palmer and Philp, "Keys To The Kingdom" 1969)

The song's lyric captures the deep feelings of two people who want to hold on to their trust in one another's insights into their futures as they face separation. Each one tells the other to leave them with the perceptiveness they will need to conquer the contests they are going off to chase.

KATHY WEST

I read into these words that the couple wants to believe they share an understanding that, while they must, for now, move on to independently overcome their doubts, they will always keep a faith in each other's strength to endure whatever lies ahead in the wake of their pursuit of happiness. If it is meant to be, the wisdom of their parting ways may ultimately prove to bring them closer.

Knowing the biblical reference to the title of this song, I felt a need to research the phrase "Keys to the Kingdom." I discovered a seven-book series written by Garth Nix[*] between 2003 and 2010 that portrays a set of challenges of a young boy Arthur who, before he dies, is approached by a stranger giving him a key that will open a house that only he imagines in his mind. Arthur doesn't know what may be inside the house, but he knows that the futures of many of his friends depend on him finding out. The house is expected to be the center of the universe, and Arthur discovers that "the Will of the Architect" was not being fulfilled as it was intended. It was, rather, broken into seven pieces by the "Architect Trustees." It became Arthur's task to fight all the Trustees, each afflicted with one of the seven deadly sins: sloth, greed, gluttony, wrath, lust, envy, and pride—"seven objects of power" given to those entrusted with various pieces of "demesnes" (leased property). Arthur is faced with reclaiming these domains by taking each Key and ultimately fulfilling the Will (of the Architect). A reference to the sin of pride as that committed on Sunday is the

---

* (Wikipedia, The Keys to the Kingdom 2010)

only possibly understandable sin. It seems to occur in the Garden of Eden defined as the incomparable garden. Lord Sunday, trying to be heroic, claims with optimistic naiveté that his only wish is to care for his garden.

The stories in this series also reference the symbolism of Judeo-Christian tradition as, according to the gospel, Jesus says to Peter:

> I will give you the keys to the kingdom of heaven, [and] whatever you bind on earth will be bound in heaven, and whatever you loose [free] on earth will be loosed in heaven.
> (Matthew 16. The Holy Bible 1999)

This allegory has an uncanny parallel to the actual, true-life drama Rick was experiencing during that last school year and was tolerating in the final months he spent in Boston.

I had left him that fall with a trust that he held the keys to his future kingdom and that what we had as a bond would remain a bond. Through the final weeks of discomfort he was feeling, I wanted him to believe that, as he planned to journey back to Los Angeles and the dreams he was about to reprise, he should do it with my vote of confidence and belief that we would hold fast our love along the way, if that was to be. I believed he had to pursue the path to finding his will to achieve the hopes for his goals as they were intended years before. Rick was fighting the sins of envy which Dog had committed when he started making life miserable for Rick in Boston, and he was only trying to care for his personal gardens by attempting to rebuild his dreams and simply leave town. His story, however, did not have a hero's ending.

Rick continued one of his last letters, telling me he wrote to our old friend Chris Irby, asking him what it would be like to visit where he lived in New England if Rick came out during spring vacation, but he said he probably would not get to see Chris. Instead, he told me this:

> I want to get out of Boston so I'd rather see you at home. Another thing . . . . I'd like to come down to Virginia as soon as it gets warmer . . . . I Miss you, Love, Rick

Rick continued by saying he had spoken with Carole and Charlie. The conversation with Carole was a little guarded, but they both agreed to try to make it a groovy summer for all.

His last comment was that he hadn't played at all for a while, which naturally made him sick to his stomach.

I could sense Rick's angst over having to bear the strain of waiting for the school year to end before he could get away. I wondered if he was anxious to get away to the new undertaking looming within the next and maybe final trip to LA, or was he really meaning to imply that he was finally ready to get away from Boston, and everything it represented, to leave it behind once and for all?

I read into this perhaps what I wanted to hear, the latter, although I was pretty certain Rick was ready to give up on school and forget about the gap, the people, and the lifestyle that Emerson had fulfilled during a time of uncertainty. He was ready for his journey on the trail of a definitive campaign toward his ultimate goals. However, I didn't hear him saying he was looking forward to getting away from me.

I put a lot of credence in him saying he actually wanted, or at least thought about, a visit with me in Virginia. That would have meant the world to me. Not only was it the first time he ever suggested he would wander the distance to see me and how I was living at school, but I would also have the chance to show him off to my friends who had heard about every blade of grass The Myddle Class had crossed in the past two years. That was huge, but I knew it was likely just a gesture of love and something that would never happen. It was the thought that counted.

I allowed myself to think that he was not going to say any final good-bye to me; he and I would just strengthen our commitment to each other, and perhaps I would get a new invitation to wind up in Los Angeles alongside him again one day to play out our destiny.

However, the scary thought was that, like for so many others who had made the effort to share the expedition and failed, it was hard to know if we could endure as a couple. The pragmatist in me had doubts if we would ultimately hold on to a faithful, loving alliance amidst the endless temptations for all-out independence and the craziness of the LA lifestyle laden with self-indulgent pressures of the music business. However, it was sure thrilling to imagine it all, and I would have been up for a repeat of the challenge.

* * *

I did meet Rick at home over spring break, and we talked a lot about all the promise a return to LA could present. We avoided the fact that I was not tagging along on this next sojourn, but that was OK. We had a good visit. We spent some time in the city. We met up with Alex Kaye, who was living in New York since leaving Gettysburg. That seemed to make Rick a lot more relaxed because we always did a lot of laughing with Alex, talking about what was now old times. Rick spent some time in NYC at a couple of recording dates as a studio musician. This made us both happy. He was back in his element with a chance to forget about school for a few days. Our time home together passed quickly, and we didn't want it to end. We were enjoying just feeling close again like we did before all the time that had passed without a tangible hold on the future. Now it was time to look at a new horizon to drive toward—even if it meant going separately into the sunrises and sunsets that loomed ahead.

In April 1969, the next thing I knew, Carole was writing telling me that Charlie had decided to move out of the home they shared for nearly a year, and he found a house in the Canyon he was moving into alone. They had agreed that freedom was needed to prevent the magic from being destroyed by what they considered problems resulting from life becoming mundane. Mundane? Did life need to be a constant high? How much stimulation did everyday life need to provide these people? Wasn't it enough to feel periodic success amidst the hectic nature of the business they were in? Or was it just too much to deal every day with knowing that if the output of their talent wasn't continuous, there was always some new talent—in a new group or a new individual artist—waiting in the wings to take the lead, and then the fairy-tale magic might just fade to dust.

Carole ended her sad news update, telling me:

> Write, you no-good so-an-so! (Only kidding—I love you enough to insult you!) Anyway, write soon and be well. Love, Carole.

I wondered as I read this latest news from Carole if Charlie didn't have an ulterior motive for leaving her to have his independence because now he had a chance to look forward to the old Myddle Class reuniting as possibly a new group of twenty-two-year-olds with all the freedom in the world, in spite of some halfhearted connections to the women in their lives. I never could really tell if Charlie shared with Carole the passion for their relationship to work out that she had from the very beginning. One could only hope that he had given her all the love and compassion he had the capacity for at his age. No one really knows what matters between two people to make or help them stay together. As much as friends or family want to hope for the best for their loved ones, it is only ever understood by the two people who share a bond how strong the glue truly is. As much as I was saddened to hear Carole say that she and Charlie were off again, I figured she was going to handle this the only way she knew how to, and that was to take it for what it was worth, hope that they could remain connected until there was no more hope, and bury herself into her work. That was what I often did; otherwise, I would have never made it through college.

* * *

As of April 15, 1969, I received a letter from Rick with a return address in Brighton, Massachusetts. He had moved into an apartment with a couple of old friends from Berkeley Heights who were attending school in Boston. There was a small menagerie of people who had followed Rick to Boston. Rick was trying to sound upbeat at first, but this letter was very sad, and it was his last.

> Kath' It's finally getting warm here . . . unfortunately, I'm so far behind in school that I doubt whether I'll have too much time to enjoy it. I am playing with Van Morrison May 1.

He went on to tell me the following:

> . . . . [I] called my father the other night . . . no reason . . . well, I wasn't ready for what followed . . . it was like Gettysburg all over again . . . seems that he doesn't dig the idea

of me living with Debbie and Marianne . . .
but it was crazy . . . he told me to leave school
now and come home and get a job . . . that I
am dirty and disgusting (that's new shit . . .)

He described that he ended that phone conversation
with his dad saying, "I told him to call me when he calmed
down."

I couldn't believe what I was seeing on paper and
hearing in Rick's voice coming through in this letter. He
hadn't sounded this nervous and frustrated in a long time.
At first, I was glad to hear that he had moved out of the
apartment and was no longer living with Dog—although
I wasn't hearing the why.

Rick's letter ended with the following:

I guess I'm just naïve . . . That crap about
people are basically honest and really want
some kind of meaningful relationships with
other people is just bullshit . . . there's a lot of
F___'d-up people running around managing
to discase everyone around them. Sorry to get
all worked up . . . but . . . it never stops . . .
Cheerful news later (if there is any). Love,
Rick

It wasn't until we spoke on a phone call after this letter
that I came to understand that Rick knew he needed
to get away from Dog's grip on him. He had started to
think Dog was looking to hurt him. He told me in this

call that his guitars were stolen from his apartment, and he suspected it had to do with Dog trying to keep him from leaving to go back to Los Angeles. He didn't want to tell me everything on the phone because we planned to meet at home in another week. He only said he wanted to get through the next month he had left in the school semester and get out of town.

After hearing how sad Rick was feeling, I went back over the end to his letter. I concluded, while he was hurt by the words he had with his father, he was, without saying so, talking about Dog—who Rick considered a friend—and how resentful Rick thought Dog had become, because now he believed his so-called friend had stolen his guitars. Both of the men Rick wanted to look up to had disappointed him beyond repair. That was frightening.

I started thinking about how I always felt Dog wanted to keep an annoying dominance over Rick in order to satisfy his own need to have Rick include him in his promising lifestyle. With evidence of that notion becoming rejected Dog had perhaps decided to wreck Rick's hopeful future by hatefully taking away his lifeline to separation from Dog. It seemed that Rick was beginning to suspect Dog was capable of this kind of contempt.

Rick and I made plans to meet back at home the first weekend in May. I was always willing to make the trip to New Jersey whenever it was important to do so—and this was as imperative a time as any because I knew Rick needed me. I felt that parental instinct that something was terribly wrong and I must see him again.

Rick flew home the first Friday of May. I always managed to find the money, time, and connections to get to New Jersey. DC was the midpoint and hub of transportation links between Virginia and New York / New Jersey because a plane trip all the way was too expensive given central Virginia was not a destination for many commuters from the northeast. Sometimes a friend of mine who had a Volkswagen Beetle would pack four kids in that Bug along with all their luggage, food, and books to make the four-hour car trip to DC that was the halfway point. Once you were in the corner of that car that you could barely fit into, you weren't moving for hours. From DC, I could take the train the second half of the way, which I always found pretty depressing because I didn't have the money to enjoy the company of people in the car that served food and drinks. The most likely alternative was to take the Greyhound bus from DC to New York's Port Authority, and as miserable as that means of travel was, it was the cheapest.

Whichever way I had planned this trip, I made it home to see Rick that weekend. He first went to spend some time with his dad and borrowed his car. He asked me to meet him at the Howard Johnson—the orange-roofed motel and restaurant on Route 22 in Greenbrook where we would often go to have their famous hotdogs or apple pie with ice cream and coffee late at night after our high school dates. I borrowed the car that had been mine but was now used by my sister, and I went to meet Rick at the Ho Jo's.

When I walked in, I saw Rick sitting in a booth waiting for me to arrive. He was hovered in a corner with his arms crossed tightly against his chest; he was very despondent. I was shocked to see him appearing fragile, so near broken, and in such despair. He didn't want to talk much about the guitars being stolen. In fact, he didn't seem to want to talk much at all. I tried to do most of the talking about my trip and how long it took to get from point to point using the various lousy means of public transportation that were available for students with no money just like the mostly lonely nomads that you would find on Greyhound buses. But it was just to make small talk because I could see pain in this guy's eyes that I didn't know I could do anything about. I thought, at the time, this was all about him losing his most prized possessions—his guitars—as devastating as that was in and of itself. But there was also the last phone conversation he had with his dad that had made him feel just terrible.

At least he was home for a couple of days, and perhaps that night they started talking things over. But I was not going to tell him how to handle that; only he and his dad could work out how they felt about Rick's situation in Boston and the fact that he was once again leaving to pursue music as a career.

I guessed it always hurt Rick to know that his dad didn't understand his passion for his music. I felt very sad for him and for myself a bit because I couldn't think of any really comforting words to say. I thought about what Rick would write in his letters to me, at the times we would be having a quarrel, when he didn't know what to say. I thought, "I don't know how to start this . . . I can't just say, 'hi hon' . . . how are you' . . . more bullshit."

We talked a little about his plans to return to Los Angeles, but he was clearly no longer excited about that. All he talked about was how he just wanted to make it through the last few weeks of school and get out of Boston before the end of May.

I wondered if I was missing something in the hopelessness written all over Rick's face. I didn't realize at the time that he might have been holding back from telling me about some kind of helplessness that went beyond losing the guitars. He was more than discouraged; he was truly dejected. All I remember about the rest of that last weekend we had together in New Jersey is the nights we spent just sitting in the car talking little and me mostly trying to ease his agony with a little lovemaking, hoping to relieve his tension.

I returned to school after this disturbing visit with Rick at home. I worried about him every day, but I needed to get back to trying to concentrate on all the reading and studying I needed to do to get ready for the end of my school year. It was time to buckle down and complete some papers that were always due the last month of classes. Exams were just weeks away, and I tried to focus on some pain and agony of my own.

I couldn't cast out of my mind the dispirited attitude Rick had portrayed when we saw each other last, and I began to worry that whatever was happening in Boston or whatever he could not resolve with his father had caused him to not be himself. He didn't offer me his usual words of encouragement and love; he no longer seemed to care how anyone else felt about whether he was leaving for LA, and he didn't seem to care if no one loved him anymore. It was as if he really needed to get away with no promises, spoken or unspoken. If Rick was short on love and caring at the moment I felt I might have to face losing him for good this time, but I couldn't put my finger on a reason why. I am reminded of how I felt back then when I hear the words to one of my favorite songs by the Eagles. Rick was trying to tell me he had given me the best of his love and, while he didn't want to give up on us, as of then he had little more to give.

Chapter Sixteen

THE WORST OF TIMES

How Was I to Know?

JUST A FEW weeks later, on a Saturday afternoon in Virginia, I was out shopping for a new outfit to wear to a party planned for the night. When I returned to my dorm, one girl told me I had a phone call around 3:00 p.m. from Carole King in California and she would be calling me back. By 6:30 p.m., I was dressed to go out; my date had called from the dorm lobby to say the guys were there to pick up me and three other girls for the evening.

I stalled going upstairs when soon the pay phone in the hallway rang, and the call was for me. It was Sue Palmer on the other end. All she said was, "Kathy, I have terrible news . . . Rick is dead." I couldn't process what I had just heard. I gave out a yell as I pleaded, "What do you mean Rick is dead? Where is he? I need to talk to him." Sue sadly replied, "You can't talk to him . . . he's gone." She proceeded to only describe briefly that Dog killed him. He called Rick to tell him to come to the apartment because he had Rick's stolen guitars. Rick went there, and nobody heard from him for a couple of days. Finally, Dave and Rick's sister Bonnie were called when the Boston Police found Dog in the apartment with Rick's dead body.

I was still in a state of shock, but we talked about a memorial service that was being planned at home and that Carol would have airline tickets waiting for me at the airport, so I should plan to get home. All my friends were huddled around me, still on the phone. They didn't quite get the whole story, but when I hung up the phone, I guess I described what I had heard. My boyfriend in Boston was just killed by his roommate. No one could believe it. These girls felt like they knew all these people whom they never met but had heard so much about. They knew I was devastated.

But our dates were upstairs waiting for us to leave for the evening. I went up to the lobby and met my date, the other Rick. I immediately told him about the phone call I had just received from California. He knew about my boyfriend, Rick, in Boston, and he knew what he meant to me. He was saddened, and he just hugged me and said, "Let me take you away from here tonight, you shouldn't be alone." So I went out for the night to the party, which I don't remember much about. I just remember sitting on a couch in the house of a friend with a whole crowd of kids around me drinking beer and trying to get me to respond to any of the fun they were having. Everyone knew what had happened, and they just didn't know what to say or do, except to let me stare into space and try to digest what I needed to do next.

As of Monday, I went to visit with each of my professors to explain the reason I needed to go home. I would not be at school for the exams that were scheduled that week. They all allowed me to take my exams when I'd return in a few days. With that, I got a ride to the airport, and I was on a plane to New Jersey with images in my head that I was going to see Rick one last time. I was remembering the day at Venice Beach in Los Angeles, the night in Boston when we celebrated my twenty-first birthday, and all the intimate nights we spent alone just sharing the love we had between us.

For the two-and-a-half-hour flight, all I thought about was everything I wanted to say to him. I wanted to let him know that I was sorry I had left Boston and left him to find out for himself that Dog was no good. But who could have known he could be this bad? This was beyond comprehension, but I was being reminded of how deeply suspicious of Dog's envy I had become just the year before.

All I could think of while I travelled home to Rick's memorial service was what I had come to learn about the disturbing personality traits often used to describe a person who superficially can resemble a normally functioning person but who internally lacks an inner core constructed on good conscience or a healthy self-concept.

Such a person might suffer from a constant identity conflict and chaos in their life could result in purposely destructive behavior that was most often self-imposed. But when harmful intentions are directed to hurting others, it could become criminal violence.

Dog's smart, often charismatic external persona was perhaps a cover-up to his apparent internal inability to care about anyone but himself and a capacity to rationalize his devious behavior. In my despair I could only remind myself of how I tried to stop his manipulations before he could hurt me or worse, hurt Rick. But, my voice was not strong enough nor heard for long enough, and now it was too late.

I could never have imagined the relationship Dog wanted with Rick would have such dire consequences. No one ever wants to believe a thing as terrible as premature death could happen to anyone, let alone to someone they love. I didn't lose him to the war or to another woman; it wasn't a car accident or an overdose. This was a permanent loss that possibly could have been avoided. Could I have been to blame? Should I have worked harder to make Rick and others understand the threats Dog had imposed not only to me but to Rick as he was allowed to win control over Rick's existence in Boston? How did no one see it coming? This was a situation I had no idea would have such tremendous impact on my life ahead.

Chapter Seventeen

GOOD-BYE MY LOVER, MY FRIEND

Memorial Services

IN MAY 1969, a New Jersey local newspaper published an obituary about Rick's death: "Memorial Services Were Held Tuesday for Richard Philp." The piece gave tribute to Rick as being well-known in his hometown as an accomplished guitarist who performed with The Myddle Class. It acknowledged that the group's imminent success, predicted by trusted people in the music industry, never happened because this tragedy caused the group to disperse.

Jane and Elayne from Emerson were among the people who attended the Millington Episcopal Church Memorial Service held in Rick's honor. I don't remember getting ready to go to the church, who took me there, or even all the others who were there. I believe I have buried this memory for many years. I only remember crying continuously. I remember Jane and Elayne coming up to me to jointly hug me and me them as if to acknowledge the common bond we shared with Rick and that we each understood our relationships with him, what he meant to each of us, and what we each meant to him.

After the service ended, I decided to go to Rick's house to see the family. I pulled up into the driveway, and I knocked on the door to the basement den where Rick and I had spent so many intimate times and where he would play his music just for me. Rick's dad opened the door and said, "Bonnie is upstairs." I said I just wanted to talk with him. He didn't say anything; he was washing the floor with a mop, and he just went back to doing what he was doing. With his head down all the time I was there, I just started to tell him how much Rick was loved by so many people and how he would be missed terribly. With my voice quivering, my hands shaking, and tears in my eyes, I told him that Rick loved him very much. I went on to tell him that it wasn't Rick's fault that we were late to his wedding; it was my fault. I told him that I got lost in the reservation trying to find my way to Mountainside. I even told him that Rick never blamed me for it but that I blamed myself. I don't know what other words came to me, but I just remember feeling like I was there for an eternity, and I couldn't stop talking.

He never stopped mopping the floor; he never looked up at me. He didn't have anything to say to me. I finally realized how deeply painful this had to be for him. The man had lost his twenty-two-year-old son, his namesake, and maybe, just maybe, his pride and joy.

Somehow I just ended it by saying how sorry I was for his loss, and I left. This was as big a loss for me as it was for Rick's family, but I was not family. I was only a girlfriend. I didn't feel entitled to stay to grieve with them. But I was always glad that I found the courage to go over to the house that day to pay my respects.

I wanted to have people come to me in the same way. I remember the many people who did, and I remember some of the people who did not ever say anything to me whom I thought should have. Maybe there was just too much suspicion over the circumstances of Rick's death for people to feel comfortable to bring up the subject, but I didn't see it like that. I only knew that I was known to have had a five-year relationship with this boy and that I was the person closest to him.

How could people just think of it as something that would pass and that life would go on? Not my life. Life as I knew it ended with that weekend. The person I was then became buried that day along with Rick's spirit. All I could hold on to were the memories of the love I had shared with a soul mate. I needed to return to school, to take my exams, to finish the semester, and plan to return in the fall. Other than that, I had no idea what I would do with myself. Who was I now without Rick Philp? At twenty-one years old, it would take me a long time to find that out. Notice I didn't say "it would take a long time before I figured it out." I don't know that I ever have.

Chapter Eighteen

ONLY THE GOOD DIE YOUNG

Trying To Understand

IN THE BOOK *Girls Like Us,* author Sheila Weller writes about the early years of three iconic female singer-songwriters who broke the '70s equivalent to the glass ceiling of recognition of women over men in the workplace. In this case, it was inside the music business. Her subjects were Carole King, Joni Mitchell, and Carly Simon. While Ms. Weller's extensive research resulted in fine details obtained through interviews with a wide range of people close to the three women she writes about, some facts of the early years of Carole King's rise to fame are left unmentioned. In particular, there is no disclosure of the fact that Rick Philp was the first to record with Carole and Charlie on the album *Now That Everything's Been Said* released as The City. Many of this album's recordings started with Rick playing lead guitar when he and I, along with Dog, spent the summer of 1968 in Los Angeles for this very purpose.

Commentary on this album applauds the synchronized jazzy riffs of the piano and guitar of the back-up band. This technique was customary of Rick's guitar prowess, which had previously been registered on Goffin and King demos and live performances of original songs he wrote with Dave Palmer, which as recordings had strong public appeal. I sense some of Rick's contributions to *Now That Everything's Been Said* were intentionally preserved, albeit respectfully replicated.

Ms. Weller does get it right when she acknowledges that during the early years when Carole and Gerry were producing the group The Myddle Class, "it featured a brilliant guitarist, Rick Philp . . ."

Dog did not only end Rick's life, he also ended the dreams that were so promising, the opportunities that might have been endless, and the gift to the world of music that could have been Rick's personal long contribution after his start with The Myddle Class.

Listening to the melodies, harmonies, arrangements, and Rick's lead guitar alongside the bass, drums, organ, and piano on the songs "I Happen to Love You," "I Shall

Be Released" (written by Bob Dylan), "You Go On*,"
"Free as the Wind," and later, "Keys to the Kingdom"
(three written by Dave and Rick) would make anyone
think of how ahead of their time these young guys were
when these recordings were made. This was only the
leading edge of their growth potential.

The successful songwriting, singing, producing and
performing that followed in a few short years by Dave
Palmer, Carole King, and the likes of Neil Diamond,
James Taylor, Eric Clapton and Jimi Hendrix compared to
their early years are only testimony to the budding talent
Rick Philp had already demonstrated. It could only have
grown into a great career as he had imagined it would.

But it was not to be. It was thwarted and stolen
away, along with the symbolic guitars, by the direst of
desires of one pathetic, peripheral individual who was
virtually insignificant to the future. I thought for many,
many years that Dog's crushed ego drove him to make
sure that if he could not have Rick, no one was going
to have him.

It took my relentless research to validate my memory
and beliefs about Dog and the events of May 1969 and

---

* "You Go On" (Palmer and Philp) was recorded by a girl group named
Bach's Lunch (I believe the lead singer was Darlene McCrea) with music
performed by The Myddle Class. It was a Carole King solo production
released in 1967on the Tomorrow label as a flip-side to a single remake of
"Will you Love Me Tomorrow." This vocal rendition of the brooding lyric
is called by some critics "sexy and ghost-like" but yet it is hailed as "one of
the greatest B-sides of all time" as B-side material was never intended to
beat out A-side song selections for DJ air-play.

finding a Web site published about Rick's Emerson College history professor, Dr. John Coffee, to see these very words written in black and white. He describes his recollection of hearing the incredible news at the time of the young coed at the school being slain by his roommate. I can now quote the words of Dr. Coffee and say that this was the bottom line. In an interview about his experiences as a teacher at Emerson, Dr. Coffee recalls Rick's death vividly by saying:

> Then there's the story of [the] Philp murder . . . [the] kid took two classes with me. His name was Rick Philp, a real nice, good looking kid, wrote brilliant papers. He roomed with this really weird kid . . . Apparently, [the roommate] had a crush on Rick who wasn't gay. Yet so long as [the roommate] didn't come on to him Rick didn't see a problem. But [he] started coming on to Rick. So [Philp] moved . . . and [the roommate] said you know, 'if I can't have him nobody can.' It was then that [he] stole Rick's guitar, and then called Rick to tell him he had found it and asked him to come pick it up. So Rick comes on back to the old apartment and knocks on the door, and the [guy] was waiting there with a baseball bat and he bludgeoned him to death . . . I remember I was making dinner and I heard the TV in the other room say Richard Philp, an Emerson College student . . . (Bryan 2004)

Finding this led me to further research what more I could learn about any impact the tragic incident of Rick's death may have had on the students at Emerson College. Indeed, the tragedy was significant enough to cause Dr. Coffee to make reference to Rick's demise in a book he coauthored to chronicle the first one hundred years of the school's history and the development of its unique culture. In the book, *A Century of Eloquence: The History of Emerson College 1880-1980,* Dr. Coffee and his researcher, Richard Lewis Wentworth, defined Emerson College as "not in the general run of colleges . . . definitely not ordinary." As requested, they take a reader through the evolution of a school designed for

> . . . characters, men and women of excellence also streaked with an eccentricity that has made them different. (Coffee and Wenworth 1982)

In the early '60s, Emerson was, like many schools (including mine), embedded in tradition: girls and boys had separate dormitories, they dressed for dinner, and they saw few minorities among the student population. But this generation of college students set out to change all of that. Our time at college was assumed to be a chance to extend our youth by years mostly enjoying the pleasures of learning, total self-indulgence, and freedom to ignore what was happening in the world outside our classrooms. Although it should not have been the mission for the college bound, it was easy to expect we would postpone preparation for maturity and the working world in which we would soon need to manage on our own.

But as at most other colleges around the country, the late 1960s became a time when students at Emerson wanted to use these precious years correcting the injustices of life. They wanted to prove they were aware of the societal and political waves of change that were brewing around their sanctuaries. This was becoming the age of "a time for every purpose under heaven."[*] It was time to turn conflict over oppression of woman and minorities into peaceful calming of the angst that was the reaction to a war we didn't need to be fighting—by seeking attention rather than daydreaming.

In his book, Dr. Coffee writes the following:

> The closing years of the decade of the sixties were difficult ones for colleges across America, and Emerson had its share of this affliction. It was an age, according to Emerson's 'Beacon', of independence [particularly being displayed by young woman] and extroversion, of protests and non-conformists . . . of LDS, or marijuana and of changing morals. (Coffee and Wenworth 1982)

Early in 1969, the then very popular with students dean of woman, Jean Jacobson, wrote a letter of resignation to then school president Chapin. In her letter, Dean Jacobson described how she had become overwhelmed

---

* (Ecclesiastes 3. The Holy Bible 1999)

by long hours trying to meet the expectations of being the one administrator willing to listen in order to understand the unrest of the students rather than to simply speak and not hear of the realizations students were harboring of inequities in the school's policies. Even after organized protests over the disguised dismissal of Dean Jacobson, students' interests were ignored, and the president accepted the dean's resignation. This did not sit well particularly with female students.

For decades, Emerson had enjoyed the opportunity to meet its expenses by the collection of high tuitions given the wealth of their student population—mostly white and Jewish—and the school had only a few black students quickly feeling like tokens following the pressures of civil rights movements.

In the spring of 1969, a small group of black female students formed an intended peaceful group, EBONI— Emerson's Black Organization of Natural Interest— focused on negotiating with the administration for improvements in its attitude toward minorities. The group organized what was called a proposal rather than demands for ten areas where the school needed to recognize a need to recruit, enroll, and offer scholarships to more blacks. The proposal cited a need for quotas and full-time positions to be held by black professionals. It also called for the addition of soul food on the menu of the school's dining halls and school holidays to recognize the birthdays of Dr. Martin Luther King and Malcolm X.

Although progress and compromises were being reached, there was a swelling of discontent as the administration's approach to the conflict resonated with attempts to discount speakers, thwart resolutions, and not allow attendance by protesters to organized meetings. Near institutional racism, one meeting culminated in a takeover of the president's office by men considered Black Panthers supporting EBONI and a group of Emerson athletes (yes, athletes) defending the president's office.

In the end, EBONI students swore to "make this a college we can be proud of," and the president conceded to aspects of the proposal requests for change, if not entirely literally, at least in spirit. However, it was pointed out, the group was considered a distinct minority, and everyone knew that as they approached the final weeks of the semester, summer would likely break the momentum, and the energy of that spring would likely be diminished by the start of a new school year. However, there was more. Dr. Coffee depicts the following:

> The anguish of that flawed and angry month of May in 1969 was not yet over. An Emerson student, in the final week of that month, was slain by his own former roommate, who was a member of the graduating class. The horror and tragedy of the event, which had nothing to do with the previous controversy, was a sobering influence on the College, and now, for the moment, all the petty controversies, the pushing and shoving and yelling, the demands and petitions, seemed somehow irrelevant. (Coffee and Wenworth 1982)

Dr. Coffee was asked by Richard Chapin, then president of Emerson College, to deliver a eulogy at the Trinity Church of Boston memorial service held for Rick's passing, which Dr. Coffee inferred every student attended. As he wrote the following, Dr. Coffee hoped to affirm a faith in his students, which may have been forgotten for a few days in May of 1969:

> Youth is a time for creativity; for trying new things; for changing your mind, for not being careful. It is a time for living life to its fullest before, all too soon in later years, we settle into what Thoreau called 'The deep ruts of tradition and conformity.' On occasions such as this one we realize not only how fragile and transient is our life, but also how precious it is. It is too valuable to take lightly. So live your life! Live it richly, and to the fullest. Make your music, and speak your mind, and leave this world better than you found it! (Coffee and Wenworth 1982)

Indeed, the death of Rick Philp at only twenty-two years old had enough meaning to his fellow students and faculty that Dr. Coffee gave it his endearing recognition in his book's accounting of a century of significantly historical events of the school that shaped its consciousness.

Dr. Coffee shared with me that when he first wrote about the history of Emerson College, many of his colleagues criticized him for hanging out the school's dirty laundry of a student's death in his book. However, Dr. Coffee was proud of the fact that he had received a note of thanks from President Chapin, offering his tardy but strongly felt gratitude joining with many others in commending him on his remarks about Rick Philp. Rich Chapin conveyed he thought that what Dr. Coffee had to say was beautiful and most appropriate, and he confessed a feeling of pride in having Dr. Coffee as a member of the Emerson Faculty.

* * *

At the time of Rick's death in late May 1969, the weekend news stories described an Emerson College student was found slain in the basement apartment at 233 Beacon Street, telling how Rick was last seen alive on the previous Thursday. A report stated the victim apparently had been strangled and suffered several fatal blows to the head from a blunt object. The Boston police reported that some rope and a broken pedestal were turned over to investigators as possible evidence of the homicide disclosing the body had been in the basement apartment for some time.[*]

If Rick didn't die immediately, he died a slow death while Dog cowered inside that apartment until the Boston Police Department authorities responded to a call reporting a disturbance. Upon entry by officers and finding Dog in the apartment with the dead body, Dog

---

[*] Emerson Student Found Slain. 1969. Used with permission of the Associated Press.

reportedly confessed to the police at the scene: "He's dead, I killed him, I killed Rick." Having told the police he took an overdose of drugs, he was taken to Boston City Hospital and was later booked on a charge of murder. Later, the medical examiner reported the victim died from multiple blows to the head.

The way I had heard it, a bloody wooden object thought to be a banister spindle was found inside the apartment along with Rick's body.

Rick was still wearing the ID bracelet I had given him for high school graduation. That bracelet was cut from his body, and his sister Bonnie later returned it to me. Apparently my letters to Rick did not survive the chaos.

* * *

Dog was allowed for the year before his trial to postpone court dates with repeated thirty-day stays in the Bridgewater State Hospital for psychiatric evaluations. A newspaper reported on Dog's 1970 trial "citing the use of drugs as one of the causes of the slaying," (Tarbi 1970) as Superior Court Judge Wilfred Paquet reduced the charge of murder to manslaughter and sentenced Dog to eight to fifteen years in Walpole State Prison for the beating to death of his roommate. The judge is quoted as saying, "he wished that college students would come to the courtroom and see real life tragedies instead of paying money to see *Hair*" (the popular Broadway musical about the '60s youth caught up in defiance, music, drugs and a cultural protest over the mistrust of its government, mostly due to the unpopular Vietnam War, racism and sexual repression. The volatile hippies' activism was manifested symbolically mostly by growing one's hair long).

After only two weeks of testimony, Judge Paquet allowed the trial to be halted, accepting a plea of guilty to the lesser charge of manslaughter as a clever defense lawyer counted on the judge's pity, saying Dog would need to live the rest of his life with the memory of what he had done.

After allowing a sixteen-member, all-male jury to hear arguments on disposition and a statement by Rick's sister Bonnie, which may have tried to establish that Rick was not gay and never used drugs, at the point of sentencing, the judge is quoted as saying the following:

> The taking of drugs and the element of self defense were two of the reasons he accepted the plea to the lesser charge. [He added] . . . it is unfortunate, that so many of our people who have a chance to gain an education spill it down the drain by the use of illegal drugs . . . It is here in the courtroom where the real dramas of life take place as in this case which involved the slaying of a friend that we see the real dangers of life. I wish more students could have seen and heard this tragedy. [The judge lashed out at the] . . . fiends who sell these drugs to college student and the society which allows the drugs to be sold.

He [audaciously] told the jurists that it [was]
their responsibility to see that something is
done about it. (Tarbi 1970)

How was it the responsibility of these jurists? They
were but one jury, one trial. Was it not the responsibility
of this and other judges to impose real penalty on this
and other offenders and make Dog pay real consequences
for his behavior and his personal choice to ignore the
devastation of his dire desires?

What was then and remains today unchecked is the
responsibilities of our systems of law and order that
allow criminals to have the benefit of doubt even in
the face of confession, motive, and hard evidence.
How was it not this judge who could have made a
difference in how much society needed to tolerate the
drugs and violence that were then (and still are) allowed
to permeate the wealthiest nation on earth, all in the
name of opportunity for rehabilitation? Rehabilitation
became a future profession for Dog as he was allowed
to walk free from this heinous crime in just three short
years. The story of his continued atrocious behavior is
told later.

* * *

The opinions and research conclusions of Hervey
Cleckley, MD, Clinical Professor of Psychology at the
Medical College of Georgia, Augusta, Georgia, as a
well-respected psychology expert are documented in his
book *The Mask of Insanity*.

Cleckley hoped to clarify, that although the labels are often used interchangeably, psychopathy is different from sociopathy which is considered a clinically defined mental illness. He attributes this distinction to the notion that criminal offenders that may not be deemed mentally ill are those that are not considered helpless but actually do know the difference between right and wrong, but choose to ignore it.

The district attorney as prosecutor in this criminal case also blamed the society, which allowed drug use to become rampant and said he felt that many of those involved in this matter were good students who became involved in an unfortunate situation.

It seems, what was unfortunate is the fact that authorities who want to be trusted by the public to pursue rights to due process didn't really want to take the time needed to consider, beside drug use, any other possible reasons for Dog's reckless misconduct. What were the conclusions of those who evaluated Dog's behavior as the results of nearly a year of repeat stays in a psychiatric hospital before his trial? Were there possibly judgments that his rage was driven by his vulnerable self-esteem, his selfish sense of entitlement to share in Rick's grand potential as a substitute for his own fear of a lack-luster future? Did he act violently out of his own sense of defeat when he knew he was being left out of the fantasies?

Why not a plea of insanity? Why drugs? I didn't know Dog to use drugs. He had just graduated with honors and was headed for a teaching career. Could repeated psychiatric evaluations have concluded that

Dog actually felt no sense of responsibility for Rick's death? By blaming drugs, he had justified inflicting his ultimate guilt-free pain on his friend with no interest in understanding his wrongdoing.

But was there no hope? It seemed the prison systems then, in efforts to evaluate the culpability of devious behavior, deemed it "politically incorrect" to think an inmate, in spite of committing a crime, is incapable of rehabilitation. Could it be possible that experts felt that therapy would never help Dog? For behavior modification to result from therapy a subject must want to look deeply inside himself to feel something needs to change. Perhaps the conclusion was that Dog liked himself just the way he was.

Short of full understanding of the offender they were facing in 1970, these court jesters took the prevalent easy path to blame, which was to consider young college students as nothing but disruptive and totally liable for the fear that began to engulf this country in the wake of the anger that resulted over events such as the four dead in Ohio. It was at the violent hands of our own country's national guard that the travesty of four students being shot to death took place on the campus of Kent State[*] University in the confusion of an intended peaceful but intimidating protest.

The '60s generation of college students were never blind to the disingenuous ways our government at the time tried to justify tens of thousands of their peers

---

[*] (Wikipedia, Kent State shootings 2010)

losing their lives over a threat of communism expanding in a faraway part of the world because of how it existed in Cuba just ninety miles off our shores.

Things never got too political at my school, except in 1969 when some kids talked about going to join a Vietnam War protest march in DC. I did not go, although I was tempted. The Vietnam War was still something very distant from my life concerns then, until I later realized that my favorite high school teacher, Mr. Chesler was a professor at Kent State University in 1970.

Well after the war had ended, I learned how some of my high school friends had suffered from severe posttraumatic stress disorder. During the Vietnam War, there wasn't, as there is today, a tolerance for this nor any money thrown at this problem when those vets returned home, so these guys were abandoned, ridiculed, and left to turn to drugs and any other means they could find on their own to forget the trauma they had experienced at war.

Many of those vets either suffered for many years with drug addiction or died from it, which, in the long run, cost the government more in moral decay and a poor image of the military than if they had realized the consequences of their decisions to go to war and dealt with these vets with dignity. After Vietnam, the military was determined not to repeat those mistakes, so now all war combat is treated as if the life of all soldiers is completely heroic when in reality that is yet the ultimate spin on misguided representation.

In 1970, the entire establishment of America's capitalistic power in the world was threatened by the segment of young men and women whose enrollment in colleges protected them from the requisite donning of fatigues and rifles, and the free speech of these thousands that remained at home, armed with drugs and music actually rocked the legal and political establishment into a fear of punishing the likes of Dog.

This youth wasn't totally aware of the power they wielded, but they certainly were not interested in tolerating the lies and deceit being imposed on them by the very keepers of the governance designed to protect the very freedoms thousands of young men were fighting to preserve.

These young college students of the late '60s were taking to the streets and the mall between Washington DC's Capitol Building and Washington Monument to be heard in protest of being ignored.

This is the same generation of college students who then knew how to protest government inequities that are again protesting on the same mall in DC in the name of the Tea Partiers. Not all extreme right-wing, conservative religious fanatics, this segment of the U.S. population, now armed with their respectful wealth effect having worked their way through forty-plus years of hard work and few entitlements, still want to be heard on their rights to not be ignored and still refuse to be fooled by ineptness on the part of big-government bureaucrats.

* * *

It seemed as if frustration, arrogance and rejection combined into a perfect storm to fuel a fire in Dog's heart when Rick prepared to escape his smothering clenches, rejected his sexually promiscuous advances, and planned to leave him behind in Boston to rejoin old friends he valued more. Dog's stress-fractured illusions snapped and turned him into a broken man. So he blamed drugs while deciding, if he couldn't have Rick, no one would. Then without a conscience, his sense of omnipotence allowed him to make the choice to beat to death another human being, a friend, who simply would not yield to his sordid demands.

I believed that this tragic incident and what led up to it had little to do with drugs. I especially knew that aside from some pot smoking, Rick was never into drugs. The use of drugs may have been a trumped-up defense by a clever lawyer to get this guy leniency from a reluctant judge, but taking of drugs was not the underlying cause of death.

Rick's death had mostly to do with the natural tendency Rick had for trusting and forgiving people, especially people who were supposed to be his friends. He had an Aquarius's sensitivity that was exemplified by his extreme tolerance of those who may have been flawed by demons they could not control, believing everyone had redeeming qualities that deserved his loyalty because he felt the conflicts of demons of his own. Dr. Coffee's accounting is correct that Dog was able to lure Rick to return to the apartment by a call to come to get the stolen guitars; Rick would have trusted the devil with that kind of lure to regain custody of those most illustrious extensions of his self. Against his sister's warning not to go to meet Dog, Rick took his ultimate risk. He knew if he could only get back his guitars and spend one last week in Boston to finish out the school year, he would soon be free as the wind and safely home.

Karma had other plans for Rick. Maybe the inevitable plan was for him to finally make it safely home to a place beyond the madness where he could play his music in peace and harmony under the protection maybe of his true heroes, starting with his mother, Wes Montgomery, and all the others that had gone prematurely before him. We can look back and ask why is it the good die young? But destiny is a strong force, and I do believe there is a higher calling in store for us all.

When I face the redeemer of my mistakes in this life on earth, I will ask to see Rick to ask him if I let him down by leaving Boston when I did. Could it have made a difference if I had stayed and fought harder for my place in his life? If he says no, then I will know that he really did love me because he would never bring me down.

Chapter Nineteen

A NEW SLICE OF LIFE FOR ALL

What Followed The Demise

IT WAS NOW close to dinner time and I asked my son if he wanted something more to eat. He said no, but he could use some caffeine. While I made a pot of coffee, my son who started listening with limited curiosity and got much more than he hoped for had one final question. This one did not have any shorter answer than the ones that came before. He asked me what became of Dog and did I stay in touch with Carole King and our other friends? Life did go on for all the people in my story and the past forty years were still quite captivating. I finished telling my story with how much of the past was still in my thoughts. I wanted to describe how the Carole King and James Taylor Troubadour Reunion tour concert took me back to a willingness to purge these memories. So I shared how it all turned out.

* * *

After Rick's death, I stayed in touch with his sister Bonnie for a few years. She finished her education at La Salle Junior College in Boston and moved back home for a while. She wrote me some funny letters about the guys she was meeting at her first job in New York City working at the well-known J. Walter Thompson advertising agency. She eventually worked her way up in that company to a very responsible position. Bonnie ultimately married an office executive much older than herself, much like her stepmother had done. She never had children, but seemed happy, although she never got over Rick's death. The memories of telling Rick he should not go back to the apartment and of being in Boston throughout all that she had to endure alone, including the murder trial must have been haunting. I guess knowing the outcome of advice not taken stays with you forever. But with all the strength she could muster, Bonnie had kind and sympathetic words for me. I remember speaking with her to say I was glad she was able to salvage the ID bracelet I gave Rick for high school graduation, which he always wore, and to thank her for returning it to me. In a card she sent to me with the bracelet, Bonnie wrote to tell me:

> I wish you will receive in greater measure all the love and happiness that you so willingly

and faithfully gave to Rick. You made his life worthwhile as far as he was concerned. Knowing that, you should feel humanly fulfilled. Use the relationship you had with Rick as guidance for your future, and I'm sure the sun will always shine for you.

While this was flattering, it made me sad because, back then, I thought it was sweet but wishful thinking.

* * *

After I returned to finish my third year of college, I went home for the summer and did little more than work day and night shifts for almost three months straight, waitressing at the restaurant of a local golf country club. I didn't have anything else to do with myself, but I made a lot of money.

In the school year of 1969-1970, I completed college and graduated after putting in a 1970 summer session to make up for the semester I had missed in the spring of 1967. It was not a problem to get it all in. I stayed in Virginia, living in the basement apartment of my psychology professor, department head, Dr. Cone. I babysat his daughter for spending money, and at the end of the summer, he asked me what I was going to do next. I said I had no real plans. He asked me if I wanted to go to graduate school, and I said sure. I had nothing to lose.

In September 1970, I moved to Richmond, Virginia, to start a postgraduate education. The state of Virginia paid me a stipend of $1,000 a semester and paid for all my tuition to go through a two-year program for a master's degree in psychology. The hook was I had to work for the state for two years—so between 1972 and 1974, I worked as a psychologist at the local state mental institution. I faced the challenges of trying to help modify the behavior of people who were mostly institutionalized for being crazy or retarded, but no one really knew which came first. I later left Virginia after getting married and lived fifteen years in Chicago working in the healthcare and pharmaceuticals industry. I tried to make a new life for myself, but throughout these years, while I tried to reach my own self-actualization, I kept in touch with Carole King.

* * *

Carole's letters continued after Rick's death and for several years beyond, but I don't remember being such a good pen pal. In mid-November 1969, Carole wrote the following:

> Dear Kathy,
> I'd been wondering about you. You seem into your own thing now—I'm glad you've grown & progressed, but I really had missed hearing from you girl. We're all glad to hear you're doing OK. I'll be in NY for Thanksgiving . . . if you're in town call me . . . Write soon, please keep in touch. Love, Carole.

I was certainly going to be home for the holiday, but for some reason, I decided not to meet up with Carole, even though I was grateful that she wanted to see me. I remember that while it was easy enough to write letters back and forth with Carole, seeing her might be very difficult for me.

I next heard from Carole after she received my birthday card in February. She thanked me for my good wishes and told me she had a lovely birthday because everyone made it last almost a week with presents and lunches and carrying on. That was the week that James Taylor played at the Troubadour and used a bass, drum, five brasses of varying types, and Carole on the piano. She was thrilled with the opportunity for her first gig as a musician. "I loved it, but it's hard work." After only one week, she was actually happy to return to being just a mom and a writer.

Carole always gave me some news about the friends we shared: Gerry and Sue didn't live together anymore, Danny and Joyce lived separately and Carole was writing with Gerry and Toni Stern—all that was good, and she was having a nice thing with Gerry at the time. Telling me she figured this all sounded very Hollywood, she expressed this outlook:

> My dear friend—I see that you haven't lost any of your beautiful soul that I remember knowing over these past five years!!! . . . make your life in future "news" . . . my love and friendship, although physically far away, still are here, and I send them to you.

I sat reading this message from Carole with tears streaming down my face, just thinking of how much I missed her and all the others that Rick and I had been so close to and shared so much with during our formative years. I had told Carole that I was reaching the end of school, and I did not know what I would do with myself. We had always trusted each other with our sensitivities, insecurities, and vacillations between hopes and ambivalence that went hand in hand with our confusions about an ambiguous, hazy future. Now I was on my own to walk the path of a personal new fork in the road while I still listened from afar to how Carole never gave up the pursuit of closure to old wounds—the very heartache I was trying to overcome. When Dr. Cone said he would recommend me to graduate school, I thought maybe furthering my education would be the perfect delay to dealing with who I might become.

I wrote to Carole to tell her I was heading to live in Richmond, Virginia, to begin graduate school for a master's degree in psychology. I guess it sounded like a quite mature, if not very focused, decision.

Carole returned a call I made to her, telling me she had been thinking about me and she was very glad to hear from me. She said I sounded uncertain about my future, but as usual, I seemed to have it all sort of planned and was taking it right on—just like I had always done in the face of uncertainty or in need of a direction. She told me about her new album coming out soon on Lou Adler's label, Ode. It would simply be titled *Writer,* and she said she would send me a promo copy, which she did.

In spite of this excitement, her biggest surprise and news she was most thrilled to tell me about was that, after many changes over five years, she and Charlie planned to be married on September 6, 1970. She said it seemed like the right thing to do, and she had confidence it would work out well. She told me how Charlie and Danny Kootch had formed a band, Jo Mama, with Joel Bishop, who had been Danny and James Taylor's old friend from New York. Joel had moved to Los Angeles and was with his childhood girlfriend and now wife, Connie. Abigail Haness was in the new group and became Danny's new girlfriend. Stephanie was no longer living with her boyfriend John Fishbach, and she was trying to renew a relationship with James.

Carole described it as "one big—family" suggesting that I could fill in the blank. With her impending marriage to Charlie, Carole was writing alone, or at least not with Gerry.

She ended her rambling with, "Life is not dull . . . I'm glad to know that you are still sentimental—I'm a hopeless romantic and I think of past days often, as I do of you."

Carole always reminded me of how much she valued our friendship, telling me, "I'm very much your friend, although separated by distance."

She wished me happiness and peace of mind and said she was glad I renewed our contact.

All the news of these intertwined relationships made my head spin, but this news of Carole and Charlie's forthcoming marriage made me very happy for them but sad for myself. Although she was making every effort to keep me up-to-date with the daily grind, like she always did with letters of news about The Myddle Class, somehow this news had me painfully thinking of what I could have had with Rick if circumstances had been different. But it was foolish to go down that road of old wishes I could do nothing about, so I was just thrilled for Carole and Charlie, and I hoped the happiness in her voice would last forever.

I received an invitation to Carole and Charlie's September 1970 wedding—it was handwritten on the inside of a card covered with a simple picture of them both. It was as bohemian as you could get, but that was Carole—she had money she would never spend from the sweet smell of final, individual success under her nose and the man she desired for so long. I could only think to be happy for her.

Later in that fall of 1970, Carole wrote to keep me informed of their latest work activities, which were picking up for Charlie. The group he had formed with Danny Kootch, Jo Mama, was having their first album released, (produced by Peter Asher) and they were soon going to open at the Troubadour. Also, the group was traveling back east to play at The Bitter End in the Village during Thanksgiving week. Carole suggested I look for them there, saying, "Please do."

Carole herself would soon be performing at the Troubadour with James Taylor. This time she would be the second act, except that James was going to play a bit in her set and she in his. She hoped his presence would ease her nervousness. Carole was not quite ready to be a solo act in front of an audience—not even in the small venue like the Troubadour. She planned to play some of her old songs written with Gerry in the early '60s, and she was introducing the new songs she had written without him. She said, "I hope people don't get into comparing them lyrically, because . . . [Gerry was] some act to follow!"

Carole's next correspondence was early in the new year. She was telling me how very excited she was about the plans she and Charlie had to buy the house on Apian Way, still in Laurel Canyon, that would be their new home together. She described it as a two-story English Tudor made of solid stone, with a huge cathedral ceiling in the living room, with an overlooking balcony, and with library shelves galore. Her further great news was that she and Charlie were expecting a baby late in 1971. Carole's little bit of "friend" news was that Stephanie was again seeing John, although they did not live together, "so John can work out his independence thing," and she didn't know where Sue was. She hoped I was feeling content when her letter reached me. She signed her letter as always, sending her love.

It was really nice of Carole to try to keep me connected by inviting me to see her or Charlie and Danny with their new group when we might all be around New York City. However, once I had received the news about the results of Dog's trial and knowing Dog was sentenced to a rather brief term in prison on a charge of mere manslaughter for killing Rick, I tried to put all the past behind me.

I never went to see Carole or Charlie's group in the city. Needless to say, I knew it would just be too painful.

* * *

In November 1971, Carole had received one of the rare letters I had decided to send her way at this time in my life when I was trying to decide what I wanted for my future. In a replying letter, she seemed glad to hear from me and said she wished she could see me. She was carrying a big baby and had another month-and-a-half to go before delivery. Carole sounded a bit melancholic—the way late pregnancy makes you feel—ready to cry at the drop of a hat or at the least little thought of anything sad or potentially sad.

She wrote she was sitting around flashing every now and then about what a lot of water had gone under the bridge since May 1965. She asked me if I still wondered, as she did, if we knew ourselves at all back then. She said it was too hard to think about it that way; she liked being in the now—now was groovy, although old and good friends were all the more precious to her now, especially as she was about to become a mother of three children. She told me she knew she would sound like a sloppy, sentimental pregnant lady, but she wanted me to know she counted me as an old and good friend, and she was glad we were still in touch.

Near the end of 1971, Carole was embarking on the release of her new solo album, *Tapestry,* and a new baby in her life after ten years of getting used to her two girls being somewhat grown up, but she still had me in her thoughts. I couldn't believe she still found my letters to be comforting and interesting to her because they couldn't have presented much excitement. I felt a bit jealous of her being pregnant, like it was admirable to be sentimental, and I wished I had an excuse for being down in the dumps.

I was living a pretty ordinary life as a graduate student with just a lot of work to deal with. I was working two jobs and trying to start a master's thesis. Yes, I kept working as a waitress at night along with my full-time day job. It was good money and a chance to hear a great little jazz trio every night at this bar/restaurant I worked at, which was inside a hotel in Richmond. It was called The Abbey, and I had to wear this short little monk's outfit that showed off my long legs. It was all pretty cool, and I worked with a lot of nice girls, although most of them were single, with children, and looking for some Prince Charming to come along into that bar to sweep them away from it all. I know I always felt the only way I could do that job was to remember that I was in school and this was temporary—I could see an end to it, but many of these other girls never could. That job is actually how I met the one guy, a baseball player from New York City that I kind of fell for and then later how I met the man I married. But that story is being saved for later.

* * *

Carole had sent me promo copies of a couple of her album releases—her first solo album, *Writer** and, of course, the original The City album, *Now That Everything's Been Said*. Rick had recorded on several of the cuts on this album in the summer of '68, but after his death, the tracks were apparently rerecorded with Danny Kootch as the lead guitarist.

Near the end of 1971, Carole's *Tapestry* album was released and it was a huge hit. She played down the potential for success that this record had, given it contained all her new independent writing along with some great tunes she wrote with Toni Stern (who I met during the summer of 1968 in Los Angeles). *Tapestry* also included several of her greatest accomplishments of writing with Gerry.

Over the next year, *Tapestry* was ranked number one for fifteen weeks by *Billboard* magazine and remains one of the longest-running albums by a female solo artist, charting for over three hundred weeks. *Tapestry* swept the 1971 Grammy Awards (televised

---

* After Carole's album with the group The City had been initially produced by Lou Adler, this first solo album was produced by John Fishbach although released on the Ode Records label. *Writer* was considered unsuccessful mostly due to Carole's choice not to tour to promote the album. Carole remained loyal to the many artists on this album, including James Taylor and Danny Kortchmar, using them as studio musicians on many recordings that followed. One year later came the release of the tremendously successful *Tapestry,* still without touring.

in 1972[*]), winning Carole four key trophies for the recognized achievements of Album of the Year, Record of the Year for "It's Too Late," Song of the Year for "You've Got a Friend," and Best Female Pop Vocalist for herself. This new mark of success in her own right put Carole back on top the way she and Gerry were a decade earlier with "Will You Love Me Tomorrow?" She is often credited for having written or collaborated on songs that have passed the test of time as being among the most memorable for a generation of listeners, and I knew her when much of it evolved.

* * *

From late in 1972 and for a few more years, I received note cards from Carole telling me about how her family was growing up. She began to write in incomplete sentences just to give me her life's latest highlights: her newest baby, Levi was sleeping, and she was taking a deserved rest herself; Gerry was remarried and living in New York; Louise and Sherry were now twelve and

---

* In 1971, Carole King's *Tapestry* album was one of the top-selling albums of all time, with sales estimated at over 14 million copies. *Tapestry* was also one of the all-time longest records on the Billboard Pop Album chart, remaining there for 302 weeks—nearly six years. Lou Alder accepted the Grammy's most prestigious awards for Carole when she did not attend as she had recently given birth to baby Molly Larkey. Adler was named Producer of the Year for the album as songs from *Tapestry* won in every Grammy category for which they had been nominated. Carole King continued a streak of albums and singles topping the Billboard charts for over five straight years.

ten years old; and ten-month-old Molly was walking. Charlie was playing string bass in the USC Symphony Orchestra, and he was proud of that accomplishment. She described herself as happy, qualifying that with the sentiment that marriage was hard work but rewarding, and she felt good that she and Charlie were willing to work at it.

Carole let me know that Dave Palmer was in Los Angeles with a new lady, Bonita. Carole was the one who first told me Dave was working with Steely Dan, whom she thought was very good. Dave later sent me a promo copy of the Steely Dan album, *Can't Buy a Thrill,* on which he sang lead on several songs—he seemed quite proud of those performances, as well he should have been.

Stephanie remained Carole's good friend and Carole was genuinely pleased to let me know that Stephanie was pregnant. She and her guy, John Fishbach, were happily expecting in July. She told me she thought of me often and wondered where all the time had gone. She again hoped I was cheerful and sent her love.

Carole had finally moved into a grove of contentment—her life seemed to be all she wanted and needed it to be. The news of her success and also Dave Palmer reaching a plateau of satisfaction with a singing and writing career only solidified for me how much these people had developed over the years and had realized the still temporary pinnacles of their achievements as they always knew they could. I could only think again of how Rick's talent would have developed along with that of Carole, Charlie, and Dave and others in this growth period—and how it all could have been so great for him—with or without me.

While I was honored to be kept a part of all this, albeit from a distance, I could hardly feel like I was as deeply attached as before. After all, I was living a very different life now.

After one last letter from Carole and a few more exchanges of notes, ultimately, my own wedding announcement to Carole in 1974 pretty much ended the correspondence. Our lives were now set on very different courses. All I could do after this period of transition was to follow her music, news releases about her success, and her concerts as she came close to where I was living with a hope to maybe see her for a short reunion. I did just that sporadically for the next twenty years.

* * *

It took me five years before I allowed myself to commit to a new relationship. I was unable to sustain several false starts that became challenged by long distances between home bases.

The first meaningful relationship I allowed myself to have after Rick was with Tony from the Bronx, who I fell hard for when I met him playing baseball in Richmond, Virginia. He begged me to get out of what he considered a godforsaken town and come to the city to be with him where he was a teacher. When I couldn't land a job, I didn't go. Tony had both brains and brawn, and he is the one that got away.

When I dated the guy whose job involved international travel, once he needed to leave for four months on a tour of Spanish-speaking countries and I said, that's over. We later renewed our friendship when in a second go-'round, he invited me to go skiing, which I had never done before. I agreed to take a beginner's lesson on a bunny slope, and then I was talked into going up a mountain to try my new skills. When I was literally dropped off at the end of the chairlift ride, I saw nothing but ice without any actual snow to slow my descent to the bottom. I slid uncontrollably until I fell at least four times within fifty yards. In one attempt to stop, I literally wrapped myself around a tree. Frightened as could be, I sidestepped my way back to the top and asked if I could ride the chairlift back down the mountain. I was told that was not allowed. So I simply walked to the side where there was nothing but mud and tree roots, and while holding the rented skis in one hand and poles in the other, I walked slowly down the mountain under the chairlift. People swinging in the chairs above me pointed and asked me, "Did you lose something?" I replied, "Yes . . . my nerve." Among the riders was my date who just kept on skiing—not to waste the day of fun he had purchased. I later married him with my eyes wide shut, but I wouldn't realize that for eight more years to come. It all started at a time of my most delusional thinking that I might manage a forever-lasting marriage and loving relationship froth with security, trust, and hopefully compatible compassion. All indications were that even without a long history, I had found love embedded enough in shared common interests, goals, and mutually respected capabilities to expect my love and devotion to be reciprocated with enduring love. If I was having this conversation with myself, I didn't think so at the time. I was tempted into a sense of safekeeping that someone might actually be willing to take care of me and I was encouraged to willingly strive to make an equal contribution of income to a lifestyle formulated in Chicago and shared among our newfound circle of friends. We bonded with coworkers all well suited for grand-scale accomplishments we would pursue in the face of business-oriented ambitions. This was, however, far from the life I thought I would lead a decade earlier. My life became absorbed in a satisfying, successful career although ensnared unknowingly in a flawed marriage. In the end, although I did have my wonderful son from that relationship, once again, I could not stay where I was not wanted. I divorced in 1982 when my child was less than two years old.

Then there was Scotty in Chicago whom I met on the day in August 1982 after I returned to work from divorce court. That evening, he and I had separately been given tickets by a mutual friend to go to see a James Taylor concert at an outdoor theater. This venue must have been one of James's favorites because I saw his concerts that way almost every two years for years to come. Scotty eventually wanted to go back home to live in Seattle. I tried to go, but I couldn't just pick up and leave my home and a good job without replacements. I came close, but that long-distance relationship fizzled.

My last effort was with Eric who was in the military. When he was deployed to the Mediterranean, as I was losing my job in Chicago and was forced to accept a job back in New Jersey, I knew that separation would not endure.

When I had invited Carole and Charlie to my wedding, she was happily mothering a new *baby, Levi Benjamin Larkey—born April 23, 1974—and sent me a warm letter of congratulations along with a gift. I followed Carole's solo career with heartfelt interest. I got to meet with her face-to-face a couple of times after concerts I attended. Once in Wisconsin in 1978 I was allowed backstage. We talked for a few minutes before she left me with my treasured memories commemorated by her signed promo picture, writing, "For Kathy, with love from an old friend, Carole." I met Carole again in Chicago in 1982 after a heavily attended concert at a summer festival and briefly for the last time in NYC after I had moved back to live in New Jersey in the early '90s. I went to her show at the Beacon Theatre, but I failed to gain access to a private party at the nearby China Club. Carole later came out to the club's main stage to the audience that packed a dance floor where I waited. She walked past me, mouthing that she had no voice left. Carole only played the piano while relying on her guitarist to sing a couple of new tunes.

---

* After having three girls, Carole sent me a book on how to predict the sex of your child. Male producing sperm swim faster than female producers which last longer. If you take your temperature to determine exact ovulation and abstain from sex a few days, you improve your chances of having a baby boy. It worked for us both.

Now in 2010, when I again attempted to gain backstage access to Carole, there were so many layers of gatekeepers between her and her fans that several letters and e-mails from an old friend went unacknowledged.

Carole married five times, rotating between residences located in the two largest cities on the two U.S. coasts as well as in the remote mountains of Idaho when she wanted to be more reclusive. I only knew the first two men in her life. After Charlie, Carole shared parts of her life with two Ricks, followed by one other marriage that I know of. I remembered Carole as frugal, happy making her own clothes, seeming to be one who might never spend the money she was capable of earning. However, I recently read she is trying to sell her Idaho ranch (at a reduced price yet still in a range affordable to few). This is the place that started out a hideaway haven—a perfect place to raise a few horses, cattle, and goats and bake her own bread, living without electricity as a treasured retreat from the hustle-bustle of Los Angeles, California. Somehow it ended up a feature story in *Architectural Digest* to show off the expenditure of some chump change.

Carole can be heard interviewed on National Public Radio justifying her long-standing dispute with Idaho neighbors and state officials with her research on the necessity to discourage overpopulation of the Rocky Mountain region because of the disruption it might cause to an ecosystem that deserves environmental preservation. What started as an interest in restricting an informal road bordering her property from use by neighbors who, for years, had unofficial access to the strip as a shortcut across the county ended up with Carole presenting her activist convictions to the U.S. Congress. At the same time, NPR posts dissenting views claiming expertise that underdevelopment of the region is actually harmful to the waters and natural habitats, causing erosion due to lack of attention, which could be corrected with minimal developer and state road spending seen as beneficial. I imagine, with mountains, only time will tell.

* * *

I had to believe in the notion of six degrees of separation when I needed to acknowledge the connectivity among mortals that began with the two bands sharing the same name, the King Bees. If it wasn't for this common thread, Rick, Dave, Charlie, and even Carole and I might not have met and befriended Danny Kootch, who led Charlie and Carole to an introduction to James Taylor, and Carole might never have had Danny fill in for Rick after his death on The City album or found herself sharing a stage with James Taylor as he developed into a new music era icon.

Dave Palmer may never have sought out Steely Dan (or vice versa) if not for the fact that in 1969, Walter Becker and Donald Fagan made an effort to be added to the list of adolescents peddling their tunes to the Brill Building brass. By then, the emblem was a bit tarnished by the imposing sounds of Motown, the Beatles, and Bob Dylan that put this sanctuary on the skids and caused most of its talent to make the exodus to the West Coast.

No group more than Steely Dan frequently changed band members, looking for the magic bullet to success. They had created a great group at the point in time when, with the hit album *Can't Buy a Thrill,* they included Dave Palmer to sing lead on several of the albums best cuts: "Brooklyn (Owes The Charmer Under Me)," "Dirty Work," and "Change of the Guard" (along with background vocals on more tracks including the band's big hits "Do It Again" and "Reelin' in the Years"). I once literally made phone calls to over twenty David Palmers in the Los Angeles phone book. Somehow, after a high school class reunion service distributed contact information on the class of 1965, I got an e-mail from Dave in 2002, and we spoke on the phone. He sent me a recent picture of himself. He had gained a healthy weight, and his beautiful blue eyes sparkled above a great smile—he looked like a young Jimmy Buffet. I got to see Dave Palmer several years ago while on a business trip to Los Angeles. We met for dinner one night and shared some stories. Dave was working in commercial casting, and he said he didn't even listen to music anymore. Recently, I learned of Dave's new passion for photography. One can see his works by viewing a Web site blog he created to share his latest accomplishments as an unrelenting artist. He describes his music of the '60s and '70s as his misspent youth; however, I wrote to tell him it was not misspent but actually has been missed by many who have always realized his talents.

Danny Kootch sustained a long-standing, prestigious reputation as one of the most sought-after Los Angeles session musicians and an impressive success as a co-writer and record producer, levitating solo careers the likes of Jackson Browne, Linda Ronstadt, Neil Young, and Don Henley among others. Danny co-wrote with Jackson Browne the *Fast Times At Ridgemont High* soundtrack hit, "Somebody's Baby." However well networked, Danny may be only second to Eric Clapton as a guitar player aimed at scouring talent in variously seminal groups of friends hunting for the chemistry needed to capture a lightning-in-a-bottle[*] solo run, only to sum up the memories of how great it might have been.

Lloyd Baskin even ended up a member of Seatrain, a follow-up group for none other than Al Kooper's Blues Project, who was a bit of a nemesis for The Myddle Class. It's a small world indeed.

* * *

For a full year before going to trial in May of 1970 Dog was allowed to postpone court dates with repeated thirty-day stays in the Bridgewater State Psychiatric Hospital. He was later credited with one year of time

---

[*] Danny Kootch is a member of the house band in the documentary film, *Lightning in a Bottle*, by executive producer Martin Scorsese and director Antoine Faqua. The 2004 Radio City Music Hall concert gave tribute to fifty years of "the power of the blues" music with performances by a slew of legendary artists focused in the genre. Headliners were B. B. King, Dr. John, Buddy Guy, Solomon Burke, Steven Tyler with Aerosmith, Gregg Allman, Clearance Brown, Ruth Brown, Odetta, Mavis Staples, Bonnie Raitt, Natalie Cole, Macy Gray, and many more. (Lightning In A Bottle, Overview 2010)

served on his sentence for manslaughter which was mostly time spent away from prison. While in the Walpole State Prison near Boston, Massachusetts, Dog was intelligent enough to invest his time in studying the penal system of his home state and became a specialist on alternatives to incarceration. His research was aided by the U.S. Office of Education's teacher corps corrections program. From this work, in 1973, Dog was released from prison and paroled, after serving only three years of his penalty. Within a short while, Dog founded a task force, which in 1975 sponsored a national symposium about his study of the growing popularity of halfway houses intended to rehabilitate former prison inmates into seamless reentry into community living. Following this conference, then Governor Michael Dukakis freed Dog from his brief parole.

This contributed to Dog's second successful scheming of the legal institutions of our nation. The pardon may have allowed Dog the added privilege of squelching the transcript and details of his 1969 indictment and 1970 brief trial hearings because there is little on these records maintained in the court archives.

Limited availability of the truth is possibly why in the 1980s Dog was able to obtain a substantial federally funded grant to gain as a co-owner a position to be the executive director for one of the country's largest halfway houses and community treatment centers. In New York City, Dog was responsible for the intended rehabilitation of released prisoners and drug addicts seeking opportunity to return to society as free men.

After a decade, an FBI investigation was launched into the facility Dog managed based on reported accusations of mistreatment from former inmates. Subsequent new legal struggles for Dog were mounted on multiple fear-filled complaints filed by residents of the halfway house, disclosing demands he made for unwanted, sadomasochistic homosexual acts. One victim claimed, as the controlling head of this operation and the one who issued the passes for residents to leave the facility, Dog himself checked the guy out on a pass in the middle of the night to take him to a cottage Dog had access to on Fire Island, demanding sexual favors. There, accusations report that Dog manipulated this latest prey with threats that he could send the weakened target back to prison if he did not obey.

One man later reported he was robbed of his chance to recover his life as he had hoped, and he was left with unforgettable memories of torture and sexual abuse that scarred him for life. Another was not able to handle the experiences and committed suicide, leaving a trail of evidence, which implicated Dog on twenty counts of sexual abuse and other cruelty, including charges of bribery directed toward the men he was chartered to protect. If he didn't get what he wanted he threatened to return the victims to prison with false reports of failed drug tests and misbehavior.

In this case, his attorney voluntarily disclosed Dog's 1970 criminal conviction trying to link it to an attempt to promote a defense of extortion by the halfway house inmates for becoming aware of Dog's sexual preferences. Fortunately, the tactic didn't work to any advantage.

In the early 1990s, Dog was again indicted and arraigned for his misconduct. He was not held accountable for the suicidal death of the one young man who left a note; however, he was convicted on the counts of bribery for demanding and receiving from at least one resident sexual favors in exchange for money, drugs, and a promise of favorable treatment considered obstruction of justice (offering to destroy urine samples and overlook disciplinary violations). The convictions resulted in more prison time to be served—this time it was federal.

In sentencing, the judge determined ways to uptick the point levels for the charges in order to maximize the duration of penalty. While refreshing to learn, it sounded somewhat like the O. J. Simpson case of burglary of his Heisman Trophy when the court threw the book at him and sentenced him to serve extensive prison time—ostensibly for burglary but mostly for previously and essentially getting away with murder.

The story of Dog as the director of one of the largest halfway houses in the country's penal system was told in the early '90s in a *Dateline* NBC investigative news report. The report focused on how it could be that the U.S. Bureau of Prisons overlooked Dog's criminal record of a conviction in 1970 for the death of his college roommate when it allowed him to co-own and lead a full facility of former prison inmates toward rehabilitation.

The *Dateline* episode, told of reportedly horrific incidents partly through interviews with several anonymous residents of the community center along with New York City parole officers familiar with the details. This story mostly reflected the astonishing findings that there could be such inadequate investigation into a criminal background by leaders of the U.S. Bureau of Prisons responsible for the halfway house program, which was highly popular for its purpose of minimizing the durations of prison stays.

When the prisons of our nation didn't have the space to comingle old and new criminal offenders, there was a rush to put them back into the streets of our communities where these people could especially hide their lonely existences amidst the culture of the large city streets. It was expected they might simply blend in with the homeless and derelict dwellers, in the shadows of tall buildings and people too much in a hurry to get to their next opportunity to score legal or illegal fast money to notice or care about the imperfect souls in their paths.

If the population of former prisoners could actually be capable of recovery and rehabilitation from past indiscretions, they certainly didn't deserve to be manipulated by one of their own—one man who wanted his friends, family, and his home community to believe that, as a college student, he was under the uncontrollable influence of drugs and therefore not responsible for his own act of violence and perhaps he had been rehabilitated. More likely, Dog never rued his actions, and he knew in his heart and mind that he had been well served by the benefit of doubt granted to him in 1970. One might wonder if Dog had simply feigned

A SONG FOR YOU

his own rehabilitation, as he appeared to not believe the residents of his home deserved anything more than to be new victims of his own obstinate, amoral personality tendencies.

* * *

Later in life, it is reported that Dog once again took to his trickery and deceitful ways, which he had apparently convinced himself were doing him no harm. He sat himself in a courtroom to appear to be a second chair alongside his longtime attorney friend to assist the defense for a man accused of bank robbery. It was later that the defendant, whom Dog and his friend were again trusted to help, discovered that Dog was not a licensed legal professional but rather a previously convicted felon. The man attempted to have his robbery conviction and sentence to prison appealed for misrepresentation by his own counsel. It was as recently as 2010 that this appeal was ultimately thrown out of court by a judge saying that the play-acting behavior was not egregious enough to vacate the man's conviction and sentence on the basis of ineffective counsel. At least this time, the court saw through the con. Could the defendant have known and been part of the scheme all along? Or was he but another wounded by the charlatan antics that became routine for Dog? When would it stop?

In recent years, at around age sixty, Dog resurrected his ability to perform as a cunning charmer as he became a poster boy for an organization touting an effective treatment for Aphasia, a debilitating speech-loss affliction he suffered following a stroke. As a spokesperson for this community it is told that for months after his stroke Dog could only communicate the words "yes" or "no" by blinking his eyes. His therapy is described as learning to compensate for disrupted left-brain control of communication by engaging right-brain capabilities to sing words and phrases, albeit through lilted speech. Dog apparently has maintained mastery of clever self-perceived importance but possibly he does it now living in his own diving-bell*-like hell.

---

* *The Diving Bell* *and the Butterfly* is a 2007 film based on the memoir by the same name by Jean-Dominique Bauby. The narrative depicts the life of the man after suffering a massive stroke, which left him with a condition called locked-in syndrome. The victim lost all his ability to communicate but for his learning of a technique to spell every letter of the alphabet by blinking one eye, which allowed him to speak his story. He died ten days after publication of his book.

Chapter Twenty

I KNOW NOW WHAT I DIDN'T KNOW THEN

Lessons Learned

I CONTINUED OVER the years to enjoy music following the old and new from the reunited Eagles ("Best of My Love" and "Hotel California"); the works of Bonnie Raitt ("I Can't Make You Love Me"), Vince Gill ("I Still Believe in You"), and Amy Grant ("House of Love"); LeAnne Womack ("I Hope You Dance"), Simply Red ("So Not Over You") and Kelly Clarkson ("The Trouble with Love Is"); as well as Sting, Phil Collins, Dave Matthews Band, David Gray, James Blunt, and Coldplay to name a few. The more than twenty-year popularity of rap music has eluded me.

When I listen to the car radio, it's usually to sports talk radio or a shock jock talk show. Occasionally on the weekends while driving, I will listen to one or two stations that play greatest hits from the '70s, '80s, and '90s. The '60s decade of music has mostly been dropped on FM radio since the new millennium, but it can be found on satellite radio for a small fortune. I still have my record collection from when I bought albums before I would buy food. After following the '60s and '70s folk rock and pop rock of Dylan, the Beatles, Jimi Hendrix, and a lot of jazz and Motown music, I was a big fan of Leon Russell, The Band, The Moody Blues, Roberta Flack, and Joni Mitchell; even Ray Charles, Michael Jackson, Isaac Hayes, Crosby, Stills, Nash and Young and of course, Carole King and James Taylor. Sometimes I just like to read the liner notes from those records to see what takes me back. I definitely planned to be in the audience at the Troubadour Reunion Tour concert of Carole King and James Taylor in the summer of 2010. The news of that possible last hooray inspired me to write this book and to remember how I fell in love for first time; that just once.

I still believe that when we feel we are in love with one person, we choose to invest our time, feelings, loyalty, and devotion in that partner and we want to believe our feelings will last and that these vows will be forever reinforced with a return of love and commitment.

It's over forty-five years later now. To think of Rick still makes me sad; to see visions of him still makes me cry. Why? Did I not grieve enough? Did I build such a fence around the pain in my heart that I couldn't love like that again? Have I held myself somewhat responsible for Rick's death all these years? Have I been beating myself up to the point that I could not fully give or receive love in my life again, as much as people who tried to love me hoped I could allow myself to feel entitled to believe their love was real? Was my love life also a casualty of the dreadful deed that took my first love away from me?

There is something special about your first love, especially when that lover was your soul mate. Rick was the true definition of a soul mate; we thought alike, and we could finish each other's sentences. We shared our moments of frankness, trust, and lack of defensiveness when we needed to be honest with our feelings. My family always dealt with each other that way; saying what was on your mind, particularly to another's face, never meant less love.

Rick and I both valued the importance of being faithful in our hearts. We both were, without knowing, parent pleasers. We mostly wanted to please the parent we felt couldn't appreciate us for who we were. I wasn't the closest child to my mother, but I worked as a waitress like her, hoping it might make her happy. Rick's mother was the parent who supported his love for music when he was young. His father wanted him to become a successful businessman like himself, so Rick was almost always dressed in a suit.

Although we felt we were disappointing to these parents who we thought didn't like us very much, we wanted to somehow believe they still loved us. What we didn't understand then was that somehow, our independence was intimidating; they weren't so much rejecting us as we were dismissing their need to be considered good parents. As self-reliant children perhaps we robbed them of their need to feel responsibility to keep us safe from harm and loneliness. I want to share a sentiment I received on my birthday recently from my loving son.

> It's Mom who teaches us who we are and helps us dream of who we can be. Mom, I can't begin to thank you enough for all that you've done for me.

In a eulogy to my mother when she passed away in 2000 after living in Las Vegas for twenty years, I wrote the following:

> Soon if you visit my Mom's grave site, you will see a headstone that says "Safely Home." Mommy has traveled safely home to Stirling, near her home, built by all the family journeymen where she raised her family, near God's home for the faithful. She had faith and taught us all to keep faith in our spirits, our family values, and our quests for living life. Mothers set examples of how to behave; how to get ahead; how to value what you have; how to love others as well as ourselves; and how to dare to be different.
>
> Mommy taught us we can all be individuals while embedded in tradition. Her favorite tradition was serving a classic Italian Catholic Christmas-eve dinner for a long table of family and friends, keeping a vigil with coffee and pastries—all night long—for all to come,

celebrate, go to midnight Mass, and return to be comforted at a time no one should be alone.

Mommy taught us to respect the world around us—to be thankful, thoughtful, generous and accepting—not only of those whose lives were similar to our own, but also mostly of those who were different from us. Our parents showed us how to teach, not lecture; how to give as well as take, gracefully; to love unconditionally, but with boundaries.

We may remember a bit more parent criticism than praise, but we always knew their love meant they would always be there for us. They always gave us a home to come to and go from as we needed—to venture out, find life beyond Stirling, but to know we could always come home—safely home.

I still remember Rick attending several of our Christmas family dinners, and he was always amazed at how nearly thirty people all talking over each other could actually know what was being said by all. The gift for keeping track of various conversations in a crowd was much like the art Rick taught me for listening to multiple instruments playing together like those of a band or an orchestra. He helped me to hear the bass alongside his guitar or the piano alongside the organ and the voices in harmony with each other.

Rick and I shared similar family values. He didn't actually reject everything his dad set as an example for him. We were both always thinking we needed to do the right thing. We were afraid to walk away from getting that college education, although we had no idea what we would do with it. We were both risk takers but always with a sense of purpose. How many twenty-year-olds would take off across the country for nearly three months with very little money in their pocket unless it made perfect sense? Did I influence his thinking, or did he teach me everything I knew then—particularly about how to love and feel loved?

We had our doubts and insecurities, and we weren't sure what else we needed in our lives to feel complete, but I know we felt conjoined by our strong feelings for the values we each embraced. We had the deep-rooted feelings you have for a first love that are anchored when a history is shared. We found comfort in the playful relaxation and silliness that lovers should feel when they don't need to fear judgmental backlash. These are the loves we remember the most for giving us our earliest sense of self-worth that comes with being important to someone. We remember the first time we fell in love because it was the first time we actualized the need to be needed, the thrill of being wanted, and the comfort that minimized our growing pains.

My cousin tells me that at our age, and with the aid of tools like Facebook many people try to look up their old flames. We still think about what it would be like to rekindle a relationship with our first true loves—whether we loved them in our teens, twenties, or even later. He said I can't do that because Rick died; I don't have the means to know what became of him, what he is doing now, who he is with, or where. I say I have the opposite feeling. That is, because I lost that love when I was so young, I can only imagine the what-if of how we might have survived all the craziness and held it together. That was in our DNA.

Our love lasted through five years of confusion, conflict, ups and downs, and pressures of so many others tugging, pushing, and pulling us in directions mostly for their own purpose and with little concern if something was what we wanted or needed.

Many young lovers survive doubts and pressures and settle in very early to their decisions of what to do, who to be, who to be with, and where to live out their lives. That's not to say that those people haven't made good choices. But few relationships had the strife and hurdles that we faced at that time. Maybe it was all about having had opportunities that few others had. For that, I am truly grateful, and although Rick was taken away from me at a very critical time in my life, no one can take away what I experienced. I have the memories and written words to savor of how splendidly sweet, tenderly-loving, witty, intelligent, and consummately talented he was and how much he cared for me. I had the privilege of being a part of the wild and wonderful times we shared and of being loved by this person too many others wanted a piece of.

This built my character, my strength, and the values I've carried with me throughout my life. Instead of asking what if, I choose to think, if I had not fallen in love with

Rick and had never come to know and love Carole and Gerry, Dave, Charlie, and all the others, what then?

What motivation drives the desires that love can impose? I expect it is the ultimate phase in self-actualization—the extent to which we know ourselves, our own needs and wants—that leads us to a lasting loving relationship. What I know is a mistake is to believe it's OK to make this choice alone. Not surprisingly, to succeed at love, the one you love must love you back.

When I returned to New Jersey from Chicago, my then ten-year-old son was entering middle school, and I could see he wondered what it would take to be popular. I used to say, "Just dress well and trust your instincts." As a young man, when he wonders what it will take to be ready for marriage, I tell him, "Don't think you are in love and need to get married just because your friends do. One day someone will seem right to you, and you will just know. When you make her laugh, you will know she loves you. When she makes you listen, you will know you love her. That's the time when the risk will be worth taking."

I have learned from the catharsis I've achieved by revisiting these memories, some happy and some sad, that if you really love somebody, maybe it never goes away, and when you lose someone you can't live without, you can let yourself go a long time feeling angry. Now that I've faced my lingering heartache, I have come to realize that the things I didn't want to have happen, I needed to accept; the things I didn't want to know, I had to let myself learn. These lessons have allowed me to recognize that perhaps now, I should finally let go of this thing.

Epilogue

WHERE ARE THEY NOW?

CAROLE KING: THE successful *Tapestry* album won Carole never-ending accolades and the status as one of the most significant female singer-songwriters in the music business winning her the four top Grammy Awards at the 1972 ceremonies. This unprecedented accomplishment took decades to beat. Today Carole maintains an image of a shy, humble, creative type who just wants to give her music to the fans. To this point in 2010, Carole, at age sixty-eight, has maintained the humility along with the chops and energy to delight as many as seven hundred thousand nostalgic fans during her sixty-night, forty-three-city international Troubadour Reunion tour with James Taylor. Just like in 1970, they exchanged participation in performing each other's classic songs of music and lyrics that the audience remembered more than the meal they ate the day before. Although her Web site, blog, and concert

promos invited fans to write e-mails, when I wrote and even
sent several personal handwritten notes to her guardians,
trying to resurface, asking for a brief chance to catch up if
I could see Carole for a few minutes before or after either
of the two performances I attended, given many layers
of caretakers between Carole and a good old friend, my
requests went unanswered. More importantly, while Carole
seemed to be in a groove of flashing back to the early
days of her and James Taylor growing into Troubadours
of the music business as solo artists in the early 70s by
performing at the LA nightclub of the same name, soon
she would return home—to writing, fund-raising and simply
remembering that time of her life. My guess is that Carole
likes living in the now. Now is groovy.

Gerry Goffin: Gerry continued a successful songwriting
career well beyond his highly popular early collaborations
with Carole. A Web site, http://www.discogs.com/artist/
Gerry+Goffin, proves the indisputable durability of
Goffin gems by listing the favorites that were repeatedly
covered at a rate of nearly one a month for four decades
by some of the most distinguished artists over the years.
One most notable is the mid-'60s song "Goin' Back"
recently recorded by Phil Collins to title and introduce
his project to reminisce about the music of the decade
by covering the most popular and magnificent songs
of Motown. Gerry remarried as recently as 2005 and
as expected, the hills of Los Angeles continue to be his
home.

Charlie Larkey: Having remarried at least once,
Charlie continued playing a variety of musical styles with

various colleagues and has been found flying airplanes over Austin, Texas—the city that touts an unofficial slogan, "Keep Austin Weird."

Dave Palmer: After the decline of The Myddle Class, Dave made several attempts to reprise his passion for singing, joining group efforts at album releases with the Quinaimes Band and Wakoo. The first group was a majority collection of Myddle Class members. The aspirations developed in 1969 when Rick and Gerry started to regroup all the talent of these friends seemed everlasting. However, it was 1971 when Dave grabbed the brass ring with Steely Dan as he was invited to perform as lead vocalist on several cuts and to front for stage-frightened Donald Fagan on the band's tour to promote the 1972 release of their first commercially successful album, *Can't Buy a Thrill*. Dave's vocal on "Dirty Work" is described in liner notes as a bittersweet rendering (and one of my favorite tracks). He was proud enough of his achievement to send me a promo copy, which I have framed in a shadow box alongside my other favorite albums of Jimi Hendrix (*The Cry of Love*), Bob Dylan (*Bob Dylan's Greatest Hits II*), The Band (*Music from Big Pink*), the Beatles (*Abbey Road*), Carole King (*Tapestry*), the Eagles (*Hotel California*), and James Taylor (*James Taylor*); his first, recorded in London. When Fagan decided to abandon the artists that contributed to this success, he substituted many for session musicians on later works, and Dave Palmer left the group. Dave wrote several lyrics to Carole King's music and still enjoys sharing in royalties of her number 1 hit single, "Jazzman." I last saw Dave in

2006—living in the Los Angeles / Studio City valley, and we shared some memories and current activities in our lives. You can check out his Web site, http://mytpearl. blogspot.com/ which displays Dave's latest achievements in photography along with links to several pretty wild videos of him singing with Steely Dan and Wakoo.

Danny Mansolino: Danny turned his love of music and instruments into a career as a technician and business owner for piano/organ tuning, repair, and restoration. If you Google Danny Mansolino, you will find references to the early songs of The Myddle Class with links to Carole King and Gerry Goffin. Multiple Web sites, including YouTube, provide fans with pictures and MP3s of the group and their songs. The incredible talent and product of these young guys is still revered as classic garage/ pop-rock and ahead of its time. There are, even now, thousands of hits to these Web site postings as listeners' comments clamor for a modern digital format of a complete collection as one was never released.

Michael Rosa: Myke likely holds the most complete set of Myddle Class recordings and has been said to remember the tragic loss of his friend Rick as something like sending a small universe of people into a tailspin and losing their way.

James Taylor: James remarried in his fifties and is parenting twin boys since 2002. James was co-contributor to the 2010 Troubadour Reunion Tour with Carole King, reclaiming his status as an icon of the '70s music era.

Danny Kortchmar (Kootch): Danny rejoined old friends Carole and James as the guitarist on the 2010 reunion tour and admits he was always in the right places at the right times. Danny reportedly still misses Rick Philp as a friend and a great guitarist whom he looked up to.

Al Aronowitz: Al died at the age of seventy-seven in 2005. Al's children share his best writings on a Web site *The Blacklisted Journalist*. You can feel like you were there as Al looks back over his career and memories of his days as a close friend and admirer of some of the greatest musical artists. Don't miss reading his reflective tribute to his memorable efforts to become a millionaire in the music business as the manager of The Myddle Class.

Scott Ross: Scott remains living in eastern Virginia with his wife of over forty years, Nedra Talley Ross, near their children and grandchildren. He has continued a successful career as a broadcast journalist and talk show host for the CBN (Christian Broadcast Network), founded by Evangelist Pat Robertson. See Scott's interviews on the Web site of the CBN 700 Club.

Dr. John M. Coffee: Rick's history professor retired from a prominent teaching career at Emerson College. He coauthored the book, *A Century of Eloquence: The History of Emerson College 1890-1990,* in which Dr. Coffee pays tribute to the slaying of Rick Philp amidst his writings of the most significant events in the school's first one hundred years. Still in Boston, Dr. Coffee serves as an officer to an elite club of historic transportation token collectors. I had the privilege to speak with Dr. Coffee about his book, and I deeply respect and thank him for sharing his memories of Rick with me.

Rick's family: Before his passing in 2009 at age eighty-seven, Rick's father had lived through the losses of his first wife, his oldest son, and first daughter. Bonnie Philp also died young. Like Rick's death, Bonnie's illness was something her father might have thought he could have controlled or should have prevented. She had struggled with a poor self-image of being overweight for many years, and in midlife, she suffered from complications of an eating disorder. Life is just not fair.

Rick's younger brother, Steve remains married, with two children and grandchildren living in New England where we met during my writing this book. I gave Steve CDs of the songs taped in 1969 by Rick and our friends which he said he was pleased to be able to listen to after all these years. Steve shared with me his fond memories of The Myddle Class, especially Rick. He still laments over how Dog robbed him, his family, and many loyal fans of Rick's music and what could have become an illustrious career to be enjoyed among all the greats, especially by all those who, along with us, loved his brother Rick and had the privilege to be touched by his brief life.

Dog: Reportedly, Dog discontinued representing a chapter of the Aphasia Society aimed at promoting awareness of the language affliction he endures from a stroke. He apparently roams free somewhere in northern New Jersey.

The End

Notes on Sources

E ARLY IN 2010 I heard about a Broadway musical that aimed to take an audience back to the history surrounding the rise to fame of Elvis Presley and several colleagues, starting with an unforgettable one night in a recording studio that merged the talents of would-be music icons. I said to myself, "I could write that!"

I decided to start a project to write my story of knowing and loving some music greats in my own past. As I started out to write about the tumultuous experiences I shared with a group of talented singer-songwriter performers, I realized I was writing a story of my first love, a love lost to tragedy. It was difficult at first to reconstruct chronological events, but I turned to a box of memorabilia and correspondence from my boyfriend, Rick Philp, and my friend, Carole King, which I had saved for over four decades. If not for the personal nature of their depictions of facts and events they shared with me

I could not have given adequate clarity and credibility to the deep love and connections we shared with each other and a special circle of friends. I hope I have delivered a flattering representation of the network of impassioned young souls that were embedded in a relentless common pursuit of success and self-development.

As I disclosed to some close friends my plan to write a book about my youth, I was surprised at how much persuasion I received with agreement that my story was a compelling one. I decided to just go for it. I deeply wish to thank my many friends, old and new, along with my closest family and colleagues who supported me in my desire to take this departure from the present and encouraged me to peel back these memories from my past. You know who you are.

I also want to thank the many educationalists, authors, journalists and providers of public service who willing offered me helpful support to my research of the human behavior and events that contributed to the darker aspects of my story.

My deepest respect goes to those music historians, producers, engineers and long-standing fans of the work of The Myddle Class, other garage bands, and many talented artists that marked early contributions to the history of the rock music business. I especially wish to thank the developers and contributors of the many Web sites maintained for sharing knowledge, insights and opinions, discographies and blog comments which helped me to validate the excitement of the formative music taken from those years that served as the foundation to my story. A special thanks is due to the keeper of the Garagehangover Web site a.k.a. Chas Kit for his high interest in The Myddle Class and its fans who sent replies to the post. Chas helped me reach out to these fans and old friends.

I am particularly grateful to Steve Philp for his willingness to meet with me after these many years so that we could each share our personal memories of Rick along with some heartache we revealed over the loss of his influence on our lives. Steve graciously introduced me to his wife and family photos which took us back to the happy times we remembered.

Sincere thanks go to the staff of the Watchung Hills Regional High School for the permission to use *Lenape* pictures from the year of our graduation. Efforts were made to identify the copyright holders of all photographs and citations used in this book but some were unreachable. I will be grateful to anyone who might wish to advise me of any oversights or corrections.

In keeping with a common interest in recalling those early years that influenced who we have all become, I hope each and every reader of my memories will enjoy sharing with me my journey going back.

Bibliography

Altschuler, Peter. *The Murray the K Collection.* REELRADIO, Inc. 1966-2001. http://www.reelradio.com/mk/ (accessed December 8, 2010).

Aronowitz, Al. "The Blacklisted Journalist:Column 83; How I Nearly Made A Million Dollars In The Rock And Roll Business." *The Blacklisted Journalist.* January 15, 2003. www.bigmagic.com/pages/blackj/column83. html (accessed April 16, 2010).

—. ""The Pre-Beatles Pop Era: 'The Dumb Sound'"." *The Saturday Evening Post* ©, August, 1963 Used by Permission.

Aronowitz, Myles. "The Blacklisted Journalist, An Obituary." *The Blacklisted Journalist.* August 2005. www.blacklistedjournalist.com/column118.html (accessed April 12, 2010).

Autographed Playbill. 2010. http://www.intrafi.com/hair/holding/ photographs/hair/AutographedPlaybill.html (accessed May 20,2010)

B. Ross, M. Gillen, D. Roberts, Jon Scott. *A Killer In Charge/ Breaking The Silence.* Investigative Reporting, *Dateline* NBC, New York: NBC News, 1992.

Bauby, Jean-Dominique. *The Diving Bell and the Butterfly: A Memoir of Life in Death*. Translated by Jeremy Leggatt. New York: Vintage International/ Vintage Books—A Division of Random House, Inc., 1998.

"Boston Police Department Journal Report." Boston, May 24, 1969.

Bryan, Emily. "Prof. John Coffee: An Emerson gem—Campus Life." *JSONS. org*. February 24, 2004. www.jsons.org/media/storage/paper139/news (accessed April 10, 2010).

"Carole King Troubadour Reunion." *CaroleKing.com*. 2010. http://www. caroleking.com/tour2010/tour.html (accessed March 20, 2010).

Clapton, Eric. *Clapton The Autobiography*. New York: Broadway Books, an imprint of the Doubleday Broadway Publishing Group, a Divison of Random House, Inc., 2007.

Cleckley, Hervey M., M.D. *The Mask of Sanity*. New York: C. V. Mosby Co., 1941, 1950, 1955, 1964, 1976.

Coffee, John M. PhD, and K. Wenworth. *A Century of Eloquence-A History of Emerson College 1880-1980*. Boston: Alternative Publishing, 1982.

Collins, T. J., Newsday staff writer. "Gay Killer Ran Halfway House/ Rebhab Director Did Time." *from Newsday* ©, January 31, 1989. All rights reserved. Used by permission.

D.C. *Let's swim to the moon—uh-huh . . . (Ondine)*. October 26, 2007. http:// streetsyoucrossed.blogspot.com/2007/10/lets-swim-to-moon-uh-huh. html (accessed October 24, 2010).

—. *Unga-wah! (Ungano's)*. November 17, 2005. http://streetsyoucrossed. blogspot.com/2005/11/unga-wah.html (accessed September 5, 2010).

Dick, Devil. "The Devil's Music: The Myddle Class—"Don't Let Me Sleep Too Long". "*The Devil's Music*. June 11, 2010. http://devildick.blogspot. com/2010/06/myddle-class-dont-let-me-sleep-too-long.html (accessed 2010).

Dion DiMucci. 2010. http://www.history-of-rock.com/dion_dimucci.htm (accessed Augusst 10, 2010).

Eagles, The. *"Best Of My Love"*. Comp. Don Henley. 1967.

"Ecclesiastes 3." *The Holy Bible, King James Version.* American Bible Society, New York. 1999. http://www.bartleby.com/br/108.html (accessed November 10, 2010).

Fan Club, The Myddle Class. "Fans To Picket For Scott Ross." *The Myddle Class newsletter—Issue #1, p.2.*, November 1, 1965.

—. "First Concert Dec. 11th." *The Myddle Class newsletter—Issue #3, p.1.*, December 1, 1965.

—. "First Record Release!" *The Myddle Class newsletter—Issue #2, p.1.*, November 20, 1965.

—. "King Bees Change Name." *The Myddle Class newletter—Issue #1, p. 1.*, November 1, 1965.

—. "The Myddle Class in Concert." *The Myddle Class newsletter—Issue #3, p.2.*, December 1, 1965.

Fass, Mark. "Law.com.—Judge Finds No Ineffective Assistance in Trial Where Defense Lawyer's 'Associate' Was Non-Attorney Felon." *ALM Media Properties, LLC.* September 8, 2010. http://law.com/jsp/article.jsp?id=1202471735396 (accessed October 6, 2010).

Felder, Don with Holden, Wendy. *Heaven and Hell—My Life in the Eagles (1974-2001).* Hoboken, NJ: John Wiley & Sons, Inc., 2008.

Forgotten Bufffalo featuring Tommy Shannon WKBW. 2010. http://www.forgottenbuffalo.com/wkbwradio/wkbwstommyshannon.html (accessed December 10, 2010).

Gerry Goffin Discography at Discogs. 2010. http://www.discogs.com/artist/Gerry+Goffin (accessed August 10, 2010).

Goffin And King—Honey And Wine: Another Gerry Goffin & Carole King Song Collection. 2010. http://www.discogs.com/Goffin-And-King-Honey-And-Wine-Another-Gerry-Goffin-Carole-King-Song-Collection/release/1945578 (accessed September 10, 2010).

Hare, Robert, Ph D. *Without Conscience: The Distrubing World of the Psychopaths Among Us*. New York: The Guilford Press / A Division of Guilford Publiations, Inc., 1993.

Jazz, All About. *Danny Kortchmar*. April 3, 2008. http://www.allaboutjazz. com/php/musician.php?id=16550 (accessed September 25, 2010).

Jimi Hendrix Biography. 2010. http://www.jimihendrix.com/us/jimi (accessed Nobember 23, 2010.

Kamp, David. "The Hit Factory." *Vanity Fair*, November 2001: 248-275.

Kaufman, Estate of Murray. "The Murray the K Collection." *The Reel Top 40 Radio Repository*. 2010. http://www.reeradio.com/mk/ (accessed October 10, 2010).

King, Carole. Personal Letters to the Author. Various 1966-1974.

Kit, Chas. *Garagehangover*. July 14, 2005. http://www.garagehangover. com/?q=MyddleClass (accessed May 5, 2010).

Kortchmar, Danny. *Bio: Danny Kortchmar*. http://www.dannykortchmar. com/webspace/Bio (accessed October 10, 2010).

Landers, Ann. *Ann Landers Talks To Teenagers About Sex*. New York: Prentice Hall, 1963.

Lightning In A Bottle > Overview. Rovi Corporation. 2010. http://www. allmovie.com/work/lightning-in-a-bottle-304391 (accessed October 10, 2010).

Marshall, Scott. *Scott Ross: On His time with Dylan, Hendrix and Clapton*. December 2000. http:www.cbn.com/700club/scottross/Scott-Who_ on_Dylan.aspx (accessed June 24, 2010).

Maslow, Abraham H. *Motivation and Personality*. New York: Harper & Row, Inc., 1954, 1987.

"Matthew 16." *The Holy Bible, King James Version*. American Bible Society, New York. 1999. http://www.bartleby.com/108/40/16.html (accessed November 10, 2010).

"Neil Bogart. Answers.com Wikipedia." *Wikipedia*. 2010. http://www.
answers.com/topic/neil-bogart (accessed December 7, 2010).

Nix, Garth. *Keys To The Kindgom* series, Sydney, Australia: Allen & Unwin,
2003-2010.

Nuttall, Lyn. *Don't Let Me Sleep Too Long—The Vacant Lot (1967)
Archives:Sources of Australian Pop Records.* 1967. www.poparchives.com.
au/1234/the-vacant-lot/dont-let-me-sleep-too-long (accessed 2010).

Palmer, David. *mytpearl.com.* 2010. http://mytpearl.blogspot.com/ (accessed
August 10, 2010).

Palmer, David, and Richard Philp. *"Keys To The Kingdom"*. 1969.

Pfenninger, Leslie. *Ode Records.* 2003-2010. http://www.onamrecords.com/
Ode_Records.html (accessed December 10, 2010).

Philp, Rick. Personal letters to the Author. Various 1965-1969.

Photography by David Palmer. 2010. http://www.mytpearl.com/# (accessed
September 10, 2010).

PlayThemAgain. *You Tube: The Myddle Class: "Don't Let Me Sleep Too Long,"
original45.* January 29, 2010. http://www.youtube.com/watch?v=s2MS8-
IoZE0&feature=related (accessed 2010).

Rob. "[bomp] rick philp—the myddle class." *Bomp List archives.* March 1,
2004. http://bomplist.xnet2.com/0403/msg00042.html.

Robertson, Pat. *Nedra Ross: "The Right Ronnette"—CBN TV—Video.* 2010.
http://www.cbn.com/media/player/index.aspx?s=/vod/SW86v2_
NedraRoss_031507 (accessed July 10, 2010).

Ronald Harwood. *The Diving Bell and the Butterfly.* Directed by Julian Schnabel.
Produced by Universal Pictures. Performed by Mathieu Amalric.
2007.

Sando, Peter. "The Night Owl Cafe: Rock and Roll Memoir#14." *petersando.
com.* 1997. http://www.petersando.com/mem14.html (accessed August
25, 2010).

Solomon, Howard. "Cafe Au Go Go Promotion © 1966; Used with permission." *Cafe Au Go Go official Web site.* http://www.cafe-au-go-go.com/index.html, circa 1966.

Soriano, Scott. *CRUD CRUD: You Go On (Bauch's Lunch, 1967).* January 2006. crudcrud.blogspot.com (accessed June 2010). sunshinetunes67. *You Tube—The Myddle Class—"Free As The Wind".* 2009. http://www.youtube.com/watch?v=dxr9VwUFXcI&NR=1 (accessed 2010).

—. *You Tube: Myddle Class-I Happen To Love You.* June 6, 2009. http://www.youtube.com/watch?v=pbgN5mAcb8I&feature=related (accessed 2010).

Tarbi, Charles. "Drugs Cited in Student Death." *The Boston Globe;*© May 29, 1970. Reprinted with permission. All rights reserved.

The Associated Press. "Emerson Student Found Slain." ©May 25, 1969. Used with permission. All rights reserved.

The City (Carole King) "Snow Queen" 1968. Lory73. 2008. http://www.youtube.com/watch?v=xPDH_6wkToU&feature=related (accessed September 10, 2010).

Von Buseck, Craig.

—. *The Scott Ross Interview: Part 1—Video.* 2010. http://www.cbn.com/media/player/index.aspx?s=/vod/ScottRoss_Interview1 (accessed July 5, 2010).

—. *The Scott Ross Interview: Part 2—Video.* 2010. http://www.cbn.com/media/player/index.aspx?s=/vod/ScottRoss_Interview2 (accessed July 5, 2010).

—. *The Scott Ross Interview: Part 3—Video.* 2010. http://www.cbn.com/media/player/index.aspx?s=/vod/ScottRoss_Interview3 (accessed July 5, 2010).

—. *The Scott Ross Interview: Part 4—Video.* 2010. http://www.cbn.com/media/player/index.aspx?s=/vod/ScottRoss_Interview4 (accessed July 5, 2010).

Weller, Sheila. *Girls Like Us*. New York: Atria Books, A Division of Simon & Schuester, 2008.

White, Timothy. *Long Ago And Far Away—James Taylor—His Life and Music*. London/New York: Omnibus Press, 2005.

Wikipedia. *Cafe Au Go Go*. October 11, 2010. http://en.wikipedia.org/wiki/Cafe_Au_Go_Go (accessed November 23, 2010).

—. *Cafe Wha?*. 2010. http://en.wikipedia.org/wiki/Cafe_Wha%3F (accessed August 10, 2010).

—. *Carole King*. May 27, 2006. http://en.wikipedia.org/wiki/Carole_King (accessed May 26, 2010).

—. *Fillmore East*. November 27, 2010. http://en.wikipedia.org/wiki/Fillmore_East (accessed December 10, 2010).

—. *Garage Rock*. October 22, 2010. www.en.wikipedia.org/wiki/Garage_rock (accessed November 10, 2010).

—. *Gerry Goffin*. November 28, 2010. http://en.wikipedia.org/wiki/Gerry_Goffin (accessed December 10, 2010).

—. *Jerry Leiber and Mike Stoller*. 2010. http://en.wikipedia.org/wiki/Jerry_Leiber_and_Mike_Stoller (accessed September 10, 2010).

—. "Joey Reynolds." *Wikipedia, the free encyclopedia*. October 24, 2010. http://en.wikipedia.org/wiki/Joey_Reynolds (accessed November 10, 2010).

—. *Kent State shootings*. August 23, 2010. http://en.wikipedia.org/wiki/Kent_State_shootings (accessed September 15, 2010).

—. *Lou Adler*. April 23, 2010. http://en.wikipedia.org/wiki/Lou_Adler (accessed July 10, 2010).

—. *Neli Bogart*. October 10, 2010. hppt://en.wikipedia.org/wiki/Neil_Bogart (accessed November 20, 2010).

—. *Richie Havens*. December 4, 2010. http://en.wikipedia.org/wiki/Richie_Havens (accessed December 7, 2010).

—. *Ronnie Spector*. December 3, 2010. http://en.wikipedia.org/wiki/Ronnie_Spector (accessed December 9, 2010).

—. *Self-actualization.* 2010. http://en.wikipedia.org/wiki/Serlf-actualization (accessed June 15, 2010).

—. *Self-concept.* 2010. http://en.wikipedia.org/wiki/Self-concept (accessed June 10, 2010).

—. "Self-schema." *Wikipedia, the free encyclopedia.* 2010. http://en.wikipedia.org/wiki/Self-schema (accessed June 10, 2010).

—. "The Drifters (American Band)." *Wikipedia, the free encyclopedia.* 2010. http://en.wikipedia.org/wiki/The_Drifters_(American_band) (accessed September 9, 2010).

—. *The Keys to the Kingdom.* December 2, 2010. http://en.wikipedia.org/wiki/The_Keys_to_the_Kingdom (accessed December 10, 2010).

—. *The Mamas & the Papas.* April 26, 2010. http://en.wikipedia.org/wiki/The_Mamas-%26_the-Papas (accessed July 10, 2010).

—. *Tin Pan Alley.* 2000. http://en.wikipedia.org/wiki/Tin_Pan_Alley (accessed September 9, 2010).

"WPTR Radio Station." *Weekly Chart.* Albany: Radio Station Promotions, August 16, 1966.

Index

344 KATHY WEST

Edwards Brothers,Inc!
Thorofare, NJ 08086
22 March, 2011
BA2011081